Financial Institutions and Services

snova
New York

Financial Institutions and Services

SME Finance: Constraints and an Information Asymmetric Perspective
Chokey Wangmo, PhD, Sardar Islam (Editors)
2021. ISBN: 978-1-68507-063-2 (Hardcover)
2021. ISBN: 978-1-68507-141-7 (eBook)

Fannie Mae and Freddie Mac: Background, Reforms and Legislation
Dominik Wurfel (Editor)
2020. ISBN: 978-1-53618-652-9 (Hardcover)
2020. ISBN: 978-1-53618-672-7 (eBook)

Housing Finance: Background, Developments and COVID-19
Lara Cunha Cardoso (Editor)
2020. ISBN: 978-1-53618-621-5 (Hardcover)
2020. ISBN: 978-1-53618-670-3 (eBook)

Financial Audits: IRS, Federal Debt and Troubled Asset Relief Program
Caroline Watts (Editor)
2020. ISBN: 978-1-53617-370-3 (Hardcover)
2020. ISBN: 978-1-53617-371-0 (eBook)

Financial Audit FY2019 and 2018: Bureau of Consumer Financial Protection and the Federal Housing Finance Agency
Lucas Fiedler (Editor)
2020. ISBN: 978-1-53617-583-7 (Hardcover)
2020. ISBN: 978-1-53617-584-4 (eBook)

More information about this series can be found at
https://novapublishers.com/product-category/series/financial-institutions-and-services/

Anthony J. Haley
Editor

Credit Reporting

Reforms, Scoring and Policies

snova
New York

Library of Congress Cataloging-in-Publication Data

ISBN: 979-8-88697-414-0

Published by Nova Science Publishers, Inc. † New York

Contents

Preface

The existing credit reporting system does not work for consumers. Too frequently, consumers struggle to access their credit reports, and when they do, too often, they find that errors can limit their financial opportunities and can be difficult to correct. Consumers need a credit reporting system that works for them, one where their reports are accessible and accurate, and errors are easy to correct.

Chapter 1 - This is an edited, reformatted and augmented version of Hybrid Hearing, before the Committee on Financial Services, U.S. House of Representatives, One Hundred Seventeenth Congress, First Session, Serial No. 117–33, dated June 29, 2021.

Chapter 2 - The consumer data industry—generally referred to as credit reporting agencies or credit bureaus—collects and subsequently provides information to firms about the behavior of consumers when they participate in various financial transactions. Firms use consumer information to screen for consumer risks. For example, lenders rely upon credit reports and scores to determine the likelihood that prospective borrowers will repay their loans. Insured depository institutions (i.e., banks and credit unions) rely on consumer data service providers to determine whether to make available checking accounts or loans to individuals. Some insurance companies use consumer data to determine what insurance products to make available and to set policy premiums. Some payday lenders use data regarding the management of checking accounts and payment of telecommunications and utility bills to determine the likelihood of failure to repay small-dollar cash advances. Merchants rely on the consumer data industry to determine whether to approve payment by check or electronic payment card. Employers may use consumer data information to screen prospective employees to determine the likelihood of fraudulent behavior. In short, numerous firms rely upon consumer data to identify and evaluate potential risks a consumer may pose before entering into a financial relationship with that consumer.

Greater reliance by firms on consumer data significantly affects—and potentially limits—consumer access to financial products or opportunities. Specifically, negative or derogatory information, such as late payments, loan defaults, and multiple overdrafts, may stay on consumer reports for several years and lead firms to deny a consumer access to credit, a financial product, or a job opportunity. Having a nonexistent, insufficient, or stale credit history may also prevent credit access.

Accordingly, various policy issues have been raised about the consumer data industry, including the following:

- How to address inaccurate or disputed consumer data provided in consumer data reports;
- How long negative or derogatory information should remain in consumer data reports;
- How to address differences in billing and collection practices that can adversely affect consumer data reports, an issue of particular concern with medical billing practices;
- How to ensure that consumers are aware of their rights and how to exercise them in the event of a consumer data dispute;
- Whether uses of consumer data reports outside of the financial services, such as for employment decisions, adversely affect consumers and should be limited;
- Whether the use of alternative consumer data or newer versions of credit scores may increase accuracy and credit access; and
- How to address data protection and security issues in consumer data reporting.

Congress has shown continuing interest in these and other policy questions surrounding the consumer data industry. In the 116th Congress, the House passed H.R. 3621, the Comprehensive Credit Reporting Enhancement, Disclosure, Innovation, and Transparency Act of 2020 (Comprehensive CREDIT Act). This bill includes legislation from other bills marked up by the House Financial Services Committee: H.R. 3614, H.R. 3618, H.R. 3622, H.R. 3629, H.R. 3642. In the 116th Congress, the House Financial Services Committee marked up two other bills: H.R. 5332 and H.R. 5330. On March 27, in response to the coronavirus (COVID-19) pandemic, the President signed the CARES Act (P.L. 116-136). Section 4021 of the CARES Act addresses credit reporting during the pandemic. The House also passed two versions of Heroes Act (H.R. 6800 and H.R. 925). Both bills would create a moratorium on furnishing adverse information to credit bureaus during the COVID-19 pandemic period, as well as for other future major natural disasters.

Chapter 1

A Biased, Broken System: Examining Proposals to Overhaul Credit Reporting to Achieve Equity*

Committee on Financial Services

Tuesday, June 29, 2021
U.S. House of Representatives,
Committee on Financial Services,
Washington, D.C.

The committee met, pursuant to notice, at 10:05 a.m., in room 2128, Rayburn House Office Building, Hon. Maxine Waters [chairwoman of the committee] presiding.

Members present: Representatives Waters, Velazquez, Sherman, Scott, Green, Cleaver, Perlmutter, Foster, Beatty, Vargas, Gottheimer, Lawson, San Nicolas, Axne, Pressley, Torres, Lynch, Adams, Tlaib, Dean, Garcia of Illinois, Garcia of Texas, Williams of Georgia, Auchincloss; McHenry, Lucas, Posey, Luetkemeyer, Huizenga, Wagner, Barr, Williams of Texas, Hill, Emmer, Loudermilk, Mooney, Davidson, Budd, Kustoff, Hollingsworth, Gonzalez of Ohio, Steil, Gooden, Timmons, and Taylor.

Chairwoman WATERS. The Financial Services Committee will come to order.

---

* This is an edited, reformatted and augmented version of Hybrid Hearing, before the Committee on Financial Services, U.S. House of Representatives, One Hundred Seventeenth Congress, First Session, Serial No. 117–33, dated June 29, 2021.

In: Credit Reporting
Editor: Anthony J. Haley
ISBN: 979-8-88697-414-0

Without objection, the Chair is authorized to declare a recess of the committee at any time.

Before I begin, I want to welcome Members to our first Full Committee hearing this Congress that has been held in a hybrid format. As I mentioned at last week's markup, I appreciate all of the Members' patience these past months, and I am proud of the work we have been able to achieve as a committee in the midst of this pandemic.

Members will note that today we are joined in person by three witnesses, while two of our witnesses will be testifying virtually. The screen showing the virtual platform in the hearing room has been formatted to ensure that the witnesses participating virtually appear at the top of the screen. I appreciate Members' flexibility, and I look forward to being fully in person in the coming weeks.

As a reminder, I ask all Members participating remotely to keep themselves muted when they are not being recognized by the Chair. The staff has been instructed not to mute Members, except when a Member is not being recognized by the Chair and there is inadvertent background noise.

Members are also reminded that they may only participate in one remote proceeding at a time. If you are participating remotely today, please keep your camera on, and if you choose to attend a different remote proceeding, please turn your camera off.

Today, this committee convenes for a hearing entitled, "A Biased, Broken System: Examining Proposals to Overhaul Credit Reporting to Achieve Equity."

I now recognize myself for 5 minutes to give an opening statement.

As the title of this hearing indicates, our current credit reporting system is broken. Good credit is a gateway to wealth, yet for far too long, our credit reporting system has kept people of color and low-income persons from access to capital to start a small business, access to mortgage loans to become homeowners, and access to credit to meet financial emergencies. That is why, even before the pandemic, the House passed two bills out of this committee, the Comprehensive CREDIT Act, and the Protecting Your Credit Score Act, that provide long-overdue reforms to our credit reporting system. We are considering those bills again with this hearing, but allow me to also explain how the pandemic has exposed just how broken our credit reporting system is.

Last week, I received a letter from a gentleman in Ohio. In this letter, he explained how he had lost his job because of the pandemic. Without his salary, and with no help from any of his creditors, he couldn't afford to cover all of his bills. Although he had never before missed a credit card payment, his credit score has suffered so badly, he wrote that, "I couldn't get credit now if I paid someone to give me credit." He closed his letter by asking what this committee was doing to protect consumers like him.

As Chair of the Financial Services Committee, it is indeed a priority of mine to protect consumers like him who are unfairly penalized in their credit reports, and it is precisely why we are holding this hearing today to ensure greater transparency, accountability, and protections for customers and consumers across the country.

We saw this coming. That is why Democrats worked to include strong credit reporting protections in the Health and Economic Recovery Omnibus Emergency Solutions (HEROES) Act and other COVID legislation that Republicans rejected. This issue is not a matter of personal failings. This is about a failed system. This is a system that fails people with perfect credit who may be victims of identity theft, this is a system that fails people who get caught in a debt trap because of predatory lending, and this is a system that fails people who don't have the means to dispute errors that reporting agencies make.

As further proof of the need for reforms, in a ruling issued last Friday the Supreme Court denied relief for thousands of consumers whom TransUnion wrongly matched with the names of those on a terrorist watch list. The credit bureaus can now label Americans as terrorists with impunity.

The Consumer Financial Protection Bureau's (CFPB's) complaints about credit reporting surged 50 percent in 2020, receiving nearly 50,000 complaints in December alone. During his campaign, President Biden supported a proposal for a public credit reporting agency, and I directed staff to prepare the discussion draft we are discussing today.

As some of today's witnesses will attest, creating a public consumer credit reporting agency would be a major upgrade over today's broken, biased credit reporting system. We need big, bold legislative solutions to transform this broken system.

So, I encourage my colleagues to join me in reevaluating how we determine creditworthiness, and in learning how we can harness new technologies to build a more fair and equitable credit system.

I yield back the remainder of my time, and I now recognize the ranking member of the committee, the gentleman from North Carolina, Mr. McHenry, for 4 minutes.

Mr. MCHENRY. Thank you, Madam Chairwoman. We can all agree that the credit reporting industry is in need of reform. While there are thousands of companies across the country that operate within the credit reporting system, there are only three nationwide credit reporting agencies. It is clear that it is an oligopoly. That means there is less consumer choice and competition to provide the best product. Reforms are certainly needed to improve this system for all participants.

For example, we should be working together to eliminate barriers to entry in this industry. We should be thinking through ways to encourage more companies to compete with the three credit reporting agencies. But instead of creating more competition in the private sector, my colleagues on the left go to the same playbook: a government-run bureau, based on anecdotal evidence and faulty data, including slanted surveys. This is part of their broader goal to dismantle the financial system as we know it. If the idea of a government-run credit reporting agency isn't bad enough, the Democrats want to house it at the Consumer Financial Protection Bureau. This would be disastrous. We should be promoting competition to create better opportunities for consumers, not allowing a single government entity to run the credit reporting process for all Americans.

We know that government-run programs are the least-effective entities to deliver services. Can you imagine the IRS, the Post Office, or the DMV compiling and maintaining your credit report? It may not be great now, but, holy cow, that would be awful.

Additionally, we know cyberattacks are on the rise. Personal financial data is some of the most coveted information by criminals. Add this to the fact that Democrats consistently want consumers to use their full Social Security number to identify themselves, it is a recipe for disaster, and more identity theft. A massive new government-run database of consumers' personal financial information would be a sitting duck for bad actors.

Finally, a government-run credit bureau raises privacy concerns. The government should not be the central repository for all financial data available on its citizens. That is a very dangerous precedent.

As my fellow Gastonian from North Carolina—a nice small town in Western North Carolina—Thomas Sowell, who grew up in my hometown, stated, "It is hard to imagine a more stupid or more dangerous way of making decisions than by putting those decisions in the hands of people who pay no price for being wrong." I agree. It is a terrible idea to give the government the power to make credit allocation decisions potentially based on political favorability. We have seen the IRS target conservative groups. We have seen Federal regulators pressure financial institutions that invest in whole industries. Why would we take the risk with individual consumers' information?

Our free market system is the envy of the world. Our choices are better than anywhere else on the globe. It encourages competition that benefits consumers by yielding solutions that better serve them. There is room for improvement. Yes, that is indeed the case, but not with government takeovers like what my Democrat colleagues are pushing today.

And with that, I would ask unanimous consent to insert two letters into the record expressing concern and opposition to the bills attached to this hearing today, including one from the Consumer Bankers Association and another from ACA expressing concerns with attempts to alter the credit reporting market, including a government-run bureau.

Chairwoman WATERS. Without objection, it is so ordered.

Mr. MCHENRY. I yield back.

Chairwoman WATERS. The gentleman yields back. Thank you, Ranking Member McHenry. I now recognize the gentleman from Missouri, Mr. Luetkemeyer, for 1 minute.

Mr. LUETKEMEYER. Thank you, Madam Chairwoman. This hearing marks yet another step taken by the Majority to move toward a socialist financial services industry. Attached to this hearing is legislation that would create a government-run credit bureau within the CFPB. This proposal would mean the government is in charge of determining if someone is creditworthy in the United States, a terrifying thought. This proposal comes only weeks after a hearing on the FinTech Task Force regarding central bank digital currencies, where the Majority proposed numerous ideas of public Fed accounts and postal banking. This is what the slippery slope of socialism looks like, ladies and gentlemen.

It is clear that the Majority is pushing for a world where the Federal Government not only decides if you can get a loan, but they are the ones who, in fact, lend you the money. I urge my colleagues to go back to their districts and ask their constituents if that is what they want for the American financial system. My guess is they would be terrified that this proposal would receive serious consideration before this committee. With that, Madam Chairwoman, I yield back.

Chairwoman WATERS. I now want to recognize today's distinguished witnesses to the committee: Mr. Syed Ejaz, a financial policy analyst with Consumer Reports; Mr. Jeremie Greer, the co-founder and co-executive director of Liberation in a Generation; Ms. Amy Traub, the associate director of policy and research at Dēmos; Ms. Chi Chi Wu, a staff attorney with the National Consumer Law Center; and Mr. Dan Quan, an adjunct scholar with the Cato Institute's Center for Monetary and Financial Alternatives.

Each of you will have 5 minutes to summarize your testimony. You should be able to see a timer on your screen or on the desk in front of you that will indicate how much time you have left. When you have 1 minute remaining, a yellow light will appear. I will ask you to be mindful of the time and, when the red light appears, to quickly wrap up your testimony so that we can be respectful of both the other witnesses' and the committee members' time. And without objection, your written statements will be made a part of the record.

Mr. Ejaz, you are now recognized for 5 minutes to present your oral testimony.

Statement of Syed Ejaz, Financial Policy Analyst, Consumer Reports

Mr. EJAZ. Thank you. Chairwoman Waters, Ranking Member McHenry, and members of the committee, thank you for inviting Consumer Reports to testify regarding Americans' experiences with credit reporting and paths towards a better credit reporting system for consumers.

The existing credit reporting system does not work for consumers. Too frequently, consumers struggle to access their credit reports, and when they do, too often, they find that errors can limit their financial opportunities and can be difficult to correct. Inaccuracies on credit reports are not a new issue. In 2012, the Federal Trade Commission conducted a study on credit reports in which 21 percent of participants found one verified error on their credit report, and 5 percent had errors so significant that they were put in a different credit risk tier. Complaints to the Consumer Financial Protection Bureau regarding credit reporting errors remain among the most frequent submissions to their database and have more than doubled since 2019.

In February of 2020, in Consumer Reports' own American Experiences Survey, a nationally-representative survey addressing a wide variety of consumer issues, 14 percent of participants who said they had checked their credit reports, also said that they had found errors. This is unacceptable. Credit reporting agencies hold information that can be used to make consequential lending, employment, and, in some States, underwriting decisions about us. Credit report errors that damage credit scores can keep people from affordable interest rates as well as employment, and, again, in some States, auto insurance.

During February and March of this year, Consumer Reports asked volunteers to check their credit report and let us know about their experiences in a project we called Credit Checkup. Nearly 6,000 people responded to our survey and shared their stories: 34 percent of participants who checked their credit report told us that they found at least one error on their report; 29 percent said they found an error relating to their personal information, such as wrong name or address; and 11 percent found errors relating to account information, such as mistakes about their account payment history.

One participant, Victoria Ross, shared her story, which captures how much the credit reporting system can impact consumers. Her TransUnion credit report mistakenly showed a PayPal account balance of around $1,200 that she had paid off, an error which led her to face unaffordably high interest rates when trying to find a car loan. Victoria filed multiple disputes, but was unable to get her credit report fixed until after Consumer Reports contacted TransUnion. Victoria's story is one of many that show how an inaccurate, unresponsive credit reporting system can cause problems for consumers.

One in 10 consumers who took our survey found accessing their credit reports to be difficult or very difficult. Many consumers shared stories of being locked out of their credit reports because of identity verification questions that they simply couldn't answer, because those questions were based off of inaccurate information.

Some consumers told us that while they were checking their free credit report, they were pushed towards products and services that they would have to pay for. Multiple people said that they were asked for credit card information before seeing their reports, and later were charged. One told us, "TransUnion ran me through an exhausting series of questions, sales offers, and ridiculous permutations until I was able to get a credit report and score displayed. Then, I found that they had signed me up for a monthly service and charged my credit card $27-and-change for the first month, to be charged monthly. I immediately canceled the subscription and had to call the helpline to get this charge removed from my card."

These stories highlight just some of the problems that consumers encounter with the deeply-flawed credit reporting system and are a fraction of the thousands of stories that Consumer Reports has collected.

Consumers need a credit reporting system that works for them, one where their reports are accessible and accurate, and errors are easy to correct. The good news is that legislation that is discussed here today can help address some of the most glaring problems. For example, the Protecting Your Credit Score Act requires all credit reporting agencies and data furnishers to match first name, last name, date of birth, and all nine digits of a consumer's Social Security number when placing their information on the reports. This bill also creates a secure portal where consumers can freeze their credit, file disputes, and check their reports, for free, an unlimited number of times.

The House can also pass the Comprehensive CREDIT Act once more. This bill gives consumers the right to appeal the results of disputed investigations, restrict the use of credit reports for employment, and implements many other commonsense reforms to the credit reporting system.

Credit reports play a central role in the lives of consumers, and the industry should focus on the needs of consumers first. A consumer-centric credit reporting system would put consumers in control of their own credit information, make it easy to access reports and scores for free, strengthen standards to ensure reports are accurate, and simplify the process for correcting errors. Congress can put consumers first by passing the Comprehensive CREDIT Act, and the Protecting Your Credit Score Act. Thank you.

[The prepared statement of Mr. Ejaz can be found on page 64 of the appendix.]

Chairwoman WATERS. Thank you very much. Next, we will go to Mr. Greer. You are now recognized for 5 minutes to present your oral testimony.

Statement of Jeremie Greer, Co-founder and Co-executive Director, Liberation in a Generation

Mr. GREER. Chairwoman Waters, Ranking Member McHenry, and members of the committee, thank you for giving us the opportunity to talk about racial bias and flaws in the current credit reporting system. My name is Jeremie Greer, and I am the co-founder and co-executive director of Liberation in a Generation, which is a national racial justice movement support organization working to dismantle what we call the, "oppression economy," and looking to build a liberation economy in its place.

Within the oppression economy, credit reporting agencies such as Experian, TransUnion, and others have anointed themselves as the gatekeepers with the power to determine who can and cannot access financial products, services, and the capital necessary to navigate the economy. They are the gatekeepers to a dual financial system that, on one hand, builds the wealth of households through products and services like affordable mortgages and low-cost credit cards, but, on the other hand, preys upon the financially-insecure through products such as subprime mortgages, payday loans, auto title loans, and predatory credit-building products and services.

Our current credit reporting system both reinforces and exacerbates the dual financial system. Far too many people of color find themselves on the wrong side of this system because they are credit invisible. According to the Consumer Financial Protection Bureau (CFPB), 15 percent of Black and Latinx consumers are considered credit invisible, meaning that they have no credit record at all, while about 13 percent are deemed to have thin or unscorable credit files.

Also, other racial and economic disparities such as income and neighborhood segregation have a huge impact on someone's credit score. For example, take income. Black and Latinx median income is about $40,000, and the median White income is about $70,000. A study by Experian and WalletHub shows that these levels of income mean that Black and Latinx households would have an average credit score of 643 and 681, respectively, which is deemed a bad or risky credit score, while the average White household would have an average credit score of 700 or 737, which is considered a good credit score.

So, what creates these disparities? A major contributor is the biased data that goes into calculating the score, for example, on-time payments, which favors things like mortgages and credit cards, but often completely disregards other forms of payments like a cellphone, rental payments, or utility payments that are more likely to be made by low-income consumers of color.

Another example is credit history. In this case, you need credit to get credit, and historic barriers towards Black and Latinx communities have held back credit from those communities for a long time and made them unable to access credit. For example, think of a child going to college, where a parent is able to open a credit card account for their child. That creates credit for the child. Many Black and Latinx households are not able to do that. They are not able to pay off their child's student loan debt. They are not able to co-sign an auto loan because of the lack of access to credit in Black and Brown communities.

Sadly, research from the CFPB shows that the reality of being credit invisible or having an unscorable account at an early age makes people suffer for both a long time and in the near term. To end this dual financial system, we must reform these credit reporting agencies, and efforts like the bills that passed out of this committee that Chairwoman Waters referenced, including a public agency responsible for protecting consumers, having accountability and transparency in the system is also critically important.

We look forward to efforts that improve our credit scoring system, and we look forward to working with the committee to create those. Thank you for allowing me the time to address you.

[The prepared statement of Mr. Greer can be found on page 93 of the appendix.]

Chairwoman WATERS. Thank you, Mr. Greer. Ms. Traub, you are now recognized for 5 minutes to present your oral testimony.

Statement of Amy M. Traub, Associate Director of Policy and Research, Dēmos

Ms. TRAUB. Thank you, Chairwoman Waters, Ranking Member McHenry, and members of the committee. My name is Amy Traub, and I am associate director of policy and research at Dēmos. Dēmos is a dynamic think tank that powers the movement for a just, inclusive, multiracial democracy and economy. One of our core principles is economic democracy, the idea that we the people must be able to exercise real power over the economic decisions that shape our lives. We focus on Black and Brown communities, that have been largely excluded from economic decision-making.

In my testimony this morning, I will make the case that credit reporting is part of our nation's financial infrastructure, and is necessary for full economic participation and thriving. I will share evidence of systemic racial inequity in credit reporting and will show that the many failures of the system arise from the structure of the industry, and, thus, require structural change. Finally, I will argue that publicly-controlled credit reporting offers the best opportunity to rebuild the system and ensure that it operates in the public interest and promotes racial equity.

Dēmos welcomes the introduction of the National Credit Reporting Agency Act, which would shift power to consumers by enabling them, for the first time, to opt out of the flawed private credit reporting system and choose a fair public option. We look forward to continuing to work with the committee to further strengthen this bill. We also support the Comprehensive CREDIT Act, which would directly reform private credit reporting, and I urge Congress to enact this legislation.

Credit reports and scores play a large role in determining Americans' access to economic security and opportunity, including access to housing, transportation, employment, and entrepreneurship. The credit reporting system is the gatekeeper to such a broad range of economic opportunities, that it forms a core part of our nation's financial infrastructure.

Yet, this privately-controlled infrastructure is failing consumers. My fellow witnesses described the outrageous inaccuracy of credit reports, the nightmare process of getting errors corrected, and numerous other failings of the system.

The most devastating failure is the way that credit reporting reproduces and spreads racial inequality. Although credit scores never formally take race into account, they draw on data about personal borrowing and payment history that is shaped by generations of discriminatory public policies and corporate practices that limit access to wealth for Black and Latinx families. Discrimination in employment, lending, housing, and education has produced significant racial disparities in credit history, so that today, credit scores disproportionately represent Black and Latinx consumers as riskier than White consumers. As a result of this disparity, whenever credit data is used in decision-making, it multiplies inequality.

Transforming credit reporting is very far from the only step needed to address racial economic inequality, but it is a powerful tool to disrupt that cycle of disadvantage. Although the vast majority of American consumers rely on credit reporting to access economic opportunity of all kinds, the credit reports of more than 200 million Americans are controlled by just three private companies: Equifax; Experian; and TransUnion. As private corporations, the aim of the credit reporting agencies is to generate profit, which they do by extracting packaging and selling data about consumers' personal borrowing and payment activity.

Since consumers are not the customers of the private credit reporting agencies, they have no market mechanism to demand accountability or fairness. Consumers cannot opt out of the system or choose to work with a competing company. In effect, by controlling credit data, the three credit reporting agencies have consumers at their mercy. They have arbitrary, unaccountable power over all of our financial destinies. The oligopolistic structure of the credit reporting industry is the reason that it is failing American consumers.

The many problems we are discussing today all stem from the fact that credit reporting is a part of our public infrastructure that is under a private stranglehold by three companies. Congress can and should continue to regulate the industry, yet without tackling the flawed structure of the industry itself, Congress and the regulatory agencies will always be playing a game of catch-up with a private industry that has no built-in incentives for accountability to the consumers whose financial fates it shapes.

This is why Dēmos has proposed a public credit registry designed to be responsive to consumer needs and equity concerns rather than the corporate bottom line. My written testimony describes why a public credit registry is needed to serve the public interest and how it will develop algorithms that diminish the impact of past discrimination, deliver transparent credit scoring, improve accuracy, and offer a publicly-accountable way to address disputes. Thank you.

[The prepared statement of Ms. Traub can be found on page 109 of the appendix.]

Chairwoman WATERS. Thank you, Ms. Traub. Ms. Wu, you are now recognized for 5 minutes to present your oral testimony.

Statement of Chi Chi Wu, Staff Attorney, National Consumer Law Center (NCLC)

Ms. WU. Thank you. Madam Chairwoman, Ranking Member McHenry, and members of the committee, thank you for inviting me to testify today. I am testifying on behalf of the low-income clients of the National Consumer Law Center.

Members of the committee, the Fair Credit Reporting Act (FCRA) is 50-years-old, half-a-century, and in those 50 years, the credit reporting system has been broken and biased. It remains broken despite multiple enforcement attempts by the Federal Trade Commission (FTC), nearly 10 years' of supervision by the CFPB, and two multi-State settlements by State attorneys general. It remains broken after 50 years of private litigation with tens of thousands of lawsuits by injured consumers, including several eye-popping multi-million dollar jury verdicts. It remains broken after two rewrites of the FCRA in 1996 and 2003 to attempt to address credit reporting abuses. It has consistently favored the interests of creditors, debt collectors, and the like over the rights and interests of consumers.

The result has been unacceptable levels of errors, a biased, Kafka-esque system that automatically rules in favor of industry during disputes, and stark racial disparities that perpetuate systemic racism. We can see how broken it is from the over 300,000 complaints to the CFPB in 2020 about consumer credit reporting. That is a lot of complaints, twice as many as 2019, and nearly two-thirds of the total complaints to the CFPB last year.

And, of course, you have the FTC's 2012 study which shows that 20 percent of consumers have a credit report with a confirmed error, with 5 percent having a serious error. That is 10 million Americans who have errors so serious on their credit reports that it could deny them credit, a job, or an apartment, literally a roof over their heads. And without firm action by Congress, it is only going to get worse.

Just this past Friday, the Supreme Court issued a ruling in a case called, *Ramirez* v. *TransUnion* that will make it even harder for consumers to vindicate their rights under the FCRA. The Supreme Court held that a credit bureau can wrongfully accuse a consumer of being a terrorist, a drug dealer, or worse, and the consumer can't even bring a lawsuit because that alone doesn't constitute concrete harm. Imagine that. They have to first have a creditor, landlord, or employer see the falsehood and suffer having their reputation besmirched and ruined in the eyes of a complete stranger before the courthouse doors will open.

As Justice Clarence Thomas said in a fiery dissent: "If this sort of confusing and frustrating communication is insufficient to establish a real industry, one wonders what could rise to that level. If, instead of falsely identifying Ramirez as a potential drug trafficker or terrorist, TransUnion had flagged him as a potential child molester, would that alone be insufficient to open the courthouse doors? What about falsely labeling someone a racist, including a slur on the report? What about openly reducing a person's credit score by several points because of his race? If none of these constitutes an injury, how can that possibly square with our past cases?"

So, Congress needs to act. Only Congress can fix this, and Congress must fix this because it hasn't gotten better in 50 years, and it is only going to get worse. Make no mistake: The Supreme Court's *Ramirez* decision will most certainly embolden the credit bureaus to act with even more impunity, favoring the interests of banks and debt collectors even more and be even more blithe about abusing and mistreating consumers, knowing that there are even fewer checks on their behavior. We need a public credit registry now so the financial reputations of consumers aren't held hostage to the profit-making interests of Equifax, Experian, and TransUnion, to fatten their bottom line. Thus, we support the proposal in the National Credit Reporting Agency Act to establish a public option credit registry so that consumers have a choice.

A key reason for the abuses of the credit bureaus is that consumers can't walk with their feet. We are captives. A public credit registry should and would allow us to walk with our feet, walk away if we are unhappy with the credit bureaus. And if the credit bureaus are allowed to continue, we need wholesale reform. We need laws, like the Comprehensive CREDIT Act, and the Protecting Your Credit Score Act.

To address the awful *Ramirez* opinion, we need injunctive relief under the FCRA, which the majority opinion in *Ramirez* specifically noted could reopen the courthouse doors. But a number of courts have held that the FCRA doesn't provide for injunctive relief, the ability to simply ask a court to order a credit bureau to fix that report.

Fifty years of abuse is enough. We need a public credit registry and wholesale reform now. Thank you for the opportunity to testify, and I look forward to your questions.

[The prepared statement of Ms. Wu can be found on page 116 of the appendix.]

Chairwoman WATERS. Thank you very much, Ms. Wu. As a reminder, all witnesses who are participating virtually should keep their cameras on for the duration of the hearing, even when they are not speaking.

With that, we will go to our next witness. Mr. Quan, you are now recognized for 5 minutes to present your oral testimony.

Statement of Daniel J. Quan, Adjunct Scholar, Cato Institute Center for Monetary and Financial Alternatives

Mr. QUAN. Thank you. Chairwoman Waters, Ranking Member McHenry, and distinguished committee members, my name is Dan Quan, and I am an adjunct scholar at the Cato Institute Center for Monetary and Financial Alternatives. I am also a venture capitalist and an adviser to Fintech startups. I am honored to be here today. It is not just my titles or expertise that makes my testimony unique. It is also because, as a new immigrant to this land of opportunity, I know personally what it is like to be credit invisible, to build credit from scratch, and to dispute an error. I also know how empowering access to credit can be. My wife and I once had to choose between groceries and prescriptions. Thanks to access to credit scores, we were able to get low-cost loans to overcome those tough times.

My testimony will focus on the public credit bureau proposal. Before I begin, we should acknowledge that our consumer credit market, the largest and the most competitive in the world, depends on a functioning credit reporting industry. The other witnesses have correctly pointed out that the credit reporting industry has many issues, but the industry is not fundamentally broken. What it needs is appropriate policy interventions and more private-sector innovations to improve credit access, and also improve accuracy, security, transparency, and accountability.

There has been a sea change in the credit reporting industry in the last 10 years. Credit bureaus have been subject to CFPB supervision since 2012, and improving accuracy has been a top priority for them. The industry is also evolving as technology advances. New credit score models, such as Experian Boost and UltraFICO, allow consumers to use their on-time bill payment history to increase their FICO scores. Some lenders are also using cash-flow data to expand access to credit. Ten years ago, consumers could only obtain one copy of a free credit report every 12 months. Today, consumers who have an internet connection or a smartphone can get free credit reports and free credit scores easily. All of the policy goals outlined in the public credit bureau proposal can be adequately and effectively achieved by improving the existing system. In addition, I am also very concerned about the negative consequences of such a government-run credit bureau. First, the public credit bureau may pose a significant threat to consumers' privacy. The Federal Government will score everyone and maintain a huge database that monitors every aspect of our financial lives: how much we owe; from whom we can borrow; how much we pay; where we live; and for whom we work. Putting so much sensitive personal information in the hands of the government, especially when consumers have no way of opting out, should be a concern big enough to override any potential merits.

Second, the cost of setting up and running the public credit bureau needs to be seriously considered. The CFPB has a workforce of about 1,500 employees and an annual budget of around $600 million. The smallest national credit bureau employs over 8,000 people and has an annual operating cost of more than $2 billion. Those are not apples-to-apples comparisons, but they give us a sense of how much the Federal Government needs to be expanded to run the public credit bureau.

Finally, the public credit bureau will crowd out private investment and ultimately monopolize credit reporting. Competition will be reduced to zero, and innovation in expanding access to credit will cease to exist.

I have the following recommendations. First, refresh the FTC Accuracy Study. The landmark FTC Accuracy Study was done over 10 years ago. Much has changed, and a new study is long overdue.

Second, impose Federal supervision of data security. Credit bureaus should be held to the same standard as financial institutions when it comes to data security. Congress needs to act quickly.

Third, reform the dispute process. The dispute process should be made easy for consumers. Consumers should have the right to dispute directly with furnishers.

Finally, protect consumers' data rights under the Dodd-Frank Act, Section 1033. Consumer-permission data access is key to reducing racial disparities in credit. Unfortunately, many large financial institutions have too often illegally created obstacles to data access. It is imperative for the CFPB to write a pro-consumer, pro-competition, and pro-innovation rule.

Thank you for the opportunity to provide this information, and I welcome any questions that you may have.

[The prepared statement of Mr. Quan can be found on page 100 of the appendix.]

Chairwoman WATERS. Thank you very much. Ms. Wu, I am deeply concerned about the effects of this devastating pandemic on homeowners and other consumers, especially those who are not able to dispute inaccuracies and errors on their credit reports. In my opening statement, I discussed the letter I received from a man in Ohio who lost his job, couldn't keep paying his bills, and, as a result, saw his credit score drop.

But it is not just him. Let me give two more examples from consumers from my home State of California, who recently submitted complaints to the CFPB about these issues. The first is a homeowner whose mortgage showed up on credit reports as, "deferred," because of COVID. The consumer said they did not sign up for payment assistance, and their bank confirmed that the account was current.

Another person complained about the lack of response from the credit reporting agency, saying, "I have been filing disputes with all of the credit bureaus, and I am getting nowhere. With COVID going on, I understand that things are taking longer, but this is not right. I am trying to clean up my credit, and I am getting the run-around from the bureau."

Ms. Wu, in your experience, how do these types of errors and inaccuracies affect a consumer's ability to access credit?

Ms. WU. Thank you, Madam Chairwoman. These types of errors you describe can be devastating to a consumer's ability to access credit. They can cost thousands, if not deny them the ability to get credit or even a job or an apartment. There are a lot of them. The reason I think you see a doubling of complaints about credit reporting to the CFPB is because of these very issues caused by the pandemic—consumers getting forbearances, but being wrongfully reported or not even getting them and being reported for a forbearance.

That is why we had advocated for a moratorium on negative reporting during the pandemic, just recognizing the devastating economic consequences. The House passed that in the HEROES Act, but unfortunately, the Senate didn't. On a long-term basis, we need the ability for consumers to dispute errors, and then, if they can't get them fixed because the credit bureaus automatically defer to the information providers, the furnishers, we need a right of appeal or an ombuds function and a right of injunctive relief to fix those credit reports.

Chairwoman WATERS. Thank you. Mr. Greer, in your testimony, you describe the current credit reporting system as a tool for social gatekeeping, used not only as the basis for credit and lending decisions, but a system that also is used by companies making employment decisions, landlords considering prospective tenants, and insurance companies practicing their policies, while individuals are held to account every time they miss a payment, and even see their credit score drop when they shop for credit.

The big credit reporting agencies have skirted responsibility time and time again for their misdeeds, as recently shown by increasing complaints to the Consumer Financial Protection Bureau in litigation during the pandemic.

Mr. Greer, given the system's impact, do you think Congress really needs to consider bold reforms, such as creating a public credit reporting agency that consumers could choose to use as an alternative to the private credit bureaus who profit off the use of their data? You heard what the opposite side was saying about how the government should not be in this business at all. Tell me what you think?

Mr. GREER. Thank you, Chairwoman Waters. I think the credit score and our credit record has become much more than a tool to use to determine whether you can purchase a mortgage or whether you can get a credit card. It has become a tool that is used to decide whether to offer employment, or to rent a car, or whether you can get a cellphone. If you are a domestic violence victim, could you get a cellphone to protect yourself from your batterer? It has taken a huge, important, and central piece of our daily lives. And because of that, entrusting it in the hands of private-sector people who are responsible to their shareholders and to their customers, and the customers are not us—e are not the customers; we are the product. The data that we provide is the product that they sell, and they sell it to financial institutions, which is why it is so important that we have a customer-centric institution.

And I think the idea around putting it in the Federal Government's hands is a good one to protect consumers, and to protect us so that we can operate within society, in the credit markets, in the employment markets, and in the rental markets. So, I think that this is critically important. Thank you.

Chairwoman WATERS. Thank you very much. A few more seconds are left here. I think one of the most egregious problems with this is deciding whether or not someone is employable, and who is impacted by that?

Mr. GREER. It is Black and Brown communities. It is communities of color. It exacerbates the barriers that communities of color already face in the employment market, whether it is criminal history backgrounds, whether it is the neighborhoods they live in, ability to get transportation to work, but then you add this on top of it. And with all of the disparities that Ms. Wu and Ms. Traub have talked about, it really drives those disparities.

Chairwoman WATERS. Thank you so very much. The gentleman from North Carolina, Mr. McHenry, who is the ranking member of the committee, is now recognized for 5 minutes.

Mr. MCHENRY. Well, let's go fix the problem. Let's not create a new problem. Mr. Quan, my question for you is, this is all about creating a government-run credit reporting bureau. That is exactly what this hearing is about. You want a government-run agency. Instead of seeing three large credit information furnishers operating as an oligopoly, you are going have a monopoly with a government agency. And rather than having three different sets to compare, as imperfect and in need of reform as it is, the idea that you are going to say, we have a problem because we have three different credit reporting agencies, and now we are going to have one, and it is going to be the government, who are you going to sue when the government puts the screws to you? Good luck with that, right? I see this as a problem, not that the challenges outlined by this panel aren't, in fact, the things that we need to address.

I think addressing it by just shoving it into a government agency is going to make things worse, not better, for my constituents and for my colleagues' constituents, regardless of what you look like. A credit score if you are poor is a bad thing across-the-board, so we need to get at the root causes of this, and we need better data provided. We have heard from the panel, and they said, let's use alternative data. I agree. We can do that in a bipartisan way. We can, in fact, make it law.

But instead, if you want this to be a government takeover, and that is what the whole debate is about, and you are not going to have any discussion about what Republicans have offered as a solution, then we are going to have a standstill here. Nothing got done last Congress on this. Nothing is going to get done this Congress on it because there is no willingness to have a bipartisan conversation about the things that are achievable in a bipartisan way.

Mr. Quan, your written testimony outlines major flaws in the concept of a government bureau being the arbiter of credit. Highlight your primary concern with that, if you would?

Mr. QUAN. Thank you, Congressman. As I have outlined in my written testimony, all of the notable policy goals in the public credit bureau proposal can be effectively achieved by reforming the industry today. We have the most competitive credit market in the world, and this industry is not broken. It has many issues. And in addition to failing to achieve these goals or, to put it another way, by more effectively achieving these goals by reforming the existing industry, I think the public credit bureau proposal has the following major problems.

First, intrusion of privacy. So, we now have a government that can really monitor every aspect of our financial lives. That is a huge concern. And if we think the government already knows too much or enough about us, I think this bureau is going to make things even worse.

When we talk about the cost and the potential waste of spending—I already mentioned some big numbers in my oral statement. Let me give you a few more numbers. According to a research firm, Standish Group, they found out between 2003 and the end of 2012, only 6.4 percent of the large Federal IT projects succeeded. Fifty-two percent were over budget, delayed, or didn't meet expectations. The other 41.4 percent were complete failures. And we have learned enough from the recent rollout of the vaccine appointment system, which the Federal Government spent $44 million on, and it never even worked, not to mention the continuously poor quality in Federal student loan servicing, and more than 10 years ago, the botched rollout of Healthcare.gov.

Mr. MCHENRY. Okay. Mr. Quan, to that point, cyberattacks are also a major issue with Federal databases. We have seen this as Federal employees, and former government employees who may be on the panel, or employees of Executive Branch agencies have had their data stolen. So, the idea that a government agency doing this will be a better steward of our data is quite questionable given the track record the Federal Government. Additionally, I think we all can agree the procurement process for IT and technology for the Federal Government needs reform as well.

So, we have a whole set of issues that are quite challenging to create a database like this before you even talk about the question of its level of security, before you talk about the cost. And I think there are enough questions here that—what I would offer to my Democrat colleagues is what I offered last Congress. Let's try to do the work that is bipartisan, that we can achieve in this sphere and make things better. Even if you still have your goal of a public credit registry, which I completely disagree with, let's do the things that are a modest improvement or a significant improvement for our constituents, that are achievable today. And I think we have some ideas put forward to the panel and I would love to have that bipartisan cooperation here in this committee.

And with that, I yield back.

Chairwoman WATERS. Thank you very much. The gentlewoman from New York, Ms. Velazquez, who is also the Chair of the House Committee on Small Business, is now recognized for 5 minutes.

Ms. VELAZQUEZ. Thank you, Madam Chairwoman. Ms. Wu, the CFPB began handling consumer complaints about the credit reporting agencies (CRAs) in 2012. Since that time, complaints about the CRAs continue to be one of the largest categories of complaints handled by the CFPB. For example, in 2020, the CFPB handled about 532,000 complaints, approximately 58 percent of which were regarding the CRAs, which was the largest category of complaints reviewed by the CFPB. What do you think such a consistently high number of complaints, year over year, says about the state of this industry?

Ms. WU. Thank you, Congresswoman. I think it says exactly what the title of this hearing says, which is that the credit reporting system is broken, and it is biased, and it needs fundamental reform. I think that is why we need a public credit registry option. The bill discussion draft makes it an option so that consumers have true, meaningful choices. If they don't like the credit bureaus because they commit so many errors and have for decades, they have the choice of a public option.

To address some of the points before about cybersecurity, are we forgetting about the Equifax data breach 4 years ago, how one of these credit bureaus lost or let hackers take the personal information of half of the American adult population? In terms of privacy, our data is with three private corporations that monetize and exploit it and don't do a very good job of making sure it is accurate, as seen by all of those complaints.

Ms. VELAZQUEZ. Thank you. I have other questions.

Ms. WU. Okay. Sorry.

Ms. VELAZQUEZ. Ms. Wu and Ms. Traub, one of my biggest frustrations with the CRAs is that they have developed a system where the consumer has little to no control. Consumers never directly sign up as a customer. They have no control over whether a furnisher provides their information to a CRA, and they cannot stop doing business with the CRA if they are dissatisfied or simply choose to opt out. Both of your organizations have supported the idea of a public CRA. Can each of you explain why you favor such a proposal and how a public CRA will provide more accountability and transparency, and provide the customer with a fairer and more beneficial system?

Ms. TRAUB. Thank you, Congresswoman. It is absolutely true that the private system is failing us, and Dēmos has proposed a public credit registry. Since consumers are not the customers of the private credit reporting agencies, we have no way to demand fairness or accountability through the market. Consumers can't opt out of the system. So, the three private credit reporting agencies really have consumers at their mercy. They have this arbitrary, unaccountable power over our financial destinies. A public credit registry, why we support it, is because it is a way to take that power for consumers, and make sure the credit reporting operates in the public interest with a lot of mechanisms for public accountability, not government control.

A transparent process for credit scoring is one important element of that. That doesn't mean everyone knows your credit score. It means everyone knows how credit scores are determined, a dispute resolution process that actually enables consumers to present evidence and see the evidence on the other side, and, as a last resort, the right to take the public registry to court over errors, as well as enhanced accountability from companies that furnish the data to the public credit registry.

Ms. VELAZQUEZ. Thank you. Ms. Traub, as you know, many low- or moderate-income (LMI) communities and communities of color access credit from alternative financial servic providers. Unfortunately, however, many alternative financial services providers do not report positive credit payments to the credit reporting agencies. Can you explain how consumers who access credit from these markets fail to gain the benefit of making positive payments, and how this can hurt them in the long run?

Ms. TRAUB. Absolutely. Thank you, Congresswoman. Right now, many types of alternative credit sources do not report, and, therefore, when people are paying their cellphone bill on time, or a payday loan on time, that doesn't turn into positive credit in the way that paying a mortgage on time would. Our proposal for a public credit registry allows consumers to opt into other types of reporting, other types of payment history. We think it is important that consumers be able to opt in because there are cases when—

Mr. PERLMUTTER. [presiding]. The gentlewoman's time has expired. We will let you either answer that in writing or somebody else will let you finish your answer.

Ms. TRAUB. Thank you.

Mr. PERLMUTTER. The Chair will now recognize the gentlewoman from Missouri, Mrs. Wagner.

Mrs. WAGNER. I thank the Chair.

Mr. Quan, what would happen to the availability and the cost of credit if we eliminated entire categories of debt from credit scores?

Mr. QUAN. Thank you, Congresswoman. That is an excellent question.

The way and the reason we have the most competitive consumer credit market is because the lenders have as much information, as accurate as possible, about the consumer. If we eliminate accurate information—while some information may be negative, may be detrimental to individual consumers, depending on the circumstances, but regardless, it is accurate—lenders would not be able to make the best lending decisions. As a result, the cost of credit will increase for everybody, and availability of credit will decrease for everyone.

Mrs. WAGNER. Thank you. Should the goal of reform be to increase the number of qualified borrowers or to lower the bar so low that it jeopardizes the system for others?

Mr. QUAN. Of course, it has to be the former, not the latter.

Mrs. WAGNER. Generally speaking, do you believe that competition creates better products and generates better outcomes for consumers?

Mr. QUAN. Of course. Without competition, lenders will have no interest in improving their products or lowering the cost. With competition, we have more expanded access to credit. More consumers can qualify for credit.

Mrs. WAGNER. Now, knowing that competition benefits the consumer, which is what is very important to my constituents in the Second District—again, cost and access—tell me, how does a one-size-fits-all, government-run credit bureau benefit the credit system or the consumer?

Mr. QUAN. Since we are talking about competition, we have heard the words, "opt in," right? So, if the consumer doesn't like how they are treated by the private credit bureau, they can opt into the government's credit bureau, which supposedly is better.

But here's the thing: A government credit bureau is backed by unlimited taxpayers' money, revenue. Private bureaus have to answer to shareholders.

They don't have unlimited financial resources. So, at the end of the day, this is not an opt-in system.

If we are not happy with the current situation of the three major national credit bureaus dominating the credit reporting industry, and we have a government-run bureau, at the end of the day, there will be only one bureau, which is a public bureau, and there will be no competition whatsoever.

Mrs. WAGNER. I agree wholeheartedly. What would you recommend as an alternative to the bills being proposed today, that would improve cybersecurity, reduce data errors, and bring about a more inclusive credit system?

Mr. QUAN. I do think regarding accuracy—we have heard all these stories from consumer groups and from the industry. And frankly, the most authoritative study on accuracy was done over 10 years ago. Many things have changed.

It is imperative that we have another study be done, either by the CFPB or by the FTC. Without evidence, we cannot make the policy. So, that is number one.

Number two, I think we should increase competition. I mentioned that technology innovation can help. I mentioned that in my last recommendation, which is that the CFPB should write a proconsumer 1033 rule. That rule will open up the opportunity for consumers to furnish their own payments data, which is not allowed currently in most cases in credit bureau furnishing. So, if that data can be used in credit underwriting, we will see more consumers potentially qualify for credit and for affordable credit.

Mrs. WAGNER. Thank you, Mr. Quan, for your very specific analysis and the alternatives that you have offered here today. I agree that if the government takes this over, we will have just a one-size-fits-all, government-run system. Competition is needed in this space, and I thank you very much for your input here today.

And I yield back. Thank you.

Mr. QUAN. Thank you.

Mr. PERLMUTTER. The gentlelady yields back. The gentleman from Georgia, Mr. Scott, who is also the Chair of the House Agriculture Committee, is now recognized for 5 minutes.

Mr. SCOTT. Thank you very much.

Perhaps the most paralyzing issue in this that we can address quickly, coming up with some answers, deals with student loan debt. And Mr. Greer, I have looked at recent data from the Student Borrower Protection Center. You may be familiar with that. It shows a widening gap between private student loan usage and outcomes between Black and White borrowers.

Black students, it says, are 4 times as likely to struggle with repayment of private student debt in comparison to their White peers, despite being less than half as likely to take out a private student loan. That is why I say the student loan issue is one—and I might just refer to some of the comments from the other side— but this is a very serious racial issue. The impact this has on a young borrower's credit score can—and does—have long-term consequences, such as making it more difficult to get a job, buy a car, or own a home. This is a paralyzing issue.

Mr. Greer, I found it interesting in your testimony—here is what you said. You said that the current system overlooks many in our community because their monthly expenses do not go toward a more traditional credit product like a home or a credit card. They don't have them. And it penalizes consumers for holding less traditional credit products or bad debt, such as unpaid student loan debt.

So, Mr. Greer, can you explain why unpaid student loans, particularly private student loan debt, even when a borrower is current on that loan, is viewed by creditors as bad, and continues to be used as a driving factor in limiting creditworthiness, especially for Black borrowers?

Mr. GREER. Thank you, Mr. Scott, for that question. It is such an important issue, and I do want to acknowledge the work that Dēmos has done on student loan debt and raising up those racial disparities that you talked about, Mr. Scott. It all comes down to, the credit bureaus treat student loan debt, because it can't be offloaded through bankruptcy in the worst case, as more harmful in their algorithms.

And I will give you a little anecdote of my own. My wife and I wanted to buy our first home, and this was about 15 years ago. We were working with our mortgage lender, and they said, "I could get you a better rate if you make a huge payment on your student loans."

Well, we didn't have a lot of money. That came out of our savings. We had to pull that money out of our savings. And so, we had to make a choice between pulling money out of savings that would have went into the home equity of the house versus making a payment to a student loan company in order to get a better interest rate.

Those are the types of difficult decisions that these credit bureaus place on consumers, that actually cut at the wealth of people who are in the housing market or people who are looking to start a business or many of the other wealth-building activities for which people need access to credit.

So, thank you very much, Mr. Scott, for raising this because it is such a critical issue and a huge problem within the system.

Mr. SCOTT. Thank you very much.

Mr. PERLMUTTER. The gentleman yields back. The gentleman from Florida, Mr. Posey, is now recognized for 5 minutes.

Mr. POSEY. Thank you very much, Mr. Chairman.

Mr. Quan, can you please explain why the information provided by credit reporting agencies is essential to the efficient functioning of lending markets?

Mr. QUAN. Thank you, Congressman Posey, for the question. Lenders need information to underwrite consumers. The information housed in the three credit bureaus, in any credit bureau, is essential for lenders to make the right decision. All of these decisions are based on the risks that they perceive. Or in other words, they have to project the likelihood of the consumer's ability or willingness to pay the debt once they loan the money.

So, the information is essential. That is why it is important to have accurate information in the database, and it is also as important to have complete information in those databases. And when I say, "accurate," it means both positive and negative. Negative information is bad for the consumer in terms of getting credit or getting an affordable interest rate. But for the entire system, negative information, if it is accurate, is very important.

Mr. POSEY. Thank you. Mr. Quan, the title of this hearing is, "A Biased, Broken System: Examining Proposals to Overhaul Credit Reporting to Achieve Equity." Does this make sense as a policy criteria for objectives for regulating the credit reporting system? What should the objectives be?

Mr. QUAN. I think both the Democrats and the Republicans have the same objective, which is, we want to make sure we have a fair system for everybody, regardless of your gender, your color, or your religion. Everyone, if they can qualify for credit, should be able to get credit.

But obviously, we are taking different approaches here. We believe, and I believe, the current system is flawed, but it is not broken. And it will be far more effective and more cost-effective to improve, to reform the current system than to tear it down and build a new one.

Mr. POSEY. Thank you. Last year, you wrote an article commenting on the President's proposal to create a public option at the Consumer Financial Protection Bureau for credit reporting. Would you share your views on that topic with us, please?

Mr. QUAN. Yes. As I have already shared in my written testimony, as well as in my oral statement, I think that is a proposal that is going to be very,

very costly to taxpayers, and more importantly, it is not going to effectively fix the problems.

And frankly, this is not an opinion of more market-driven people like me. Even Georgetown Professor Adam Levitin, who is a very well-known scholar in the legal field on consumer finance issues, wrote a blog post earlier this year questioning the viability of a public credit bureau. All of the problems we have today will not be fixed by a public credit bureau.

Mr. POSEY. Thank you. Do you think the current credit reporting system operates with intentional bias to exclude certain groups from accessing credit?

Mr. QUAN. I would not say they have this intention to exclude people of color. We do have a problem, which is that 45 million Americans, many of them probably disproportionately Blacks and Hispanics and people of color, don't have access to credit because they don't even have a file in these databases.

That is why it is important for all of us to have a very conducive environment to promote and to facilitate innovation. And innovation is already happening. In my written statement, I already mentioned UltraFICO and Experian Boost. They are allowing consumers to furnish their payments data from utility bills and streaming subscriptions to credit bureaus to be factored into their FICO scores. And we have seen from Experian Boost that 69 million points have been boosted.

Mr. POSEY. You have advocated for innovation in financial markets, including Federal reporting, especially the incorporation into credit files of new data sources to help the, "credit invisibles," get access to credit. Could you please tell us how the private sector is responding to this challenge and what could be done to encourage even greater innovation?

Mr. QUAN. Sure, yes. I just mentioned there is UltraFICO. There is Experian Boost. And this innovation would not take place if we didn't have open banking or open finance in the United States. Or more specifically, consumers must have the right to permit third parties to have access to the bank account data, such that the data can be used in a credit scoring system.

And we have seen other innovations here. I can give you two more examples—

Mr. POSEY. I am going to thank you. My time has run out, Mr. Quan. Thank you very much.

Mr. QUAN. Yes, thank you.

Mr. PERLMUTTER. Mr. Posey's time has expired. The gentleman from Texas, Mr. Green, who is also the Chair of our Subcommittee on Oversight and Investigations, is recognized for 5 minutes.

Mr. GREEN. Thank you very much, Mr. Chairman. I greatly appreciate the opportunity to be heard, and I greatly appreciate the staff for what they have done to assist with what I am about to bring to the attention of our committee.

H.R. 123, the Alternative Data for Additional Credit FHA Pilot Program Reauthorization Act, is something with which we were successful. It became Section 2124 of the Housing and Economic Recovery Act of 2008. It did not get funded, and as a result, we are bringing this back, because we believe this is something that should be funded, and it will be of great benefit.

And I am appealing to all of my Republican friends across the aisle from me, all of them, I am willing to work with all or anyone who would like to work with me on this. I am very much interested in being bipartisan, very much interested in working with people, regardless of who they are. So if someone would like to work with me on this project, I would greatly appreciate your making yourself known to me.

More specifically, we know that in this country, depending on who is counting and how you count, we have about 45 million people who are credit invisible or unscorable. And as a result, they don't get the opportunity to make the purchases that many of us take for granted.

This piece of legislation would allow your utilities—light bill, gas bill, water bill, phone bill, cable bill—to be scored. Mr. Greer, you have spoken of this, of these utilities being scored. This bill allows you to opt in and score these utilities. And if they benefit you, then you can take advantage of that benefit and have the credit that most of us take for granted.

Mr. Greer, H.R. 123, give me your thoughts on what I am sharing with you at this time in terms of doing this, making this change such that we can do this with HUD. HUD would have the pilot program, and we would use a commercially-available credit reporting model. Your thoughts, Mr. Greer?

Mr. GREER. Thank you, Mr. Green, for raising that, and for your work on this important issue.

I say, one, you emphasize the importance of opting in. I think that is a big, important point and that consumers should have the choice around what data is being used to assess their credit score. The second point I would like to make is that this conversation about alternative data is already a part of the system. It is just that the negative stuff is what is being reported. If you don't pay your utility bill, it gets reported. If you don't pay your cell phone bill, it gets reported.

What I would like to see is if we are going to use alternative data, let's make sure that we are bringing in the positive payments. Because if I miss a payment on my utility bill, my utility gets cut off, I am going to get dinged for that. But what is not going to show up is the many months beforehand that I paid my utility bill on time.

And I think that it is important that we opt in and that we make sure that we are reporting the positive activity that is happening with people, in addition to the negative activity that is already being reported.

Mr. GREEN. And let me add something. We would also want to make sure that people understand that this is additional credit, not just alternative, meaning we will take this in lieu of other things. This is additional credit that can be added to your credit score to help you.

Ms. Traub, would you comment on this as well, because you did bring up the need for this type of credit score?

Ms. TRAUB. Yes, I think it is important that consumers be able to opt in to using alternative types of data, as Mr. Greer said. I also think that a public credit registry could look into which types of data it is inappropriate to include.

For example, medical debt has been shown—and we should do more studies to show this more conclusively—not to be predictive of people's ability to pay other types of debt. When someone takes on a mortgage or a credit card, they have a chance to think about, what are the terms, do I want to take on this debt?

When you are sick or your child is sick and needs medical care, needs to go into the hospital, you don't how much it is going to cost. You may not care how much it is going to cost at that point; you just want your loved one to get the care they need and be okay. And then, you are saddled with hundreds, thousands, maybe even millions of dollars in medical debt. Should that go on your credit report?

Mr. GREEN. My time is about to expire, ma'am. Let me just ask you, without question, reservation, or hesitation, do you agree that additional credit scoring is important, what you call an alternative credit scoring?

Ms. TRAUB. Yes. I think we need to look at different things that should be included and excluded from credit scores to make them more fair and predictive.

Mr. GREEN. Okay. Thank you very much.

I yield back the balance of my time. I believe my time is over.

Mr. PERLMUTTER. The gentleman's time has expired, and he yields back. The gentleman from Missouri, Mr. Luetkemeyer, is now recognized for 5 minutes.

Mr. LUETKEMEYER. Thank you, Mr. Chairman.

It is interesting that we believe that the government can do something better than the private sector. I heard several of the witnesses today talk about all of the errors that are made by the private sector credit bureaus, and I am not defending them. They are not perfect. They are human. They make errors.

But if you believe the government is going to make less errors than the private sector, which has to be responsible for being able to have good information and can be sued for it, which the government cannot, you are either naive or misinformed or worse. And I can tell you right now, as the ranking member on the House Small Business Committee, the Paycheck Protection Program (PPP), which was administered through the banks, had huge, huge advantages over the Economic Injury Disaster Loan (EIDL) program. With the EIDL program, which is completely administered by the SBA, almost a third, a third of the loans are fraudulent.

If you expect the government to be able to put together a program that is going to be error-free, you are on the wrong planet. Along that line, the government is going to have more errors, I believe.

Mr. Quan, I have a question for you on this. Listen very carefully. I believe the information you are going to get is very poor information because it is not going to be complete. Government delays everything. Think IRS. Do they do anything in a timely fashion? No.

This is another agency that is going to be rife with fraud, rife with delays, with incompetent and incomplete information, old data, delays in getting it fixed. And what does that mean? That means if you are a lender, are you going to rely on this information? I don't think so.

If you are a lender, if you rely on just this agency alone, because it is poor information, I would think you are going to increase the cost of the loans you make on this information and probably have less access to credit.

Mr. Quan, am I wrong?

Mr. QUAN. You are absolutely right, Congressman.

Mr. LUETKEMEYER. Thank you for that.

Along the lines of, why would anybody want to do this, why would we want the government to get into having more information like this, Ms. Traub gave us the answer. She said it is about control. Control of what? Control of information. Control of who gets loans, who gets financed.

Guess what? Again, think IRS. You are using and weaponizing another agency here against people whom they disagree with either politically or for any other reason.

Think Operation Choke Point. Here we go again. The government is picking winners and losers and picking out people who may be doing nothing wrong. They have a legal business, have a legal right to access to credit, and yet the government is getting in the middle of this and scoring them in a way that is detrimental to their ability to get loans and whatever.

Am I wrong on that, Mr. Quan?

Mr. QUAN. You are also absolutely right.

Mr. LUETKEMEYER. Thank you very much for that.

The other thing I want to talk about here a little bit is lenders. We are talking about credit scores this morning. Why? Because people need access to credit. The lenders need this information to be able to judge accordingly whether somebody is worthy of loaning money, be it for a home, a car, a business, or whatever. They assess risk. The interest rate is always reflective of risk. And the more information they have, the better they can assess the risk.

If the lenders have an incomplete amount of information, this is why you see the private sector credit bureaus trying to find more ways right now, even though they are not required to take some of these different things like rent payments, utility payments, telecom payments, service streaming payments.

Those are all being used right now by a lot of the different private-sector folks to assess risk, to be able to assess an individual's ability to get credit. Those are important things. I support those. We had a bill out of here not too long ago, a year or two ago, that actually increased that. I supported that. I think it is a good idea. The more information you have, the better the lenders can look at an individual and assess that risk and give people more access to credit. It is very important.

So, at the end of the day, it is behooving to the lenders to be able to get as much information as possible, and it is behooving to the private sector folks because they are in competition against each other—believe it or not, they are in competition because lenders pick and choose which one of these they want—to be able to get as much information as possible, and who can be more predictive about the ability of somebody to pay back that loan.

That is a really, really important thing, and I think we are missing the point when we are sitting here looking at the individual. The reason the individual wants this information out there is so they have access to credit, and we have forgotten all about that.

When you give that information to the government to allow them to oversee all this, you have just opened a whole other can of worms, and I think you really have denigrated the individual's ability to get access to credit.

With that, I see my time is up, so I yield back.

Mr. PERLMUTTER. The gentleman yields back. The gentleman from California, Mr. Sherman, who is also the Chair of our Subcommittee on

Investor Protection, Entrepreneurship, and Capital Markets, is now recognized for 5 minutes.

Mr. SHERMAN. Thank you, Mr. Chairman.

I join with Mr. Luetkemeyer at least in being a bit concerned about a Federal credit reporting agency. That concern is borne in part by my former chairmanship of the Asia Subcommittee, where we see the Communist government of China creating a social credit score based on politics. As much as I fear and I am concerned about what the credit rating agencies can do to consumers, I am even more concerned about what the government can do. I am also concerned about any bill that would take a system where the banks pay and instead provide the service for free or at the cost of taxpayers.

We in Congress and the Federal Government have had an eviction moratorium, so people who couldn't pay their rent didn't, and thank God, they are not homeless.

Mr. Ejaz, are these people going to have terrible credit reports because landlords are reporting their failure to pay rent in a way that hurts their credit score?

Mr. EJAZ. Thank you so much for your question.

For part of my answer, I will defer to Chi Chi Wu, but we at Consumer Reports are concerned that when the relief that was passed with the Coronavirus Aid, Relief, and Economic Security (CARES) Act and all of the policies that were passed in order to address consumer concerns during COVID-19, when those expire, consumers' credit reports may be affected significantly.

Ms. Wu actually—and I will pass it to her—called this the, "pandemic paradox," where scores have somewhat stayed afloat throughout COVID-19, but once relief expires for folks, we will start seeing the impact on folks' credit reports, and it is best to get as ahead of that as we can.

Mr. SHERMAN. I have put forward proposed revisions that we have not passed to say that those who couldn't pay because of COVID should not have their credit scores reduced, and I think that we do need to revisit that if—but I want to go on to another question.

And that is, we have this recent lawsuit against TransUnion for inaccurately reporting that certain individuals are on the Office of Foreign Assets Control's (OFAC's) Specially Designated Nationals and Blocked Persons List. It is usually called the, "terrorist watchlist."

Now, it is one thing when a credit rating agency says that someone didn't pay a medical bill. Okay, they may get confused. They may make a mistake.

Things happen. But when you incorrectly report that they are on the terrorist watchlist, that is a much bigger deal.

Unfortunately, the court, throughout the lawsuit, claimed that only plaintiffs concretely harmed by the defendant's statutory violation have Article III standing. And of course, many in the class did have that concrete harm, but many others that were in the class did not.

Ms. Wu, did TransUnion violate the Fair Credit Reporting Act by stating that Mr. Ramirez was on the terrorist watchlist?

Ms. WU. Absolutely, TransUnion did. They failed to use reasonable procedures by tagging an innocent man as a potential terrorist. But the Supreme Court said that even though TransUnion violated the Fair Credit Reporting Act, those consumers for whom the information wasn't shown to a third party, couldn't even get through the courthouse doors, and this was a California lawsuit. That is why we think Congress needs to provide for injunctive relief, ecause the court did say if there is injunctive relief, that might be a way to get through the courthouse doors.

Mr. SHERMAN. So, the court said that if they had added something erroneous to your report, but nobody had seen it, then, you couldn't have a day in court?

Ms. WU. That is correct. You could get it, and you could panic, and say, "Oh, my God. They think I am a terrorist."

Mr. SHERMAN. Right.

Ms. WU. But there was no remedy.

Mr. SHERMAN. No remedy for the psychological harm unless there is, in fact, defamation communicated to a third party?

Ms. WU. That is correct.

Mr. SHERMAN. Again, if this was accusing people of not paying a medical bill, that is one thing. With the terrorist list, you have to be a lot more careful. And I should point out that people of certain ethnic and religious groups are the ones who are going to have the names that are going to be on the list. So, this did not affect people randomly in our society. This affected anybody who has a name that is similar to another name.

Mr. PERLMUTTER. The gentleman's time has expired.

Mr. SHERMAN. I yield back.

Mr. PERLMUTTER. The gentleman yields back. The gentleman from Michigan, Mr. Huizenga, is recognized for 5 minutes.

Mr. HUIZENGA. Thank you, Mr. Chairman. I appreciate it.

Mr. Quan, I am just wondering, can you give us a sense of the overall trend of credit scores, especially during the pandemic?

Mr. QUAN. Thank you, Congressman.

Overall, I think that Experian has reported that during the pandemic, because of the CARES Act interventions, consumers' credit scores actually have increased slightly by, I think 7 points.

Mr. HUIZENGA. Okay. So, we didn't see them erode. We actually potentially saw them increase a bit, correct?

Mr. QUAN. Correct. And also, we are seeing some kind of deleveraging, especially in credit card debt. So, people are paying off their debt because of the government assistance.

Mr. HUIZENGA. And somewhat, it may be argued and pointed out, limited opportunities to go out and actually spend money on anything. I think a lot of us were a little frustrated with that as well.

So, obviously, there are lots of calls for a government-run credit reporting bureau that somehow would increase competition and accountability. What is your take on that? Does it actually increase accountability and increase competition? I think that is one of the more bizarre claims.

Mr. QUAN. No. In terms of competition, no. There is not going to be an increase in competition, and it is actually more likely that competition will be reduced to zero. Again, as I said in my written testimony and also in my oral statement, the private sector has problems, of course, but they actually have this profit motive so that if they don't treat customers better, someone else may do a better job. The customers will go somewhere else.

And lenders need accurate information. So, it is not in anyone's interest to have inaccurate information. When you have a government bureau, there will be no competition, because they are backed by unlimited tax revenue, and the private sector cannot compete.

Mr. HUIZENGA. Yes, and obviously, nobody wants inaccurate information. I find it fascinating, my predecessor's questioning about the no-fly list and the terrorist watchlist. Apparently, those on the other side had no qualms about having people on that when it was time to, oh, go purchase a weapon, for example. That seemed to go out the window. But as long as it was dealing with credit, now suddenly, they are very interested about who is falsely getting on that watchlist.

But, Mr. Quan, predictive data assists lenders in providing borrowers with access to affordable credit, and I am curious if you had discussed the consequences to consumers if a risk-based pricing system was rejected?

Mr. QUAN. Oh, there will be a disastrous outcome for every consumer, not just the low-income consumers who have difficulty in accessing credit. Risk-based pricing, basically what it means is the lenders allocate or make decisions on credit based on the risks they perceive. And this is how the private sector works. If you have a higher risk, that means you probably have a lower chance of paying me back. That is why as an investor, as a lender, I am going to have to charge you a higher rate to compensate for the risk I am taking.

And if we get rid of risk-based pricing, what is going to happen is lenders will have no incentive or interest in treating anyone who has more means to pay back or more willingness to pay back, and everyone will get charged the same price. At the end of the day, what we see is low availability of credit and higher cost of credit for everybody.

Mr. HUIZENGA. And let's take it one more step, okay? What about the regulators who go in to those lenders and have to look at the quality of their lending to determine whether they are in compliance or not? Has anybody looked at the effects that might have?

Mr. QUAN. That is a great point. I look at student loan lending, and the Federal Government hands out loans to anyone without even questioning whether they will have the ability to pay it back. So, the Federal Government essentially is the biggest subprime lender in this country.

If the Federal Government was supervised by the OCC or the FDIC or the Fed, it would fail the safety and soundness exam.

Mr. HUIZENGA. In my last 30 seconds here, do you have any confidence that the Federal Government is going to be able to keep all of this data secure? We saw that the Securities and Exchange Commission had a breach. They are now building the consolidated audit trail, which is going to hold all of our personally identifiable information.

There are a lot of people on both the left and the right, who have previously expressed doubt about the security of this information all being in one spot, basically one giant vault, which becomes a target. So, do you have any confidence about that?

Mr. QUAN. You said it very well. I have no confidence whatsoever.

Mr. HUIZENGA. Okay. My time has expired, and I yield back.

Mr. PERLMUTTER. The gentleman yields back. The gentleman from Missouri, Mr. Cleaver, who is also the Chair of our Subcommittee on Housing, Community Development, and Insurance, is now recognized for 5 minutes.

Mr. CLEAVER. Thank you very much, Mr. Chairman.

Mr. Ejaz, if given the choice, would you choose the University of Kansas (KU), or the University of Missouri (MU)?

Mr. EJAZ. Excellent question. I would choose MU any day.

Mr. CLEAVER. I know it is a difficult question, but I had to ask it.

Mr. EJAZ. Thank you.

Mr. CLEAVER. There are a lot of scoring models that use statistical analysis to assign a score to a person. One particular company used 50 versions, 50 versions of a score for a person that can be sent to lenders.

Does that make any sense at all, 50 different versions?

Mr. EJAZ. Thank you for your question.

It is true. There are so many different credit scores that any one person can have. The reason for this is because lending product categories can differ, and the private sector believes that different scores should be applied for different types of products. But it is true that the "credit score" that I think is in most people's head is more of an approximation of what the variety of your credit scores say, as opposed to being your true credit score.

Mr. CLEAVER. So what is the logical reason—this is to any of you—that we don't have a uniform system of creditworthiness?

Ms. WU. That is a great question, if I may, Congressman? It for sure confuses consumers that there are so many different kinds of scores out there. You have FICO. You have Vantage. You have different generations, different product types.

One thing a public credit registry option could do is give a standard score so that consumers know where they stand. And it gets even worse because the credit bureaus also sell these, "Fake-O scores," that no lenders use, and people get confused. They think they have one score, they go to buy a car, and their car loan rate is different.

So, certainly something a public credit registry could do is to standardize it so there is more clarity.

Mr. CLEAVER. Anybody else?

[No response.]

Mr. CLEAVER. Okay. That's fine. I wanted to move over to the credit invisibility to find out if there is anything that you would recommend to this committee that we need to do to help bring credit-invisible individuals into the scoring system, although it is messed up, too. But what would you recommend? Does anyone have any recommendations?

Mr. QUAN. Congressman Cleaver—

Ms. WU. If I may, Congressman? I think the thing that has been hammered on is consumer choice. One of the most important things about credit invisibility is consumers should have the choice to be able to supply their rental, cell phone payments, and bank account histories because the system for too long has stripped consumers of the ability to make the decision. The consumer should have the choice.

Alternative data can be helpful, but it can also be harmful. We have to proceed with caution. Some of the most promising data— and here is where, for example, Mr. Quan and I agree—is bank transaction data, because it can show ability-to-repay. It has a shorter timeframe, so you are not locked into that 7 years for bad credit information.

And one important thing is to give consumers control and the ability to share that when they want to, but turn it off when they don't.

Mr. QUAN. Congressman Cleaver, if I may jump in here, I, 100 percent, agree with Chi Chi on this issue. I think it is really about consumers' control. That is why I think it is very important that we have a functional open banking system in the United States, where consumers are in the center of the data flow, so they can consent, they can permit any third party that wants to have access to their data. So, they know exactly who is using their data, how long it is going to be there, and for what purposes.

All of the innovations in the private sector regarding using cashflow data, using bank transaction data, is already happening. But the key thing is really about having a good rule of the road, which, again, I am mentioning the CFPB here, but you have them write a pro-consumer, pro-innovation, open access 1033 rule.

Thank you.

Mr. CLEAVER. Thank you. I yield back, Mr. Chairman.

Mr. PERLMUTTER. The gentleman's time has expired. The gentleman from Kentucky, Mr. Barr, is now recognized for 5 minutes.

Mr. BARR. Thank you, Mr. Chairman.

Mr. Quan, I think you stated it well that the impact of eliminating risk-based pricing would have a very negative impact on low- and middle-income borrowers. It would eliminate access to credit and drive up the cost of credit. A recent study from the United States Chamber of Commerce corroborates your testimony and found that eliminating risk-based pricing and replacing it with a uniform pricing model would raise prices on consumers and limit the availability of credit and other financial services, especially to low- and middle-income borrowers.

And that makes sense, right? If lenders can't accurately predict a borrower's ability to repay, they need to raise prices or limit options to account for the increased uncertainty. A prohibition on using predictive data would not make the system more equitable but would instead dramatically exacerbate inequalities that the authors of these bills say that they want to fix.

Speaking of inequalities, Mr. Quan, are you aware of any of the three major private credit reporting bureaus using race-conscious criteria?

Mr. QUAN. No, I am not aware of that.

Mr. BARR. To your knowledge, is there any evidence to the contrary that these credit reporting bureaus use only race-neutral criteria, payment history and the like?

Mr. QUAN. That is my understanding, sir.

Mr. BARR. And yet, one of the Majority's witnesses says that the current system of private credit reporting bureaus is plagued with, "systemic racial inequity."

Let me ask you this question, Mr. Quan. How would excluding certain predictive credit data from credit reports harm a low-income, but financially responsible, African-American consumer with a high credit score?

Mr. QUAN. You really touch on a very important point. And I think I will also give the credit to the other witnesses, who are really highlighting the important fact that a lot of Americans, especially people of color, have challenges getting into the mainstream credit system. That is because you have to have credit in order to build credit. So, if you don't have credit, how can you build credit?

That is why it is important to have this new source of data, payment data, alternative data—rent payments, utility payments—for the lenders, available to lenders to use to bring access of credit to these people.

Mr. BARR. My point is that whether you are White, Black, or Hispanic, whatever your racial minority is, if these credit bureaus are using race-neutral criteria, and maybe you are a low-income individual, but if you pay your bills, and you have a positive credit score, a positive credit history, your credit score is going to be higher. And if you eliminate the risk-based pricing, the cost of credit is going to go up, and that is going to harm that borrower regardless of their racial profile. Isn't that correct?

Mr. QUAN. That is absolutely correct. It doesn't really matter what color your skin is, or what religion you believe in, if you can pay back the loans, your score will go up, if you pay back the loans on time.

Mr. BARR. Thank you, Mr. Quan. Let me ask you about this national credit bureau idea. We have talked about it ad nauseam here. But what incentives does a private credit reporting agency have in competition with other private credit reporting agencies to get credit data accurate and get it right?

Mr. QUAN. If the credit bureau cannot provide accurate data to lenders, lenders will stop using their services, period. Because what lenders want is really accurate data for them to make better lending decisions. So, there is a natural competition among the three bureaus to make sure the data is accurate.

Mr. BARR. And Mr. Quan, what incentives would a single government bureaucracy have to fix errors?

Mr. QUAN. I wouldn't even call it an incentive. It is just their ability. I am not a technologist here. So, whatever best method is available to the private sector, the government can use that, too. There is no reason for me to believe the government is able to do a better job in improving accuracy while the—if we believe accuracy is a big issue today.

Mr. BARR. And just one final question on this alternative data issue. Obviously, utilization of alternative data by these private credit reporting agencies is helping Americans gain access to credit. But I think I heard one of the other witnesses say that positive data should be reported, but not negative data reported. How would that impact the cost of credit if the data was only selected in that way?

Mr. QUAN. If we believe accuracy is important, accuracy means complete data, whether it is positive or negative. If you specifically ignore negative data, that is not accurate. So, we have to make sure we have accurate and complete data available for lenders.

Mr. BARR. Thank you. I yield back.

Mr. PERLMUTTER. The gentleman's time has expired. The gentlewoman from Ohio, Mrs. Beatty, who is also the Chair of our Subcommittee on Diversity and Inclusion, is recognized for 5 minutes. I think she just exited. We will go to Mrs. Beatty in a few minutes.

The gentleman from Illinois, Mr. Foster, is now recognized for 5 minutes.

Mr. FOSTER. Thank you, Mr. Chairman.

Your credit score is often one of the most important metrics affecting how you interact with the financial services industry. Particularly with respect to housing, which is a basic human need, your credit score affects your ability to rent or own a home. It determines whether or not you can finance a car or a home, and it is even examined by the State bar associations when law school graduates apply to become attorneys.

So despite the obvious great importance of your credit scores, a Consumer Reports survey indicates that 34 percent of Americans report finding errors in their credit profile. The Consumer Data Industry Association (CDIA), however, claims that figure to be false and boasts a 98 percent accuracy rate.

However, the studies cited by the CDIA, conducted by the FTC, and the Policy and Economic Research Council (PERC), seem to indicate t23.9 percent, and 19.1 percent error rates, respectively. And so, there are some significant disagreements over these accuracy figures. And I was wondering if anyone could speak on what really is the best knowledge on that?

Mr. EJAZ. I am happy to take that. I can start with it. And thank you for your question.

The PERC study was done in 2011. As well, the FTC study that we cited today, or the panel cited today, was done in 2012. And I absolutely join Mr. Quan in asking the FTC to take another look at this.

At Consumer Reports, we put out a survey that volunteers could fill out. And yes, 34 percent found at least one type of error. I still think that despite those other two studies being done almost 10 years ago, that there is still an indication of many, many problems, and I am sure Chi Chi can say more.

Ms. WU. Yes, if I could just make two points about these accuracy studies? Number one, whether it be 2 percent or 20 percent, when you talk about 200 million files, that is millions of people affected, so, even 2 percent would be 4 million people. The FTC found 5 percent, or 10 million people.

I agree that another study done by the FTC would be helpful, but we need reform now. The FTC study actually took almost 10 years because it was so complicated, and they wanted to do it right and systematically and rigorously. We can't wait 10 years for reform. American consumers can't spend the next 10 years continuing to be abused by the credit bureaus.

Mr. FOSTER. Thank you.

And now, when you look over the different types of errors that happen, one of the most common seems to be simply identity errors, where you are getting the wrong information about the—or the right information about the wrong person. For example, the Equifax website has a FAQ page called, "What can I do if I believe my credit file is mixed up with someone else's?" That leads me to believe, as well as hearing from my constituents, that there are identity errors.

Now, some States are rolling out something that many people feel will be transformative to eliminating not only identity errors, but also identify fraud, which is these mobile IDs, mobile driver's licenses sometimes, which allow you to download the information on your REAL ID-compliant driver's license onto your cell phone, and authenticate yourself online for any transaction.

And if we had a high-quality way of authenticating yourself when you enter into a contract, when you successfully pay, when you start a bank account, what fraction of the errors would go away if we had a high-quality digital ID in this country? Does anyone have a feeling for that?

Ms. WU. The issue with the credit bureaus and mixed files isn't just about what kind of identity. It is matching. It is how you make sure A matches to B. And the problem with the credit bureaus is that their matching criteria is overly loose. Social Security numbers are unique identifier numbers, but the credit bureaus use only 7 out of 9 digits, and they use a partial match of a name and a partial match of address.

So, that is how they have any two different people mixed up. You can have the most rigorous identification, but if you make your criteria too loose, you are going to mix people up. And they make the criteria too loose deliberately, because that is what lenders want. They would rather have false positives than false negatives. It is all about the incentives, and that is why it is important to have reform and a public credit registry option.

Mr. FOSTER. Yes. I think that what you really want here is accuracy. And if you look at countries like Estonia that have a highquality, secure, privacy-preserving digital ID, these problems largely disappear. And I think that we should join the States that are rolling out these advanced identity products which were also rolled out recently by Apple and Google Android as something that they will support, and this could be transformative at least in eliminating this class of identity errors from messing up a person's credit rating.

I hear the gavel, so I yield back.

Mr. PERLMUTTER. The gentleman's time has expired.

The gentleman from Texas, Mr. Williams, is recognized for 5 minutes.

Mr. WILLIAMS OF TEXAS. Thank you, Mr. Chairman.

I have bad news for everybody in here. I am a car dealer, I am a borrower, and I am also a lender. And I use risk-based pricing every single day. Making sure that we have a complete and accurate picture of an individual credit history allows us to offer the best rates possible to our customers.

If we begin to hide information, like we are talking about today, lenders like myself will be forced to price in this additional uncertainty that we might not get a return on capital, and the price of credit will go up for everybody.

The bottom line is, if you pay your bills, you have a good credit rating. If you don't pay your bills, you don't have a good credit rating.

I listened to Ms. Wu. She said that people have been abused for 50 years. I have been in business for 51 years, and I have never abused anybody.

I thank everybody for coming here today. Now, the response of my Democratic colleagues to problems within the big three credit reporting bureaus is to centralize power and to create a public option within the CFPB.

This belief that the Federal Government can somehow run a credit reporting agency more effectively and efficiently than the private sector is garbage. It is ridiculous. It is the Post Office. It is Amtrak. It is the Small Business Administration (SBA).

Not only will you force consumers to hand over all their data to the Federal Government, but it will also remove all incentives for the private sector to innovate and come up with new models that will better predict the creditworthiness of borrowers.

So Mr. Quan, quickly, can you discuss how the incentive structure we talked about today to compete and innovate would change for the private credit bureaus if a public option is created?

Mr. QUAN. Thank you, Congressman Williams. You are absolutely right. When the government takes over, there will be no incentive whatsoever for the private sector to compete with the government. They cannot compete and come up with better ways, and more innovations, because the government, again, would monopolize credit reporting, and there would be no competition. There would be no innovation whatsoever.

Mr. WILLIAMS OF TEXAS. And with no competition, the consumer is—

Mr. QUAN. Worse off.

Mr. WILLIAMS OF TEXAS. —put in a bad position.

If making it harder for the private sector to compete wasn't bad enough, placing this new public credit reporting agency within the CFPB is also extremely problematic, and it is just a ridiculous idea. Since its inception, my Republican colleagues and I have been pushing to reform this rogue agency and make it more accountable, whether by creating a bipartisan board so the CFPB is not run by a single director, providing greater clarity to their enforcement capabilities so that businesses are not penalized for practices that were never previously identified as illegal, or bringing the agency under the normal appropriations process.

All of these reforms have been blocked by the Democrats, which ensures that this agency will operate on a partisan basis for the foreseeable future. If the Democrats' proposal were to be signed into law and public options created within the CFPB, I am concerned that the new agency would be hijacked for partisan political objectives, such as removing all student loan information or unpaid medical debt from credit reports.

You borrow the money, so shouldn't you pay it back, for crying out loud? You tell the person, I am going to pay you back, but you don't want to pay it back.

So, Mr. Quan, given the discretion that the CFPB currently operates under, how would it be possible to ensure that this new public option would not be used for political purposes rather than working to ensure that lenders are provided with the best information available as they attempt to accurately price risk and give the customer the best price?

Mr. QUAN. Thank you, Congressman, for the question. I think it is best in the current system that lenders make the choice, make the decision of who they want to lend money to and at what cost, assuming, of course, that they follow the Equal Credit Opportunity Act (ECOA).

If we let the government dictate whom they should lend to, at best, the criteria for underwriting will be influenced by the Administration, whether it is Republican or Democrat. And at worst, the Federal Government will be deciding who is creditworthy.

I think this is the worst outcome. We have government decide who is worth credit, and the private market is the best way to advocate credit, not the government.

Thank you.

Mr. WILLIAMS OF TEXAS. In the end, the private sector will get it done better. The government will pick winners and losers. They do every single day, and it will trickle down into less product, higher prices for the consumer, and it will also go to less employees, and, again, the government control will be putting a stick in the economy. So, the private sector is much better.

I yield back. Thank you.

Chairwoman WATERS. Thank you.

The gentlewoman from Ohio, Mrs. Beatty, who is also the Chair of our Subcommittee on Diversity and Inclusion, is now recognized for 5 minutes.

Mrs. BEATTY. Thank you, Madam Chairwoman, and thank you to the witnesses and to my colleagues.

We have heard a lot today about credit unions and who is affected by credit reports and the data that is collected. The Consumer Financial Protection Bureau issued a report in 2014 entitled, "Consumer credit reports: A study of medical and non-medical collections."

In that report, the CFPB found that over 50 percent of credit reports that had collections were related to medical collections. We have also heard that most of those dollar amounts were somewhere around $200, and the highest were all under $490.

We also noticed that a company called NerdWallet compiled data from all of the Medicare compliance reviews of U.S. hospitals conducted by the Office of the Inspector General.

We found that almost 50 percent of Medicare medical claims contained medical errors that resulted in an overpayment of something like 26 to 27 percent. We have also heard that some individuals have said those numbers were closer to 70 or 80 percent.

So, Ms. Wu, with a system with error rates for medical debt so high, could the argument be made that it is not beneficial to include these debts at all in credit scores?

Ms. WU. Thank you for the question, Congresswoman, and absolutely, yes. The argument could be made that medical debt for medically-necessary services should not mess up anyone's credit report. People get sick. It is not under their control. It is bad enough that we have a health care system where people go into unmanageable debt just to stay alive and stay healthy. For it to mess up their credit reports is unconscionable.

Mrs. BEATTY. Thank you. I am also Chair of the Subcommittee on Diversity and Inclusion, and I spent the last 2 years advocating for companies to diversify their workforces and their senior leadership.

When I look at the three credit reporting agencies, they are a perfect example of why this work is so important.

So, Mr. Greer and Ms. Traub, I am going to ask you this question. When I look at TransUnion, only 9 percent of their senior leaders and 10 percent of their board are underrepresented minorities, and 30 percent are women, and we can keep going with Equifax and Experian, all the same. Even with Experian, astonishingly, they have virtually no racial diversity on their boards or in their senior leadership.

Several of our witnesses have discussed the inherent inequities that exist in the current credit reporting system. Do you believe that the makeup of the leaders of these companies has a direct effect on the inherent inequities in the credit reporting system?

Mr. Greer?

Mr. GREER. Yes. Thank you, Congresswoman Beatty.

I absolutely do. All of this conversation about accountability has been, who is more accountable to whom? I will say this, and I have been called naive many times; my wife and my son call me naive all the time.

But I would rather have this body hold some institution accountable, the folks on this dais up here, because the folks on this dais more accurately reflect the population of the people who are consumers in our marketplace than the shareholders and the people who run these companies. Nearly 90 percent of shareholders across our economy are White. And I haven't looked at Equifax, TransUnion, and Experian's shareholders but my guess is that it reflects that number.

Like I said, when we talk about accountability, the folks in this room are more accountable to the consumers who are impacted by these companies than the companies are themselves.

Mrs. BEATTY. Thank you. I think I only have 30 seconds left. Ms. Wu, can you explain to this committee why it is important to include a credit score with the annual credit report?

Ms. WU. Yes. Consumers should have access to free annual credit scores so they can see their standing, so that if they want to get a credit card, buy a car, get a mortgage, or even rent an apartment, because landlords use them, they know where they stand.

Mrs. BEATTY. Thank you. I have introduced a free credit score and consumer act. It is also in this comprehensive credit. So thank you, and I yield back.

Chairwoman WATERS. Thank you very much.

The gentleman from Arkansas, Mr. Hill, is now recognized for 5 minutes.

Mr. HILL. Thank you, Chairwoman Waters. Thanks for convening this hearing. And thank you for our panel's participation, both in person—and I'm delighted to be here in person—and online as well, and thanks for talking about the importance of the credit system and how that has enabled millions and millions of Americans over the past several decades to have more access to credit, and more opportunity to fulfill their lives with a home or a car or something that they need to benefit themselves.

So, our credit system is fundamental to our households having access to the credit they need for their future.

Mr. Quan, have credit reports helped more families have access to credit?

Mr. QUAN. The answer is, yes.

Mr. HILL. Have credit reports helped community banks avoid credit losses by adding them into their underwriting process?

Mr. QUAN. The answer is, absolutely, yes.

Mr. HILL. Do you support the concept of consumers offering additional data? I don't ever use the words—I am like Mr. Green of Texas—"alternative data." I like the words, "additional data."

So, Mr. Quan, do you support the concept of consumers offering additional data in order to strengthen their credit report, say, their telecommunications or cable or rent or utility bills?

Mr. QUAN. Absolutely, yes.

Mr. HILL. In the past two Congresses, Keith Ellison—now the great consumer advocate and attorney general for Minnesota, and a former member of this committee—and I had that exact bill for Congress. It was a bipartisan bill that was called the Credit Access and Inclusion Act, and I still promote it. I still introduce it. I still support it. It has no bipartisan support like it did in previous Congresses.

In fact, it passed on the House Floor, I think, on the suspension calendar, and it allows a consumer to add their utility payments or rental payments as a way to boost their credit score.

Have you had a chance to look at that bill in the past, Mr. Quan? Mr. QUAN. Yes, I have.

Mr. HILL. Is that headed in the right direction?

Mr. QUAN. I think from a policies perspective, the answer is, yes.

However, Congressman Hill, I also want to remind you that the private sector is already innovating. Some lenders, mostly venture-backed, are incorporating on-time payments, streaming services, rent, et cetera, into their underwriting systems so that more consumers can qualify for better rates.

Mr. HILL. So, you are saying the private sector is innovating and actually offering that as a way for people to have higher credit scores and more credit availability?

Mr. QUAN. That is correct.

Mr. HILL. Gosh, that is good to hear. Well, I think it is a good idea. It was a bipartisan idea, and I hope it will be a bipartisan idea in this Congress as we proceed.

The flip side of this is, some of my friends on the other side of the aisle in this Congress, while they like the idea of additional data helping consumers, they have argued quite vociferously what I think is an economically illiterate concept, that actually, the government should prohibit negative history on credit reports. Should the government say that CRAs cannot give us negative credit information, Mr. Quan?

Mr. QUAN. Maybe, I will answer your question another way. We have all heard of this term GPA inflation, right, so, if everybody gets a 4.0 in their GPA, and everybody gets a perfect honors SAT score, how will schools decide whom they should admit?

And it is the same thing here. If we suppress all of the negative information in consumer reports, and everybody gets an 850 FICO score, the FICO score will be useless. No lender will use the information whatsoever.

Mr. HILL. In the long run, it strikes me that that would mean lenders would make mistakes and lend money to people who possibly couldn't pay it back, and then they would have a credit default, and their credit score would go down if people had misleading credit scores. Isn't that a possibility?

Mr. QUAN. Absolutely. You are absolutely right.

Mr. HILL. So in the long run, I think an idea like that really hurts consumers and households. It reduces access to credit, and possibly raises the cost of credit.

Could it also harm community banks that don't have fancy upscale consumer underwriting systems like JPMorgan Chase? Could that hurt the banks if they had a false reading on a credit score when they offer consumers credit?

Mr. QUAN. Not only for consumers, but also this is going to have safety and soundness concerns. The banks cannot really issue or loan out high-quality loans. Then the OCC, the prudential regulator, will have concerns.

Mr. HILL. Thank you. I appreciate your time. We are for safety and soundness of our banks on this committee. I yield back.

Chairwoman WATERS. Thank you.

The gentleman from California, Mr. Vargas, is now recognized for 5 minutes.

Mr. VARGAS. Thank you very much, Madam Chairwoman. I really appreciate you bringing this issue before us. I especially appreciate all of the witnesses today.

Consumers have to have more control over their data because consumers are not the customers. As been said here today, the interests are not really aligned with the credit reporting industry.

Mr. Quan said that you need to treat the customers better, or they are going to go elsewhere. The problem is that the consumers are not the customers of the credit reporting agencies. That is not the case here. That is why these interests are not aligned.

Now, I wish we could get to a bipartisan solution. I do think that this begs for a bipartisan solution. It has been very difficult, I think, because so many of my colleagues and friends on the other side have really been radicalized over these last few years.

They attack the government and they point out every wrong thing that the government does. And of course, everyone makes mistakes. The government does, too. But they attack it vociferously and anxiously and, really, sometimes heartlessly.

But it is interesting, the Social Security Administration has all of our Social Security numbers. In fact, it has had mine since birth. And to my understanding, they have never had a breach, and they have held it very securely for years.

Now, I could be wrong about that, and there has been a breach, but I don't think there has been, not that I am aware of.

So it is sad that we can't get to a bipartisan solution, and I do think that this begs for it. But again, the radicalization that I see on the other side—they keep calling everything socialism, communism, or whatever.

In fact, recently, one of the saddest things I have seen in politics was, we had a very well-decorated military officer, the Chairman of the Joint Chiefs of Staff, General Milley, called, by the leading political commentator on the right, "a pig," and, "stupid," just because he is an intellectual.

And what do I hear from my friends on the other side about this? Nothing. Silence. This would have never happened 10 years ago, and it certainly wouldn't have happened when Ronald Reagan was in office, I can tell you. That is why it is harder and harder to get to bipartisan. They think we are radicalized. We are not. They are, and they have to change, and I hope they do.

Now, they also seem to overlook some of the data breaches. I looked up—with just a very quick Google search, the biggest data breaches of the 21st Century: Zynga, 218 million users' accounts were breached; Yahoo, over 3 billion; NetEase, 235 million user accounts; MySpace, 360 million; My FitnessPal, 150 million; Marriott International, 500 million; LinkedIn, 165 million; Heartland Payment Systems, 134 million; Dubsmash, 162 million; and, of course, Equifax, 147 million customers.

You seem to overlook that and say the Federal Government is terrible. They can't do this. They overlook the facts of all these breaches.

So I wish, again, that we could get to a bipartisan solution. Maybe we can. It shouldn't be so radicalized.

Mr. Greer, you previously stated that according to the Consumer Financial Protection Bureau, about 15 percent of Black and Latino customers are considered credit invisible, with no trackable credit record.

So what additional information or alternative data or additional data should be collected for these individuals to have a more ample report, a better report, that really treats them holistically?

Mr. Greer?

Mr. GREER. Thank you for that, Congressman Vargas.

Yes, and some of it I talked about in the testimony were things that are painting the fuller picture of their financial lives, things that they pay bills on regularly. And we are not talking about taking data out. We are talking about adding data like cell phone payments, utility payments, rental payments, and again, the ability to opt in to doing that.

The other thing is I think we need to recognize that people of color, Black and Latino, particularly immigrant populations, cannot access credit markets, and if the credit bureaus continue to weight current credit held as something that drives credit decisions, the Black and Brown communities are always going to be behind because we have been systematically held out of accessing credit, which this committee has dealt with for a long time and continues to deal with.

Mr. VARGAS. Thank you. And again, I hope we do get to a bipartisan solution. But the fever has to break on the other side, and I hope it happens soon.

I yield back.

Chairwoman WATERS. Thank you.

The gentleman from Georgia, Mr. Loudermilk, is now recognized for 5 minutes.

Mr. LOUDERMILK. Thank you, Madam Chairwoman. I appreciate everybody on the panel being here for this discussion. It seems that this is a discussion that we quite often have, and it is something for which I think we do need a bipartisan solution.

What my good friend, Representative Hill, proposed in the past, I think, is a good starting point, if we could get some buy-in from some of the members on the other side of the aisle here as we once did.

One of the bills included for discussion in this hearing, to me, is incredibly troubling, and it is the one that has been discussed here of creating another government entity, one that would be a government-run credit bureau.

The problem is I think this is based on the false assumption that the government would do a better job of handling consumer data and credit reports than the private sector does.

We are in a period right now where the approval and trust of government is at an all-time low. The American people do not trust their government. They do not think the government operates in their best interest and, in fact, a record number of people believe that the government already has too much control over their lives.

Now, adding another entity of government with even more control over their lives would be counterproductive, in my opinion, and in the opinion of many Americans.

If you think the consumers are frustrated with credit bureaus now, I can only imagine what would happen if every American had to deal with a bureaucracy equivalent to the IRS, which has the lowest approval rating of all government. In fact, if you remember, the IRS, while it does have some accountability, supposedly, to this Chamber, to Congress, engaged in targeting a certain group of people with audits just a few years ago.

So, clearly, government doesn't always operate in this vacuum where it doesn't consider politics. In fact, politics becomes a very important part of government.

Every time someone would need to borrow money, apply for a job, or rent an apartment, they would have to wait on the Federal Government to respond. If you think that is a good solution, look at the Veterans Administration right now and how well they service our veterans with the backlog that they have.

I think this is a ridiculous solution to a problem. I think that it has been brought up with the cybersecurity issues and, yes, virtually every Federal agency has experienced a significant data breach.

If you look at how much of our data is spread out across various government agencies, we don't even have Federal standards for data privacy. But yet, we want to expand the operation of government. I think that is a bad situation.

Mr. Quan, can you elaborate on why the private sector, while not perfect, is so much better-equipped to handle and improve consumer credit reports than the government is?

Mr. QUAN. Thank you, Congressman, for the question. As I mentioned before, the best way to achieve equity in credit access is through innovation and also a conducive environment where innovation can flourish.

The private sector is already coming up with solutions to address the problem. The public credit bureau doesn't add any value to it because everything in the proposal about allowing consumers to use more data in the credit scoring system is already happening. We do not need the government to do the job that the private sector is already doing. The private sector is already innovating to allow more consumers to get access to credit.

Mr. LOUDERMILK. I am going to ask another question that has been asked in a different way. But, Mr. Quan, would removing negative but accurate information from consumer credit reports increase costs and reduce access to credit across-the-board?

Mr. QUAN. That is absolutely right, because at the end of the day, what we want is accurate and complete information. "Accurate" means that if it is positive, it should be there, and if it is negative, it should also be there.

When we have that kind of information it is best for the lenders to make the right decisions. And at the end of the day, the cost of credit won't go down and the availability of credit will go up.

Mr. LOUDERMILK. Mr. Quan, I do think that some improvements should be made to the system such as adopting alternative data and updating credit files more promptly. Can you comment on those proposals?

Mr. QUAN. Absolutely. I think sometimes consumers see an error in a report where they already paid off the debt but it has not been reflected in their credit score or credit report. That is because furnishers are not sending out their real-time information as frequently as they should be. So, again, I will say that innovation can play a role here. If furnishers can more frequently report the data, then the information for the consumer can be more real-time, or as close to real-time as possible.

Mr. LOUDERMILK. Thank you. I yield back.

Chairwoman WATERS. The gentleman from Florida, Mr. Lawson, is now recognized for 5 minutes.

Mr. LAWSON. Thank you, Madam Chairwoman, and I would like to welcome everyone who is testifying here on the committee.

This is a very important subject that we are discussing, especially in dealing with consumer credit and how it affects people who apply for jobs for their—in order for them to get a job.

Ms. Traub, in your testimony before the Colorado Senate Judiciary Committee in 2012, you stated that 6 out of every 10 American employers now look at job application credit reports when hiring for some or all positions.

Employment credit checks have become commonplace among employers who are looking for ways to predict if a candidate is honest, if they have the ability to manage money responsibly, and if they are likely to steal.

In your research, have you found any evidence of the validity of this practice before the prevalence of using credit reports in a hiring decision? If not, what is the harm in the continued use of credit checks in employment?

Ms. TRAUB. Thank you, Congressman. I am aware of no proven link between personal credit reports and either someone's performance of a specific job or criminal behavior.

In fact, a spokesperson from TransUnion admitted, "We don't have any research to show any statistical correlation between what is in somebody's credit report and their job performance or their likelihood to commit fraud." And yet, we still see a lot of employers, many employers across the country, using credit checks as part of their hiring screening process.

To answer your question about the harm of this practice, the harm is that job applicants can be rejected for jobs that they are very highly qualified for, and this is a loss for employers who might be missing out on really excellent employees because they are screening for a factor that is irrelevant, and also, a huge loss for job seekers who might be able to pay off their bills if, in fact, they were able to secure work.

In the study you referenced that I conducted for Dēmos, we found that one in 10 survey respondents who were unemployed had been informed they would not be hired for a job because of information in their credit report.

And we know that as a result of discriminatory policy, Black and Latinx consumers are more likely to have poor credit, as we have been discussing, than White consumers. So, checking credit history can become just another covert, and perhaps unintentional, means of racial discrimination in hiring, compounding discrimination that happens in lending.

There is also harm, actually, when employers sometimes will say, "Oh, well, we ask people to explain the source of the bad credit. We let them explain that."

Medical debt is a major cause of flawed credit, as we have heard today. No one should have to explain the details of their cancer treatment or their child's struggle with drug abuse to get a job. That is not relevant.

Similarly, divorce and domestic abuse are closely connected with flawed credit. These are also matters that job seekers shouldn't have to expose to a potential employer just to get a job.

Mr. LAWSON. It is very interesting, and the bill that I filed deals with these restrictions and, really, I think it is a bipartisan bill, because what you just said is not beneficial to determine whether it is going to affect a person's job performance.

As a little bit of follow-up, this restricting credit check for employment decision, as a part of Ms. Pressley's comprehensive package, the bill simply cracks down on a company using credit reports when they hire a new employee. There are two exemptions for national security purposes in instances where credit checks are required by local, State, and Federal law.

Bad credit does not always correlate, as you say in your statement, to proof of job performance. We have all made a poor financial decision. I know I have before, and we need to stop punishing people and start helping people move forward.

And I really think that this is a great thing to do, and I represent a community in which a lot of students get out of school and try to get jobs and so forth, and run into these types of situation, and it really keeps them from doing what is—well, my time is running out, so I yield back.

Mr. AUCHINCLOSS. [presiding]. The gentleman from Ohio, Mr. Davidson, is now recognized for 5 minutes.

Mr. DAVIDSON. I thank the chairman. And I thank our witnesses. I appreciate your attention to this matter, and frankly, I appreciate the Majority for calling attention to the power that credit reporting agencies have over our lives, and, I think, rightly recognize that there are problems when a credit reporting agency can effectively block people from access to banking, access to credit, all kinds of things.

And I think that is really why we should be especially cautious about giving even more power to the Federal Government. The Federal Government has not been a trustworthy wielder of its power.

Historically, the government has used its power to engage in practices that are abusive, things like redlining, where bank regulators have done that. Most recently, Operation Choke Point was kind of a different version of that.

But, sadly, there is a long history in our country of somebody saying, effectively, you are not going to bank those people, are you?

Now, who those people are has changed over time, but we should be using the power of government to stop that, not enable it, and that is, I think, what would happen here.

In fact, that is the goal of China's effort to use their power of their government to decide who gets credit, and in the opinion of their government, they are just making sure the right people get credit.

But the reality is that they are using it as a means of control. They are using their whole financial system as a means of control, particularly with what they are doing to Uighur populations.

But they are doing it to anyone who would speak ill of the government or any of their leaders, or who wouldn't comply with other norms.

In fact, if they cross China's version of their woke heresy code, they are, effectively, canceled. And we read this in all sorts of dystopian futures where people who are on the wrong side of the power structure are denied access to the financial sector.

And, thankfully, Fintech is offering alternatives to more power for more government. Fintech is truly creating this with payment systems, with crypto currencies, and with distributed ledger technology, in particular. It is also more secure.

Ms. Traub, in your testimony, you lay out the case for a public credit registry. You break your argument down into seven supposed benefits this social system would bring.

One of them, you claim, is that the government would offer enhanced data security. You go on to state that, "Americans already trust their government with extensive personal financial information through the Internal Revenue System, which has a strong record of data security."

First of all, Americans don't really trust the IRS. I think that is a gross mischaracterization. In fact, if you don't trust them, you go to jail. So, that is a bad system. And second, they have also been breached.

So Mr. Vargas, yes, they have been breached, most recently for 720,000 taxpayers who had their Social Security numbers stolen by hackers. And that is without accounting for what has been compromised but hasn't even yet been measured by the SolarWinds hack.

What we know is that true blockchain enables a much more secure architecture. We know that our current cybersecurity systems are broken at the government level, and at the private-sector level, and reinforcing the same failed systems with more power for those that keep implementing them is inherently flawed.

Mr. Quan, I am curious if you could comment on the dangers of this consolidation of reporting, maybe with respect to what China seeks to do and how Fintech today offers alternatives?

And before you answer, could you also comment on how the current system, in a way, is rightly criticized because we have privatized profits and have socialized risks, so some of the reforms on liability are important?

Mr. QUAN. Thank you, Congressman.

I think you are absolutely right in your statement that when we have a government-run credit bureau, consumers will surrender their rights to the government to decide who is creditworthy, who can get access to credit.

So, this is another bad situation for anyone. The best way is, as flawed as we think the credit system is today, it is still best handled by the private sector.

And I also want to mention that our system is not fundamentally broken. Otherwise, we would not have the most competitive and the largest credit market in the world. So, let's reform the system.

Mr. DAVIDSON. Good points. My time has expired. I think that your point is well-taken, and I yield back.

Mr. AUCHINCLOSS. The gentlewoman from North Carolina, Ms. Adams, is now recognized for 5 minutes.

Ms. ADAMS. Thank you, Mr. Chairman, and to Chairwoman Waters and the ranking member, thank you for hosting the hearing. Thank you to the witnesses as well.

One of the common themes that we heard today is the incredible damage that inaccurate information can wreak on an individual's life and that is why the TransUnion case that we heard so much about is so disconcerting.

Mr. Ejaz, according to the study that you conducted for Consumer Reports, 34 percent of volunteers identified at least one error on their credit report, and per the CFPB, of the nearly 300,000 credit reporting complaints they received in 2020, over two-thirds involved incorrect information on their credit report.

So, Mr. Ejaz, and then Mr. Greer, can each of you briefly describe the impact of inaccurate information on consumers' credit reports?

Mr. EJAZ. Sure thing, and thank you for your question. Inaccurate information on credit reports can do a variety of things for consumers. First, if it is inaccurate personal information, while it may or may not impact their credit score, it can make it difficult for consumers to verify their identity with credit reports.

And in our survey, this is actually what we found. Around 10 percent of folks who filled out our survey said they found it to be difficult or very difficult to access their credit report and that is because when you go to check your credit report, you have to verify your identity with the credit bureaus. And if the bureaus' design security verification questions based off of the information that is on your report, and if that information is inaccurate, those questions can be unanswerable, and that is what some folks had found.

But even more serious than that are the 11 percent of folks, of volunteers who filled out our survey, who found account-related errors. These are errors that can impact your credit score.

And as we have discussed at length today at the hearing, a low credit score can keep you not just from affordable credit but also access to employment, affordable homeowners and auto insurance rates in some States, and housing. And I am sure Mr. Greer can follow up.

Ms. ADAMS. Mr. Greer, do you want to add to that?

Mr. GREER. Sure. Before I do, I want to mention that I do want to thank Congressman Davidson for acknowledging the harms that the Federal Government has done to Black and Brown communities. He referenced redlining.

But what I do want to note, and it is a difficult thing that we cope with, but what the government also did was it passed the Fair Housing Act, because it has a role in protecting the rights of people. And I think the conversation today about the bureau is a perspective that people have on the government's role in also protecting people's rights.

As it relates to inaccurate information, I agree. I don't have a lot more to add to what the other witnesses said, other than that when these—one thing I think it is important to note is that communities of color often have fewer resources available to them to fight back against powerful corporations when it comes to setting the record straight on what is in their credit report.

I just want to acknowledge that, and that if we are talking about a system that is truly equitable, we are addressing the capacity challenges that communities of color face compared to others when disputing inaccurate information.

Ms. ADAMS. Okay. Thank you. I thank both of you. And that is why I proudly introduced H.R. 4113, the Improving Credit Reporting for All Consumers Act. I think it would really, really help.

So, Mr. Greer, what do you think should be done to ensure that consumers receive a resolution to errors or inaccuracies that they dispute?

Mr. GREER. I am not going to spend a lot of time on this, because I think Chi Chi has some really good ideas, and Amy as well. But I do think that some accountability for a real answer—it was referenced how long people might have to wait if the government were in charge.

Well, people are waiting today, a long time, to get resolution on their credit disputes. So, I will just leave it at that, and leave it to other witnesses who may want to weigh in on that.

Ms. ADAMS. Okay. Ms. Wu?

Ms. WU. Thank you, Congresswoman. Thank you for the question. The credit reporting dispute system is broken. It is biased. It automatically rules in favor of creditors and debt collectors when there is a dispute.

Consumers need a right of appeal. They need a higher power to go to when they can't get relief for errors. What your bill does would be a wonderful idea of creating a right of appeal within the credit bureaus, an independent unit so that consumers, when they are not satisfied, it also provides for injunctive relief, as I said earlier. That would allow them to go through the courthouse doors and ask a judge to please order the credit bureau to fix their report.

Ms. ADAMS. Thank you very much. And, Mr. Chairman, I am going to yield back about 10 seconds, and I will just pass that on to the next person. Thank you.

Mr. AUCHINCLOSS. The gentleman from West Virginia, Mr. Mooney, is now recognized for 5 minutes.

Mr. MOONEY. Thank you, Mr. Chairman.

Mr. Quan, I would like to address the proposal from the Democrats to create this government-run consumer credit agency under the Consumer Financial Protection Bureau (CFPB), an organization which has many challenges of its own including its very existence.

I have a long list of concerns with a government-run consumer credit agency. If this proposal were enacted, the Federal Government would be responsible for keeping records of billions of consumer transactions. That is an enormous responsibility.

So, Mr. Quan, you outlined concerns with putting so much sensitive personal information in the hands of one government entity in your testimony. Can you talk about the risk of cyber attacks associated with having one sole public credit reporting agency?

Mr. QUAN. Thank you, Congressman, for the question.

You are absolutely right. TransUnion has about 3.1 billion tradelines in their database, and the other two agencies probably have a similar number of tradelines. So, this new government agency will house all of these tradelines, trillions of bits of information, and they are inviting cyber attacks.

If consumers are not convinced that the private sector is doing a good job in protecting their data, there is no reason for us to believe the government is going to do a better job of protecting their data.

Mr. MOONEY. Okay. Thank you, Mr. Quan.

A centralized credit reporting agency would be a target for cyber attacks that could jeopardize sensitive information for our constituents.

Additionally, hackers and criminals will use any technological advantage they can to steal sensitive information. There is no way that a government agency would be better equipped than the free market to use the latest technology and stay ahead of cyber incursions.

Furthermore, putting consumer credit reporting solely in the hands of the Federal Government has far-reaching implications. Credit reports contain sensitive personal information, and credit scores have tangible power over our lives as consumers.

I am very concerned that creating a public consumer credit bureau would be an enormous concentration of power in the hands of the Federal Government.

That kind of power could be mismanaged by a reactionary bureaucracy, whereas free market competition incentivizes looking forward, anticipating the needs for consumers in advance.

So, I agree with Ranking Member McHenry in his earlier comments where he mentioned that competition and choice for all consumers offers the best path forward. We do not need another government takeover of an industry.

That is reminiscent of a socialist-run country, not America. I know that is an agenda for many on the other side of the aisle to socialize this country. That does not work well. That has been shown.

Rather, I would actually quote Ronald Reagan, who once said, "Government is not the solution to our problems. Government is the problem."

And with that, I yield back.

Mr. AUCHINCLOSS. The gentleman from New Jersey, Mr. Gottheimer, is now recognized for 5 minutes.

Mr. GOTTHEIMER. Thank you, Mr. Chairman, and thank you to our witnesses for being here today.

Each year, 15.4 million Americans are victims of credit card fraud, around 42,000 people every day. The FTC has found that one in five consumers have verified errors in their credit reports, and one in 20 consumers have errors so serious they will be denied credit or forced to pay higher interest rates.

That adds up to 42 million Americans with errors in their credit, and another 10 million with errors that can be life-altering. As the nation continues our economic recovery, and Americans get back to work, and our lives return to normal, I think we can all agree that it is more important than ever that all Americans have access to credit. Crucial to this access is accuracy in credit reporting.

Ms. Wu, one of the most common errors in credit reporting is data being mixed up between consumers. What do you believe drives these errors and what steps should credit bureaus be taking to lower them?

Ms. WU. Thank you for the question, Congressman.

The problem with mixed files stems from matching criteria—how you match a consumer to a file at a credit bureau. A lot of people have the same names—John Smith, Jane Doe.

The unique identifier is the Social Security number, but the credit bureaus match based on seven out of nine digits or they do partial name matches, or, in the case of *Ramirez* v. *TransUnion* that we have been talking about today, they used name only. They matched based on name, and you can imagine that a lot of people have the same name, especially minority consumers.

So, what you want to do is tighten up that criteria. Match based on all nine digits of the Social Security number. Make sure you match on something like Social Security number and date of birth, and that is what you need to do and that is what your bill does.

Mr. GOTTHEIMER. Thank you, Ms. Wu.

I believe that fixing these errors is less about someone with an incorrect report receiving a monetary reward and more about actually fixing the reputation and whether the financial system views them as trustworthy or not. However, the FCRA does not give consumers the right to injunctive relief to fix errors to their credit reports.

Ms. Wu, do you believe that consumers should have access to injunctive relief to remedy errors in their credit reporting file to increase accuracy? And how might we convince more stakeholders to support access to injunctive relief so consumers can fix these errors?

Ms. WU. Absolutely, Congressman. That is an important insight. Injunctive relief is critical. Because at the end of the day, what consumers want is they want their credit reports fixed and they want it done right, and because of the *Ramirez* v. *TransUnion* decision, they can't even get through the courthouse door unless the information is hanging out there and complete strangers see it.

But injunctive relief could get them the right to go through a courthouse door and ask the judge, to ask the credit bureau to, "Fix my credit report, please." Because basically, at the end of the day, that is what they want.

Mr. GOTTHEIMER. Thank you. One year ago today, as you brought up, in the last Congress, the House passed bipartisan legislation, the Protecting Your Credit Score Act.

This legislation would create an online portal to provide consumers with unlimited free access to their credit reports and credit scores, the ability to freeze their credit, the ability to easily dispute errors and fraud, and the ability to secure and track their data, all to boost transparency and to help Americans secure their financial health.

This legislation was needed then and it is clear it is still needed now.

I just want to thank all of the witnesses for being here today. I appreciate your work. I yield back.

Mr. AUCHINCLOSS. The gentleman from Tennessee, Mr. Kustoff, is now recognized for 5 minutes.

Mr. KUSTOFF. Thank you, Mr. Chairman, and thank you to the witnesses for appearing today.

Mr. Quan, I ask this in part because my district is partly rural. In 2018, the CFPB published a report entitled, "The geography of credit invisibility." It examined the relationship between geographic location and credit invisibility.

I am summarizing but, essentially, the report found that rural areas had the highest proportional rate of credit invisibility compared to other geographic areas.

Could you give me your opinion, Mr. Quan, on what are the primary reasons for the high level of credit invisibility in rural areas?

Mr. QUAN. Thank you, Congressman.

I think you are absolutely right about these findings. I think it is very unfortunate that people living in rural areas have challenges accessing mainstream credit as a result, and this is really a catch-22. You have to have credit in order to build credit. If you don't have credit, you cannot build credit.

So, how do you start? One way the private sector comes up with is a system or a new algorithm that allows lenders to use nontraditional data sources such as rent payments, utility payments, and teleco payments.

If that information can be used, we have seen some early evidence that consumers' credit scores can get a boost from the addition of this new information. So if more lenders are using this new source of data, I believe this problem will be—I am not sure it will be 100-percent addressed, but it will be addressed.

Mr. GREER. Mr. Kustoff, could I address that question?

Mr. KUSTOFF. Let me follow my train of thought. If I could, Mr. Quan, and maybe you just said this, but in your written testimony, you talked about the potential of new algorithms, also known as alternative data, and how that could benefit customers. Do you think that the use of that alternative data can help increase credit visibility in, specifically, rural communities?

Mr. QUAN. The answer is absolutely, yes. We have seen some early evidence that the newer scoring algorithm, whether it is from Experian Boost or UltraFICO, is exactly doing what you are hoping these new algorithms are doing.

But also lenders, especially those venture-backed lenders, are using cash-flow data without even going through FICO scores to really factor into these new data sources to help increase the chances of consumers to qualify for credit.

Mr. KUSTOFF. Thank you, Mr. Quan.

Mr. Ejaz, first of all, I want to tell you that I rely on Consumer Reports often for my product reviews for cars, and I cite it often. So, I appreciate the work that you all do at Consumer Reports.

As a general rule, under the current system, does Consumer Reports recommend credit freezes for individuals?

Mr. EJAZ. We recommend that consumers take advantage of credit freezes when they fear that their identity may have been stolen.

Mr. KUSTOFF. Would you recommend it or does Consumer Reports recommend it as a general rule to people?

Mr. EJAZ. Yes. They should take advantage of credit freezes.

Mr. KUSTOFF. And if I can maybe follow up and take it one step further, does Consumer Reports have a position about credit freezes for minors, in other words, those under the age of 18 who may or may not have credit files? I suppose they have some profile with the credit reporting agencies.

Mr. EJAZ. I can get back to you in writing about specifically that part. We do recommend that consumers, especially after the Equifax hack, check their credit report and also assess their financial life, and if they fear that their identity has been stolen and, people have been opening credit accounts in their name, to take advantage of security freezes.

Mr. KUSTOFF. And taking that one step further, and this may be something else you need to get back to me on, is whether Consumer Reports has any thoughts, under the current system if somebody 18 years or older wanted to get a credit freeze, is there a process through the three credit agencies, their websites, where they can enact a credit freeze online.

That is not true for those who are minors. There are additional steps, and I would be interested whether—again, under the current system, whether Consumer Reports has any guidance or any recommendations for parents of minors who want to try to get credit freezes. Is there an easier way to do it, or should there be an easier way to do it with the three agencies?

And with that, I will yield back. Thank you. Mr. EJAZ. Thank you.

Mr. AUCHINCLOSS. The gentlewoman from Massachusetts, Ms. Pressley, is now recognized for 5 minutes.

Ms. PRESSLEY. Thank you very much, Mr. Chairman, and thank you to all of our witnesses for sharing your expertise today.

In this country, our credit reports are our reputations. They determine where you can live, where you can work, and how much it will cost you to finance everything from a car to a college degree.

But our credit reporting systems are fundamentally flawed. They are rife with inequities and disparities which stifle the upward mobility of millions of workers and families. The pandemic and the economic hurt it has wrought has only further shed light on the ways in which our credit reporting systems are a flawed measure of financial health.

In fact, despite the devastating financial hardship that families and communities have faced over the past year-and-a-half, national credit score averages have increased to record highs.

Ms. Wu, can you speak to this paradox, and why it underscores the need for Congress to extend payment pauses and other financial protections established throughout the course of this pandemic?

Ms. WU. Thank you, Congresswoman, for the question. It has been an interesting paradox. Despite the economic devastation of COVID-19, credit scores have not plunged, and there are several reasons for that.

Number one, of course, is the stimulus and Federal unemployment benefits. You give people money, they are able to pay their bills. Their credit scores stay high, which shows that credit scores are really about economics, and not moral responsibility, as some may put it.

Another reason credit scores have held up is the protections in the CARES Act for things like forbearances, student loan pauses, and credit reporting protections when creditors do agree to accommodations.

Again, these are very important, but they are about to expire. Like the eviction moratorium, they are about to expire, and millions of consumers will no longer have their protections.

And so, it is really important for consumers to come out—coming out of forbearance is to have the right to have loan modifications so that this doesn't hurt their credit profile and put them at risk of foreclosure.

Student loan protections are about to expire. Millions and millions of consumers are going to have to start paying that again. It is going to be a problem and a struggle, which is why student loan forgiveness is so important.

Ms. PRESSLEY. Thank you, Ms. Wu.

So, how much financial damage would you say we avoided because of these protections?

Ms. WU. I think we avoided a great deal of financial disaster, especially for low- and moderate-income persons. This has been a K-shaped recovery. The folks here have done okay. It is the folks there that we need to protect.

We need to protect renters because they still owe the back rent. The moratorium kept them from being evicted, but they owe the back rent, and eventually that will show up in the form of debt collection items.

Ms. PRESSLEY. Thank you. There is no doubt that these protections did help prevent many from being pushed further towards the brink. So we must act to extend these protections to ensure an equitable and just economic recovery.

But we also have to work to advance bold, sweeping, and systemic reforms to our credit reporting system. Reforming our credit system is, I think, an issue of both racial and economic justice, which is why I was so proud to reintroduce the Comprehensive CREDIT Act, a package of reforms that will overhaul the credit reporting system and provide much-needed relief to workers and families across our country.

This bill would restrict the use of credit scores for most hiring decisions. It would ban the reporting of any debt as a result of medically-necessary procedures, and establish a credit rehabilitation process for private student loan borrowers facing hardship.

Ms. Wu, in light of the ongoing economic challenges facing our families as a result of the pandemic, why are these reforms particularly timely?

Ms. WU. Thank you, Congresswoman, and thank you for reintroducing the Comprehensive CREDIT Act. It is bsolutely critical and important, and the COVID-19 pandemic shows that because it is average credit scores that have stayed afloat, but there are going to be people in that downward slope of the K who have had their credit profiles hurt, and those folks should not be shut out of jobs because of this credit damage.

The time limits for this negative information should be shortened from 7 years to 4 years, which is something else your bill does. And for people who got COVID and are left with these huge medical bills—the New York Times has documented all of these patients with huge medical bills. Those medical bills should not impair their credit reports and hurt them economically for years to come.

Ms. PRESSLEY. It is absolutely clear that our workers and our families can no longer afford inaction with our broken credit reporting system.

Thank you, and I yield back.

Mr. AUCHINCLOSS. The gentleman from Indiana, Mr. Hollingsworth, is now recognized for 5 minutes.

Mr. HOLLINGSWORTH. Good afternoon. I appreciate all of our witnesses being here. We have a lot to get through, so I hope everybody can keep their answers relatively short.

Ms. Wu, I have certainly appreciated many of your responses. Your passion for these issues can be seen even by a casual observer.

You mentioned in your written testimony that we should, and I think I am quoting here, "restrict the use of credit reporting information in rental housing and ban it for insurance." I wondered if you might expand on that. I know that is not the main point of your testimony, but certainly, that sentence stuck out to me.

Do you think that credit report information for insurance is not predictive or why would we want to ban that?

Ms. WU. Thank you for the question.

The use of credit scores in insurance is just simply illogical. What does your credit record have to do with your driving record? There is really just no causation.

Now, there is a correlation, but correlation does not make causation. And we also know, as the other witnesses have pointed out, that there are massive racial disparities in credit scores. So, the use of credit scores in insurance also results in Black and Brown drivers having to pay a lot more for insurance.

Mr. HOLLINGSWORTH. Ms. Wu, is it your assertion that credit reporting has no predictive power and is simply a proxy for race, because an abundance of research indicates the exact opposite of that. And I would imagine these insurance companies are interested in getting the most predictive power possible for the risks that they are taking, but not including these, just by virtue of being proxies for race, but instead, because they are valuable indicators in potential risk, going forward.

Ms. WU. Again, it is about correlation. People with impaired credit, for example, their finances may be more constrained, so they may be filing claims more often. People with more resources, maybe if they get into a fender-bender, they don't put in a claim, because they can pay a few hundred dollars out-of-pocket. But people with more constraints on their finances, who may have lower credit scores, may need to file a claim, because they can't afford to do that. It is correlation.

Mr. HOLLINGSWORTH. Ms. Wu, I guess just to summarize there, because I was trying to understand the argument, your statement is that they may cost the insurance company more, but the insurance company should be prohibited from underwriting the potential risks that they are going to have higher payouts on account of writing that policy?

Ms. WU. The way insurance works is that consumers should be able to file claims when they have an accident.

Mr. HOLLINGSWORTH. For sure. No one doubts that.

Ms. WU. And so, they shouldn't be penalized for that, and there is also this idea that credit is supposed to be some measure of moral responsibility.

Mr. HOLLINGSWORTH. No one talked about that.

Ms. WU. We know from the pandemic that is not true.

Mr. HOLLINGSWORTH. Ms. Wu, I did not say that. I have never said that.

Just for clarity, I absolutely agree with you that people should be able to file claims. But I disagree with the notion that somehow the potential loss for the writ insurer should not be a part of the risk that they are underwriting in doing that policy, correct or incorrect?

If there are going to be higher claims in the future for whatever motive or reason there may be, they should be able to charge more for the premium for writing that particular insurance; that is how insurance works.

Ms. WU. But these are folks who haven't filed a claim yet. By that logic, insurance should be rated on income, because people who have less income might be more likely to file claims.

Mr. HOLLINGSWORTH. For clarity, that is why it has predictive power, because they are trying to predict what their potential losses might be and, thus, match the risk with the price that they are charging. The FTC and

Georgetown University have done their own research into this and found that credit scores actually are predictive, and not a proxy for race, as I mentioned.

I know that this hearing and other hearings have mentioned the University of Michigan study, which is entitled, "Auto Insurance and Economic Mobility in Michigan: A Cycle of Poverty," and have used that as a rationale for banning credit score data in auto insurance underwriting. Frequently, what is referred to is Detroit being at a much higher cost to insure cars than other States, however, all of the other States that are compared also use credit scoring. So, there is nothing unique about the use of credit scores in Michigan versus other States that would lead us to believe that is the problem in Michigan, where insurance costs are much higher.

Instead, what study after study has found is that it is predictive in the potential loss for insurance, and insurance companies are charging for the risks that they are taking, and in taking more risks, they have to charge more.

And with that, I will yield back my time.

Mr. AUCHINCLOSS. The gentleman from New York, Mr. Torres, is now recognized for 5 minutes.

Mr. TORRES. Thank you, Mr. Chairman.

In *TransUnion* v. *Ramirez,* the Supreme Court, in an act of judicial usurpation, held that the courts, rather than Congress, ought to decide which legal rights are enforceable in Federal court and which harms are concrete enough to establish Article III standing.

My first question is for Ms. Wu. To what extent does the Court's recent decision in *TransUnion* v. *Ramirez* undermine the enforceability of the Fair Credit Reporting Act?

Ms. WU. Thank you for that question, Congressman.

The Supreme Court's decision in *TransUnion* v. *Ramirez* really undermines the ability of consumers to seek redress in a court for credit reporting errors. It basically says that the fact that there is an error, no matter how bad—and being accused of being a terrorist is a pretty bad error—you can't go to court unless a creditor, or an employer, or someone else has actually seen it, and your reputation has already been besmirched by the error.

Mr. TORRES. And what can and should Congress do to strengthen the Fair Credit Reporting Act in light of the Supreme Court's decision weakening it?

Ms. WU. Congress can and should act to address *Ramirez* by passing the right to seek injunctive relief under the Fair Credit Reporting Act. Even though the *Ramirez* decision rested on constitutional grounds, it left open the possibility that if you are asking a court for injunctive relief, you may be able to show standing, because you are trying to prevent the risk of harm of having a credit report with this terrible error in it being shown to third parties.

Mr. TORRES. I am one of four Representatives of the Bronx, where 30 percent of residents have no credit history. I have constituents who have been paying their bills in full and on time for decades, constituents who have shown themselves to be objectively creditworthy, but none of that is captured in traditional credit scoring models.

If we had credit scoring models that consistently captured alternative data, do we have a sense of how much more of the population would have a credit history and a credit score?

Mr. Ejaz?

Mr. EJAZ. I am not aware of what that difference would be. I am happy to look into it and follow-up in writing. But it is definitely a significant issue.

Mr. TORRES. And Ms. Wu, I know the National Consumer Law Center has concerns that alternative data, if applied improperly, can do more harm than good. Can you share your thoughts on how to harness the power of alternative data to produce greater access to credit, without doing more harm than good?

Ms. WU. Yes. Thank you, Congressman.

It depends on what data you are using and how it is used. Rental data, as you pointed out, can be helpful, can be promising, as long as there is consumer choice; again, consumer choice is key, because there are 10 million Americans who are behind on their rent, and they may not want their rental information put into the system. But tenants who have been paying regularly on time and don't have that concern should be able to opt-in.

We do have concerns about gas and electric, utility-payment data, because I am from Massachusetts, and you are from the Bronx, and those winter bills can get pretty high and people can get 30 or 60 days behind, so that could hurt them. But, again, consumers can have the choice if they want to opt-in, because if they don't have those negative marks, they should be able to opt-in to the system.

So, it is always about consumer choice, as well as having alternative scores that are sort of second chance, instead of feeding the information into the credit bureaus wholesale, where it might hurt some people.

Mr. TORRES. And in addition to an opt-in requirement, could there be a requirement that only favorable alternative data be reported, because obviously, a bad credit history would be worse than none at all.

Ms. WU. Yes. Positive data certainly would be helpful. And as some of the other speakers, witnesses have pointed out, the negative data shows up in the form of debt-collection items already. So, mandating the positive data would be helpful and would balance that out.

Mr. TORRES. And what do you think is the single, most-important thing we can do in Congress to ensure that everyone has a credit score and a credit history?

Ms. WU. I think giving consumers the choice to have it included would be the single, most-important thing.

Mr. TORRES. I see my time has expired. Thank you.

Mr. AUCHINCLOSS. Does the gentleman yield back?

Mr. TORRES. I yield back. I surrender.

[laughter]

Mr. AUCHINCLOSS. The gentleman from Ohio, Mr. Gonzalez, is now recognized for 5 minutes.

Mr. GONZALEZ OF OHIO. Thank you, Mr. Chairman, and thank you to the witnesses for their testimony.

First off, let me start by saying I think we do need to, more critically, look throughout our committee about how to expand access to credit and banking services; without each, it is difficult for low-income Americans to achieve financial success. I have said that, I think, since one of our first hearings last Congress, when we had the agencies here.

And I do think that we need more innovation, and we need more competition, and we need a healthier credit space, for sure. That said, the bill that we are being asked to consider, I am hard-pressed to find a worse idea, frankly, than to federalize and, ultimately, socialize credit reporting in this country.

Unfortunately, it is sort of part and parcel for our friends on the other side of the aisle who like to solve a lot of pressing issues, which is, if you don't like what is happening, just have the Federal Government take it over and see what happens. We know that typically doesn't work very well. It is less secure, with far less innovation, and ultimately, I would argue, lead to worse outcomes economically.

But I will ask Mr. Quan for his thoughts on some of those things. Mr. Quan, what sort of impact do you believe creating a Federal reporting agency would have on innovation and investments into new technology by the private sector to promote access to credit?

Mr. QUAN. Thank you, Congressman, for the question.

You already hit the nail on the head. When the government gets involved, the new credit bureau, backed by the government, will be backed by unlimited taxpayer revenue. So, the private sector cannot compete; as a result, innovation will disappear naturally.

And as we all know—this is Economics 101—government involvement will crowd out private investment and all of the innovations we are seeing today, the innovations I have mentioned, whether it is the UltraFICO score or Experian Boost or the cash flow based on underwriting, will disappear. And there is no evidence the government is doing a better job or can do a better job in adopting or developing new technologies to improve access to credit.

Mr. GONZALEZ OF OHIO. Thank you. I couldn't agree more.

Based on the conversations that I have had with my constituents, customer service across the different Federal agencies isn't necessarily a strong suit of the Federal Government. I think today, right now, for example, those who are waiting for passports are completely out of luck because of the backlog. We have been solving passport issues for a long time and this is the worst that our office has ever seen it. That is just passports.

But what is your assessment of the ability of the Federal Government to operate a credit reporting agency and the likely customer service implications for such a project?

Mr. EJAZ. Again, you have already given a very good example, using passports. The CFPB's customer complaints portal, I think the witnesses have mentioned, is in the range of 300,000 to 400,000 customer complaints related to credit reporting. But in reality, the CRA is receiving far more than that; they are receiving millions, not just complaints, but disputes.

And there is no reason for me to believe the government, which has no expertise or any kind of experience to handle that kind of complaints volume, what we are going to end up having is a system that is probably going to be worse than what we already have now.

Mr. GONZALEZ OF OHIO. So, less innovation, less competition, worse service. Sounds great, guys. I am really, really excited about this bill.

Final question, in your testimony, you mentioned concern over future data breaches at the credit reporting bureaus. I agree, we have seen that in a lot of different sectors of the economy. And there is no reason to believe that this isn't going to continue, unfortunately.

In your estimation, what more should Congress be doing to prevent another significant breach of a credit bureau?

Mr. EJAZ. I believe that credit bureaus should be held to the same standard as financial institutions. For example, if you are a critical service provider to financial institutions, you are examined by the credential agencies under the Bank Service Company Act. We should have a similar regime that applies to the credit bureaus.

I am not saying having Federal supervision will permanently fix the cybersecurity issue; the cyber risks will always be there. But without appropriate Federal supervision, I am just not confident that consumers will feel confident that their data is secure with private sector bureaus.

Mr. GONZALEZ OF OHIO. Thank you.

I see my time is up, and I yield back.

Mr. AUCHINCLOSS. The gentlewoman from Pennsylvania, Ms. Dean, is now recognized for 5 minutes.

Ms. DEAN. Thank you, Mr. Chairman, and I thank our witnesses for your important information today.

I would like to follow up on Mr. Scott's questioning earlier during this hearing about student loan debt, particularly, private student loan debt. Many borrowers remain trapped in abusive or predatory lending arrangements and credit agencies still view this as bad debt, hurting the future economic horizons for those borrowers. I am a former professor, so I care an awful lot about student debt.

Ms. Wu, in your testimony, you speak about consumers being unfairly penalized in their credit reports when they are victims of student loan abuses. Can you describe that situation more specifically to us, and provide us with an example of how that has long-term consequences?

Ms. WU. Thank you for the question, Congresswoman.

Yes. So, private student loan debt is certainly a problem and it is a problem that affects Black and Brown borrowers disproportionately. Unfortunately, it is also tied to the issue of for-profit schools and other institutions that take advantage of Black and Brown students, promise them the sun and the moon, give them substandard educations, and then saddle them with private student loan debt, which ends up on their credit reports, maybe as defaults and delinquencies or just a lot of unmanageable debt. And, unfortunately, the student loan pause from the CARES Act also didn't help private student loan borrowers.

The Comprehensive CREDIT Act does have some provisions to help with private student loan debt in terms of rehabilitating those, but certainly, the credit reporting consequences are only one part of that.

Ms. DEAN. That is what I was going to follow up with, Ms. Wu. We know that during COVID-19, the pandemic, many private student loan borrowers did not get any relief. So, I do lift up Ms. Pressley's Comprehensive CREDIT Act.

Could you describe how the lack of that economic relief has impacted private student loan borrowers?

Ms. WU. Unlike borrowers for Federal student loans, private student loan borrowers have had to keep paying those loans. Federal student loan borrowers have had a pause and suspension of their obligations. So, those private student loan borrowers who have suffered economically during the COVID-19 pandemic, either still have to pay their loans or have negative items on their credit report from not being able to pay because of the economic fallout of COVID-19. And this could follow them for another 7 years.

Ms. DEAN. Exactly. It is such an obvious inequity. We treat one set of student borrowers one way and another set, in an economic collapse, another way.

Ms. Traub, I am going to try to fit in a question, if I may, with you. I appreciate your testimony that credit reporting is part of infrastructure. It is a resource needed to fully participate in society. And while credit reporting does not take race into account, can you describe how systemic racial inequities fail to allow equitable access in this essential infrastructure? Can you give us a little more on that topic that you offered us in your testimony? Ms. TRAUB. Thank you, Congresswoman.

We can look at where credit discrimination comes from, because you are right that credit scores and credit reports never, explicitly and directly, take race into account. But we know for decades we had economic policies in this country that enabled White families to build wealth but excluded Black and Brown families.

Wealth is passed down over generations, and access to that generational wealth shapes our behavior. It shapes people's borrowing and payment behavior today. And so, people without access to generational wealth need to borrow more to go to college, to buy a home, sometimes, just to make ends meet. And then, there is also ongoing discrimination. So, it is not a surprise, really, that we see racial disparities turn up in credit reports.

And I want to be clear that we need to fix a lot more than credit reporting to achieve racial equity, but fixing credit reporting, I believe, would improve one system that spreads inequality every time that it is used.

Ms. DEAN. I appreciate that.

Would anybody else like to speak to that issue of systemic racism in the credit reporting system, as we say, not explicitly, but implicitly?

Mr. GREER. Yes. Thanks for that.

I would just like to emphasize the point that she made that there are systemic and historical barriers that have been baked into our current lending systems and our lending structures. And it was referenced earlier, things like redlining that have held credit away from Black and Brown communities.

And we would be, and I guess this is another term we have been using a lot today, naive to believe that is not making its way into our credit reporting system.

Mr. AUCHINCLOSS. The gentlewoman's time has expired.

Ms. DEAN. Thank you. I yield back.

Mr. AUCHINCLOSS. The gentleman from Wisconsin, Mr. Steil, is now recognized for 5 minutes.

Mr. STEIL. Thank you very much, Mr. Chairman.

Some of my colleagues today have argued for the removal of predictive information from credit reports. I see this really as an attack on risk-based pricing, in which lenders attempt to assess the creditworthiness of a prospective borrower and adjust prices to compensate for that risk. Risk-based pricing is a foundational concept in our financial system and undermining the practice will increase the level of risk across the financial system and reduce credit access.

Mr. Quan, would you agree that making it harder for lenders to assess risk will effectively socialize that risk, and then, how would that impact lower-income and marginal borrowers, specifically?

Mr. QUAN. Thank you, Congressman, for the question.

I have repeatedly said that we need accurate and complete information in customers' credit files. "Accurate" means that whether the information is positive or negative, the information should be there.

So, if we remove or if we intentionally suppress negative information—our service helps consumers who have negative information, but by and large, lenders who do not have the best information available when they make decisions to credit—

Mr. STEIL. Let me dive in, because I think we have hit the point a handful of times here today. But let me shift gears ever so slightly for you, Mr. Quan, if I can.

People with low credit scores, thin credit files, young people, recent immigrants, members of underserved communities can all benefit from improved access to credit. And, unfortunately, I think much of today's hearing is focused on ways to weaken the credit scores and obscure the risk, when, to me, these ideas would increase costs and reduce access, especially for today's underserved borrowers.

Hollowing out credit reports won't help a single mom in Janesville, Wisconsin, get a mortgage. It won't help a family business in Racine, Wisconsin, get a small business loan.

So, instead of excluding data from credit reports, should we look at ways to include more predictive data that may help bring more Americans into the financial services system?

Mr. Quan, let me put a pin on it here. My colleagues on the other side of the aisle have argued that we need to get a government-run credit bureau to come up with new algorithms to address credit access.

Do you agree with that assertion, or is the private sector unwilling or unable to specifically innovate in this area? Could you comment on that?

Mr. QUAN. Congressman, you are absolutely right. The private sector has already come up with new algorithms, and they are so-called new. There is nothing new there; it has been around for a number of years now, and, frankly, those innovations are happening mainly because of: number one, there are mission-driven companies that are trying to solve the problem; and number two, and more importantly, this is a capitalistic society and there is a profit motive behind it. This is a market that is unaddressed and now it is being addressed by innovation. And lenders can make money and now, also, they can fulfill their social mission. So, the government—

Mr. STEIL. Mr. Quan, these hybrid hearings are challenging. I look forward to all of us being together in person, but I appreciate you being here. I think you hit the nail on the head. The private sector is looking at this.

Let's do some concrete examples. Experian Boost, UltraFICO, some of these opt-in alternatives, if these models and businesses expanded, would it improve credit access for individuals, in particular, some of those who are currently underserved?

Mr. QUAN. The answer is absolutely, yes.

We are still in the very early stages. Experian Boost has boosted 69 million points in FICO, and this is not VantageScore, this is the FICO Score, this is especially in FICO 8.0, which is the score that most vendors use today. So, there is a clear evidence that this innovation is driving access to credit, to expand access to credit.

The low-income consumers, new immigrants, people like me who wouldn't be able to get access to credit early in my days in the United States, now, we have a chance to get credit.

Mr. STEIL. I appreciate that.

Let me just sum it up like this. One of my takeaways from today's hearing is that credit reporting can easily be politicized, and with that in mind, I am concerned about proposals to centralize credit reporting in a government-run agency.

I am not sure my colleagues have fully considered the implications of providing a government agency with even more of our personal financial information, and then granting that agency the power to effectively withhold access to credit. A government-run system raises the prospect of politicized credit-access decisions, a loss of financial privacy, and heightened cybersecurity risks. Many Americans don't want the government to exercise this power, especially if it is based on what they buy and which bills they prioritize.

Our credit reporting agencies are not perfect, but American consumers stand to benefit far more if we improve our existing, competitive, private-sector system, than if we centralize the financial data at a government bureaucracy.

I urge my colleagues to reject the proposal, and I yield back.

Mr. AUCHINCLOSS. The gentlewoman from Michigan, Ms. Tlaib, is now recognized for 5 minutes.

Ms. TLAIB. Thank you so much, Mr. Chairman.

I so appreciate this hearing because credit scoring has been something that impacts my community directly, as the third-poorest congressional district in the country.

Mr. Greer, would you agree that racism is profitable?

Mr. GREER. Yes.

Ms. TLAIB. Thank you. I would like to submit for the record, Mr. Chairman, a great op-ed from Rashad Robinson, "Corporations profit off of racism."

Mr. AUCHINCLOSS. Without objection, it is so ordered.

Ms. TLAIB. Thank you.

Mr. Greer, you talk about oppression economy in your testimony, and I think that is really powerful, because what we are hearing are words that corporations use: risk-based pricing; assessments. We all continue to hear these kinds of really interesting terminologies, but I can tell you, personally, with auto insurance, for example, rates in my State are the highest in the nation. People will say it is all of these different factors, but credit scores are actually used to calculate whether or not a person is a safe driver: Credit scores.

So, when we talk about structural racism and we talk about this hearing, we have to really talk about the human impacts of what this means. They are selling our data, the credit scoring agencies, for profit, to auto insurance agencies which are using non-driving factors as proxies: marriage, whether or not you are married; your education level. All of these things, again, have nothing to do whether or not you are a safe driver. But they use words like risk-based pricing or assessments.

Mr. Greer, when you think about those kinds of measures of using these as proxies, and I am talking specifically about the auto insurance industry, the use of credit scores, how has that really impacted communities of color?

Mr. GREER. Right. I am really thankful for all of the work that you do, Ms. Tlaib. Not just for the people in your district, but for the people of color across the country.

But this idea is to create a class of people who can be exploited, who can have their auto insurance be much larger than it would be in another part of the country, or if they were another type of person. So, the reason why, and I think this has been documented, that auto insurance is higher in your community is because it is largely Black, Latino, and Arab-American people who are living in your community, and because our economy has been built on a system that exploits racism as a way to draw profits, this is how that plays out in that sector.

Ms. TLAIB. Mr. Ejaz, do you know what credit scoring has to do with driving records?

Mr. EJAZ. It has nothing to do with driving records. Credit scores and reports, in my view, should only be used to assess creditworthiness and, as a general rule, should not be expanded beyond that.

Ms. TLAIB. Ms. Traub, it is interesting, when somebody's credit score is lower and they use it towards calculating their auto insurance. Do you know that auto insurance rates actually go higher, so if you are poor, you are paying higher rates, even though you are a safer driver.

Did you know, Ms. Traub, that if you had a DUI, but a better credit score, you are paying less in auto insurance than somebody who has no DUI record, but a lower credit score, did you know that?

Ms. TRAUB. That is correct, Congresswoman, and it is terribly unfair.

Ms. TLAIB. That is a form of structural racism. If you look at who is impacted, it is low-income communities.

So, I want to get to your next thing, which is medical debt. Ms. Wu, you know how passionate I am about this. I don't want medical debt to be used similar to, if you buy a car and you miss a payment. Medical debt is basically, you are sick, you have to get treatment, and this is medically-necessary debt, and it ends up on your credit report for years.

Given the credit reporting agencies' poor track record, what kinds of things is your organization doing to expose the fact that medical debt in our credit reports actually impacts or expands economic disparities in communities like mine?

Ms. WU. Thank you, Congresswoman, and thank you for your passion on this particular topic.

The proposal you had that medically necessary debt should not show up on credit reports is one of the most important aspects of the Comprehensive CREDIT Act. The CFPB has found that over half—it is up to 58 percent—of debt-collection items, third-party debt-collection items on credit reports are for medical debt. It is a massive amount.

And COVID-19 really exposes how not only this is just a terrible, unjust problem, but it also runs along racial lines, because we know that Black and Brown Americans have suffered more under COVID-19. And The New York Times has documented how COVID-19 has resulted in these huge medical bills for some of the patients, and then this stuff ends up on their credit reports.

It is just wrong.

Ms. TLAIB. Yes. Mr. Chairman, if I may?

We are pushing for legislation, hopefully, and you all can take a look at it, of reducing markings on credit reports from 7 to 4 years. I know it is a good compromise. I, of course, don't want the credit reports being used, but I think moving it from 7 to 4 years can directly, dramatically, help our communities.

But right now, I think this hearing was critically important to expose at least—

Mr. AUCHINCLOSS. The gentlewoman's time has expired.

Ms. TLAIB. Thank you.

Mr. AUCHINCLOSS. The gentleman from South Carolina, Mr. Timmons, is recognized for 5 minutes.

Mr. TIMMONS. Thank you, Mr. Chairman.

I am opposed to the bill to create a public credit registry, and I believe it is a big government solution in search of a problem.

Mr. Quan, picking up where my friend from Wisconsin, Mr. Steil, just left off, risk-based pricing helps to make credit affordable for all. As our economy is recovering from the pandemic, do you believe transitioning away from risk-based pricing would help consumers?

Mr. QUAN. Think about what happened 10 years ago, the last financial crisis this country experienced. Lenders took more risks. They lent money to people who couldn't afford to pay it back. That is because of the lack of risk-based pricing that caused the last financial crisis. So, risk-based pricing is very critical to have today as we recover from this pandemic.

Mr. TIMMONS. Sir, thank you for that.

As a follow-up, could you discuss the impact that suppressing or keeping negative information out of credit reports has on the safety and soundness of our financial system?

Mr. QUAN. Lenders need accurate and complete information to make lending decisions. If we intentionally suppress accurate, but negative, information from customers' credit files, lenders will not be able to make the best decision they can; as a result, there will be an increase in defaults and we will have an unsafe and unsecure financial system.

Mr. TIMMONS. And that would likely result in everyone's premiums going up for the insurance they are currently paying for; is that correct?

Mr. QUAN. Absolutely. Everyone's price will go up, as a result.

Mr. TIMMONS. Okay. Thank you.

Moving on, I know cybersecurity has been a popular topic of conversation today, but I would be remiss if I did not chime in as well, especially, given that today we received news of another mass breach, this time at LinkedIn.

We have seen several government agencies hacked in the past, putting Americans' data in the hands of cyber criminals as well. Creating a one-stop shop of consumer credit information and a brand new Federal agency that has no experience in this particular area is just asking for trouble. Congress has always had challenges, as well.

Mr. Quan, what level of risk to the average consumer would the public credit rating agency, as proposed by the Majority, pose to the American people?

Mr. QUAN. The risk would be unthinkable, because all of a sudden, all of the information would be concentrated, centralized by one government agency which has no experience and no expertise in safeguarding that information. And as you mentioned, there are so many government agency breaches.

My data, when I was working for the government, was breached because of the OPM data breach. So, there is no evidence that the government is able to do a better job than the private sector in safeguarding our information.

Mr. TIMMONS. Sure. But I would imagine suing the Federal Government and getting a few trillion dollars for the breached, the parties that had their data breached, would be a good solution.

Mr. QUAN. That would be—

Mr. TIMMONS. So much money to give away.

Mr. QUAN. Congressman, absolutely, I agree with you. Look at the Equifax settlement, $575 million, up to $700 million. But who is going to pay for it? Shareholders.

So, if you are investing in Equifax, bad luck. But if the government was responsible for that $700 million—that is how much the Troubled Asset Relief Program (TARP) was originally for. So, of course, today we are handing out trillions of dollars—$700 million may be something like a drop in the bucket, but still, that is taxpayers' money.

Mr. TIMMONS. I have a feeling that the government would settle for far more than the Equifax breach. So, it's a bad idea. Thank you.

Mr. Chairman, I yield back.

Mr. AUCHINCLOSS. This committee is going to adjourn in order to make votes; unfortunately, that means we will have to curtail questions.

I would like to thank our distinguished witnesses for their testimony today.

The Chair notes that some Members may have additional questions for this panel, which they may wish to submit in writing. Without objection, the hearing record will remain open for 5 legislative days for Members to submit written questions to these witnesses and to place their responses in the record. Also, without objection, Members will have 5 legislative days to submit extraneous materials to the Chair for inclusion in the record.

This hearing is now adjourned.

[Whereupon, at 1:32 p.m. the hearing was adjourned.]

Written Statement of Syed Ejaz, Analyst, Financial Policy Consumer Reports

Thank you for inviting Consumer Reports[1] to testify regarding Americans' experiences with credit reporting and the paths towards a credit reporting

---

[1] Consumer Reports is an expert, independent, non-profit organization that works for a fair, safe, and just marketplace for all consumers and to empower consumers to protect themselves. Based in Yonkers, NY Consumer Reports works for pro-consumer policies in the areas of financial services and marketplace practices, antitrust and competition policy, privacy and data security, food and product safety, telecommunications and technology, travel, and other consumer issues, in Washington D.C., in the states, and in the marketplace. Consumer Reports is the world's largest independent product-testing organization, using its dozens of labs, auto test center, and survey research department to rate thousands of products and services annually. Founded in 1936, Consumer Reports has over 6 million members and publishes its magazine, website, and other publications.

system that works for consumers. The existing credit reporting system does not. Too frequently, consumers struggle to access their reports, and when they do, too often they find errors that can limit their financial opportunities and can be difficult to correct.

Inaccuracies on credit reports are not a new issue. In 2012, the Federal Trade Commission conducted a study on credit reports, in which 21 percent of participants had at least one verified error on their report, and 5 percent had errors so significant that they were put in a different credit risk tier.[2] Consumer complaints to the Consumer Financial Protection Bureau regarding credit reporting errors remain among the most frequent submissions to their database and have more than doubled since 2019.[3] This is unacceptable. Credit reporting agencies hold information that can be used to make consequential lending, employment, and underwriting decisions about us. Credit report errors that damage credit scores can keep people from affordable interest rates, as well as employment and in some states, affordable homeowners and auto insurance.

During February and March of this year, CR asked volunteers to check their credit reports and let us know about their experience in a project we called Credit Checkup.[4] Nearly 6,000 people responded to our survey and shared their stories. 34 percent of consumers who participated in Credit Checkup told us that they found at least one error on their report. 29 percent said that they found incorrect personal information such as a wrong name or address and 11 percent found incorrect account information such as an account they didn't recognize or mistakes about their account payment history.

One participant, Victoria Ross, shared her story which captures how much credit reporting errors can impact consumers. Her TransUnion credit report mistakenly showed a PayPal account balance of around $1,200 that she'd already paid off, an error which led her to face unaffordably high interest rates when trying to find a car loan. Victoria filed multiple disputes but was unable to get her credit report fixed until after Consumer Reports reached out to

[2] Federal Trade Commission, *Report to Congress Under Section 319 of the Fair and Accurate Credit Transactions Act of 2003* (2015) ii: https://www.ftc.gov/system/files/documents/reports/section-319-fair-accurate-credit-transactions-act-2003-sixth-interim-final-report-federal-trade/150121factareport.pdf.

[3] In 2020, the CFPB received 66,900 closed complaints regarding dispute investigations and 280,822 closed complaints regarding consumer or credit reporting. See: Consumer Financial Protection Bureau, *Consumer Annual Report* (2021): https://files.consumerfinance.gov/f/documents/cfpb_2020-consumer-response-annual-report_03-2021.pdf.

[4] On June 10, Consumer Reports published the results of the survey in a report called "A Broken System: How the Credit Reporting System Fails Consumers and What To Do About It." A copy of this report is attached.

TransUnion. Victoria's story is one of many that show how an inaccurate, unresponsive credit reporting system can cause problems for consumers.

One in 10 consumers who completed the survey found accessing their credit reports to be "difficult" or "very difficult." Many consumers shared stories of being locked out of their credit reports because of identity verification questions that they could not answer because the questions were based on inaccurate information.

Some also told us that while checking their free credit report, they were pushed to purchase products and services from the bureaus. Multiple people said that they were asked for their credit card information before seeing their reports, and later were charged. One told us:

> TransUnion ran me through an exhausting series of questions, sales offers, and ridiculous permutations until I was able to get a credit report and score displayed. Then I found that they had signed me up for a monthly service and charged my credit card $27 and change for the first month, to be charged monthly. I immediately cancelled the 'subscription,' and had to call the helpline to get this charge removed from my card.

These stories highlight just some of the problems consumers encounter with a deeply flawed credit reporting system, and are a fraction of the thousands collected by CR. Consumers need a credit reporting system that works for them - one where their reports are accessible and accurate and errors are easy to correct. The good news: two of the bills discussed today can help address the most glaring problems.

The Protecting Your Credit Score Act requires all credit reporting agencies and data furnishers to match the first name, last name, date of birth, and all nine digits of a consumer's Social Security numbers when placing information on their reports. This bill also creates a secure portal where consumers can freeze their credit, file disputes, and check their reports for free, an unlimited number of times.

The House can also pass the Comprehensive CREDIT Act once more. This bill gives consumers the right to appeal the results of dispute investigations, restricts the use of credit reports for employment, and implements many other common-sense reforms to the credit reporting system.

Credit reports play a central role in the financial lives of consumers. And the industry should center the needs of consumers first. A consumer-centric credit reporting system would put consumers in control of their credit information, make it easy to access credit reports and credit scores for free, strengthen standards to ensure reports are accurate, and simplify the process for correcting errors. Congress can put consumers first by passing the Comprehensive CREDIT Act and the Protecting Your Credit Score Act.

A Broken System: How the Credit Reporting System Fails Consumers and What to Do About It: Findings and Recommendations from the Consumer Reports, Credit Checkup Study, Syed Ejaz, June 10, 2021

Acknowledgments

The author would like to thank Anna Laitin, Christina Tetreault, Michael McCauley, and Scott Medintz for their assistance in developing this paper. Thanks also to David Friedman, Jamison Pfeifer, Camille Calman, Wendy Greenfield, and Jen Shecter for their helpful feedback on several drafts of the paper. Several other Consumer Reports staff members offered invaluable input and advice, including Marcus Jones, Karen Jaffe, Tess Yanisch, Chris Griggs, and Tim La Palme.

The author is grateful to Chi Chi Wu of the National Consumer Law Center, who took the time to peer-review this paper. The author would also like to thank the National Consumer Law Center, U.S. PIRG, the National Association of Consumer Advocates, Consumer Action, and Americans for Financial Reform for assisting with the promotion of the Credit Checkup survey project.

Finally, thanks to the consumers who participated in the Credit Checkup project and shared their stories with us.

Executive Summary

The COVID-19 pandemic has affected almost every aspect of the U.S. economy, fundamentally reshaping the lives of millions of consumers. Many remain out of work or struggle to make ends meet, forcing some to turn to family, friends, state and federal governments, banks, and creditors to stay afloat and find financial relief. Now, as the U.S. economy emerges from the financial impacts of COVID-19, consumers need the most critical pillars of the economy to work in their favor.

One of those pillars is the credit reporting system, which is used not only by financial institutions as the basis for credit and lending decisions—its original purpose—but also by companies making employment decisions, landlords considering prospective tenants, and insurance companies pricing their policies.

Unfortunately, several aspects of the credit reporting system appear to be fundamentally broken. CR's current study, as well as previous research on the topic, suggests that credit report errors are all too common. The credit reporting system was originally designed to serve the interests of financial institutions and continues to function in much the same way—despite its massive and growing effects on the economic welfare of ordinary consumers.

The credit reporting system, in short, treats consumers primarily as its *product,* not as its customer. During February and March 2021, CR asked Americans to check their credit reports and let us know about their experience, in a project we called Credit Checkup. Nearly 6,000 people responded to our survey and provided valuable feedback. The information they provided highlights how the current system fails to serve consumers, and points to several reasonable reforms needed to address and rectify these problems.

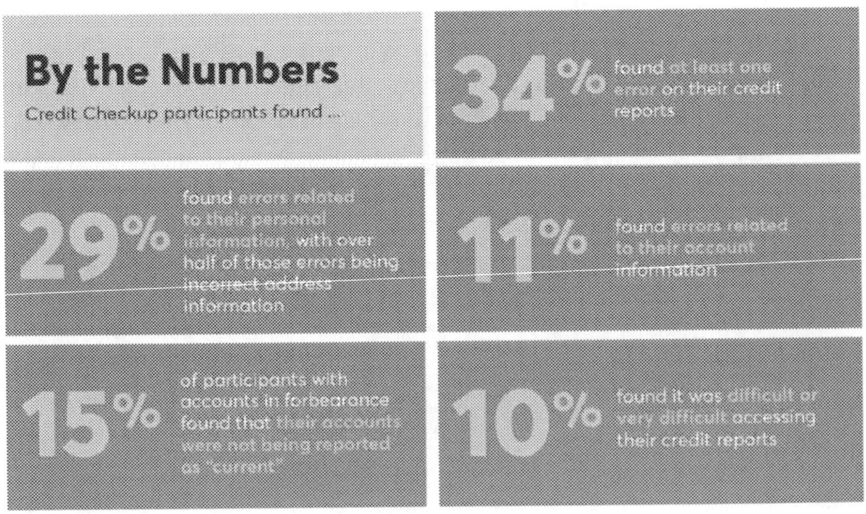

Key Findings

Consumers Are Finding Errors on Their Credit Reports

More than one-third (34 percent) of consumers who participated in CR's Credit Checkup survey reported that they found at least one error on their report, with 29 percent saying that they found errors in personal information and 11 percent finding account information errors.

Consumers, through No Fault of Their Own, Are Struggling to Access Their Credit Reports

One in 10 consumers who completed the survey found accessing their credit reports to be "difficult" or "very difficult." Many consumers gave accounts of being locked out of their credit reports because of identity verification questions that they could not answer.

Credit Bureaus Sometimes Push Consumers to Purchase Products and Services That Should Be Available Free through AnnualCreditReport.com

Consumers are legally entitled to access their credit reports free once per year, which they can do at the websites of credit reporting agencies (CRAs) and at AnnualCreditReport.com.[5] Multiple consumers report being asked for their credit card information before seeing their reports, and later being charged.

The Credit Reporting System Is Confusing to Navigate and to Understand

Some consumers are confused about why their credit scores are not included with their credit reports and why they are being shown advertisements for paid credit monitoring services while checking their free credit reports.

Marketplace and Policy Recommendations

The credit reporting system simply does not work for consumers. They do not have access to or control over their own information, and even the first step of checking a credit report for accuracy can be difficult to accomplish. In this chapter, we make four key marketplace and policy recommendations.

1. *Strengthen accuracy requirements for credit reports and improve enforcement of existing laws.* Consumer reporting agencies, lenders,

[5] For this project, CR took advantage of the fact that the three big consumer reporting agencies have expanded free access to reports. During the pandemic, they have made free reports available weekly: https://www.cdiaonline.org/wp-content/uploads/2021/03/CDIA-Release-FINAL.pdf.

and debt collectors must be required to abide by stronger standards to ensure that the information contained in credit reports is accurate and that all consumer disputes are properly investigated. The Consumer Financial Protection Bureau and the Federal Trade Commission should use their full authority to establish stronger accuracy regulations and penalize companies for any violation of the Fair Credit Reporting Act (FCRA).

2. *Provide consumers control over their own credit information.* Consumers should have control over their credit information. Access to reports and scores should be free at any time; credit reports should be "frozen" by default, meaning that an individual's credit information cannot be used to open new accounts without the consumer first unfreezing their credit. And consumers should be able to directly compare their reports, freeze and unfreeze their credit, easily file disputes, and correct errors.
3. *Redesign the identity verification system used by Equifax, Experian, and TransUnion.* Consumers should not be locked out of their reports because of bad or very old information being used to verify their identity. They should not be blindsided by questions they cannot answer when trying to access their credit reports.
4. *Rein in the role of credit reports in consumers' lives.* Credit reports should be used for the purpose for which they were developed—to assess creditworthiness. They should not be used for any other decisions about a consumer, such as insurance pricing. Credit reports should not be used in decisions regarding anything other than a consumer's creditworthiness.

Background

The Credit Reporting System

A credit report is a record of a consumer's history of paying their debt obligations. Though originally intended only to help lenders determine a consumer's creditworthiness, credit reports are now often used by prospective landlords, potential employers, and in some states insurance companies to make a variety of decisions about consumers. A credit report is also the source document used to determine the consumer's credit score, which is supposed to be a numerical approximation of the consumer's creditworthiness. As such, credit reports are enormously consequential financial documents that can greatly influence a consumer's ability to access employment, housing, affordable credit, and affordable auto and homeowners insurance.

Credit reports are housed by consumer reporting agencies (CRAs), also known as credit bureaus. Three major credit bureaus—Experian, Equifax, and TransUnion—dominate the credit reporting system. These three for-profit companies hold credit files on over 200 million U.S. consumers.[6] There are also a number of specialized CRAs that gather information such as payment history for TV and cell phone plans, public records data, eviction information, and criminal records.[7] However, Equifax, Experian, and TransUnion are the CRAs most commonly referenced by lenders, landlords, potential employers, and insurance companies, and are therefore the focus of this paper.[8]

The CRAs earn revenue in a variety of ways, including by selling consumer credit reports to lenders, landlords, employers, and other institutions.[9] They also earn revenue by charging consumers for enhanced access to their own credit reports and for services such as credit monitoring. The level of access consumers have to their own credit information varies by agency, especially among the smaller and more specialized CRAs, but federal law requires the three major CRAs to provide consumers with free credit reports once per year.[10]

The CRAs obtain information on consumers from *data furnishers.* Any institution where consumers have credit accounts or are responsible for payments can be a data furnisher. The FCRA does not require any person or institution to furnish information to the credit bureaus.[11] Furnishers can pass information to the CRAs at any time they wish.[12] Consumers have no control over which furnishers report information to the CRAs. The most common furnishers are lenders and debt collectors.[13]

---

[6] Consumer Financial Protection Bureau (CFPB), *Key Dimensions and Processes in the U.S. Credit Reporting System,* 19, (2012): https://files.consumerfinance.gov/f/201212_cfpb_credit-reporting-white-paper.pdf.

[7] CFPB, "List of consumer reporting companies": https://www.consumerfinance.gov/consumer-tools/credit-reports-and-scores/consumer-reporting-compani es/companies-list/.

[8] Id.

[9] Hurley and Adebayo: *Credit Scoring in the Era of Big Data,* 8, Yale J.L & Tech (2016): https://digitalcommons.law.yale.edu/cgi/viewcontent.cgi?article=1122&context=yjolt.

[10] Federal Trade Commission (FTC), "Free Credit Reports": https://www.consumer.ftc.gov/articles/0155-free-credit-reports.

[11] Experian, "Mortgage Company Not Required to Report Payments": https://www.experian.com/blogs/ask-experian/mortgage-company-not-required-to-report-payments/.

[12] TransUnion, "How long does it take for a credit report to update?": https://www.transunion.com/blog/credit-advice/how-long-does-it-take-for-a-credit-report-to-update.

[13] CFPB, *Key Dimensions* 14.

While a consumers' credit report provides the base information for developing a credit score for that consumer, credit scoring models are developed by credit scoring companies that are distinct from CRAs.[14] The two most commonly referenced credit scoring companies are the Fair Isaac Corp. (FICO) and VantageScore. As with CRAs, many alternative credit scoring companies exist; some use data not conventionally reported to the CRAs,[15] such as payment history for TV and cell phone bills, and public records data.[16]

Consumers have multiple credit scores, which vary based on the type of credit the consumer is being evaluated for, the company that created the algorithm that calculates the score, and the version or "generation" of the credit score. Consumers are not always shown the scores lenders use to make lending decisions. The most common consumer-facing credit scores can range from 300 to 850, with 850 being considered "exceptional" and 300 being considered "very poor."[17]

Credit Reports

Credit reports contain a variety of personal and financial information about a consumer, and may include the following:

- *Personally identifiable information:* Credit reports include a consumer's name, date of birth, Social Security number, current and former addresses, employers, and phone numbers.[18] Additional information might include personal statements submitted to the CRAs by consumers themselves, information regarding security freezes, and power of attorney status.[19]
- *Accounts and payment history:* Credit reports include details on each account that data furnishers provide to the CRAs. This includes the type of account, balance, account status, credit limits, and whether payments have been made on time.[20]

---

[14] VantageScore was first established by the three major CRAs but is not managed by any CRA.
[15] CFPB, "Using alternative data to evaluate creditworthiness": https://www.consumerfinance.gov/about-us/blog/using-alternative-data-evaluate-creditworthiness/.
[16] Ibid.
[17] Experian, "What Are the Different Credit Scoring Ranges?": https://www.experian.com/blogs/ask-experian/infographic-what-are-the-different-scoring-ranges/.
[18] Equifax, "What is a Credit Report and What Does it Include?": https://www.equifax.com/personal/education/credit/report/what-is-a-credit-report-and-what-does-it-include/.
[19] myFICO, "What's in your credit report?": https://www.myfico.com/credit-education/whats-in-my-credit-report.
[20] Equifax, "What is a Credit Report and What Does it Include?".

- *Collections, bankruptcies, inquiries, and other information:* Credit reports also include information on accounts that are currently past due or assigned to a debt collector, which can significantly affect a consumer's credit score. Both "hard" and "soft" credit inquiries are also noted on credit reports. Hard inquiries are recorded when a consumer's credit report is checked for the purpose of making lending or credit decisions, and can affect the consumer's credit scores. Soft inquiries, which do not affect credit scores, are recorded when credit reports are pulled to conduct a background check, to review existing account information, and to fulfill requests for consumers' annual credit reports.[21] Bankruptcy information is also on credit reports and can stay on them for up to 10 years.[22]

Laws and Institutions Protecting Consumers in the Credit Reporting System

The Fair Credit Reporting Act, enacted in 1970, is Title VI of the Consumer Credit Protection Act and grants consumers certain rights regarding their credit reports and scores. These rights include a consumer's right to know whether their report has been used to deny them credit, the right to obtain a credit score, the right to know what is in their credit report, the right to seek damages for violations of the FCRA, and the right to dispute incorrect information.[23] The CRAs are required to follow "reasonable procedures to assure maximum possible accuracy."[24] They are responsible for fixing errors and are typically required to do so within 30 days of receiving a dispute from a consumer. In practice, however, this provision is typically satisfied by the CRAs accepting the furnisher's findings, resulting in no changes to the consumer's credit report.[25] There is no way for consumers to appeal the result of a dispute investigation beyond filing another dispute. The FCRA is enforced federally by the Consumer Financial Protection Bureau and the FTC.

---

[21] Experian, "What Are Inquiries On Your Credit Report?": https://www.experian.com/blogs/ask-experian/credit-education/report-basics/hard-vs-soft-inquiries-on-your-credit-report/.

[22] Experian, "How to Remove Bankruptcy from Credit Report": https://www.experian.com/blogs/ask-experian/removing-bankruptcy-from-your-credit-report/.

[23] While the Fair Credit Reporting Act provides consumers the right to obtain their credit score, it does not outline how scoring companies should provide the score nor how much they can charge for scores. See FTC, https://www.ftc.gov/system/files/documents/statutes/fair-credit-reporting-act/545a_fair-credit-reporting-act-0918.pdf.

[24] Fair Credit Reporting Act, § 607. Compliance procedures [15 U.S.C. § 1681e] (1970).

[25] Ibid.

The Equal Credit Opportunity Act prohibits people and institutions from considering race, color, religion, national origin, sex, marital status, age, and whether or not the consumer is receiving public assistance when making credit and lending decisions.[26] The ECOA is enforced by multiple federal agencies, including the CFPB and the FTC.[27]

Likelihood of Errors on Credit Reports

Credit report errors have been studied and documented for a long time. In its American Experiences Survey, a nationally representative survey addressing a wide variety of consumer concerns, Consumer Reports asked 1,040 American consumers in February 2020 and 2,223 American consumers in January 2021 whether they had checked their credit reports, whether they had found errors, and, if they had found errors, whether the errors had been disputed and corrected. In February 2020, 14 percent of consumers who had ever checked their credit reports said they had found errors, and 53 percent of those who had disputed errors were able to get them corrected.

This year's survey results were largely consistent. In January 2021, 12 percent of consumers who had ever checked their credit reports said they found errors, with 57 percent able to get their errors corrected after filing a dispute.

All these findings are also consistent with a 2012 FTC study on credit reporting accuracy, which found that 21 percent of consumers had at least one verified error in their credit report that was corrected by a CRA, and 5 percent of consumers had errors so significant that they were put in a different credit risk tier altogether.[28] This point is echoed by the complaints found in the CFPB complaint database. Complaints regarding credit reporting errors have remained among the most frequent submissions to the database and have more than doubled since 2019.[29] All told, the 2012 FTC study estimated that 21 percent of all consumers with files in the credit reporting system had at least one verified error in their report.[30]

---

[26] FTC, "Your Equal Credit Opportunity Rights": https://www.consumer.ftc.gov/articles/0347-your-equal-credit-opportunity-rights.

[27] Ibid.

[28] FTC, *Report to Congress Under Section 319 of the Fair and Accurate Credit Transactions Act of 2003* (2015) ii: https://www.ftc.gov/system/files/documents/reports/section-319-fair-accurate-credit-transactions-act-2003-sixth-interim-final-report-federal-trade/150121factareport.pdf.

[29] CFPB, Consumer Response Annual Report (2021) 22: https://files.consumerfinance.gov/f/documents/cfpb_2020-consumer-response-annual-report_03-2021.pdf.

[30] FTC, *Report to Congress* 6.

In addition, the January 2021 CR survey, which had a sample large enough to explore racial and ethnic differences, found significant racial and ethnic differences in reported credit report error rates. A higher percentage of Black, non-Hispanic adults who had ever checked their credit reports found errors (26 percent) than did Hispanic adults (14 percent), English-speaking Asian adults (9 percent), and white, non-Hispanic adults (8 percent).

Types and Causes of Credit Report Errors

Mistakes on credit reports can include accounts or loans that have been paid off but appear unpaid, individual loans that are listed multiple times, and debts that are incorrectly reported in collection. Even seemingly small errors, such as misspelled names, wrong addresses, and incorrect birth dates, can cause problems for consumers.

The most common errors in credit reports occur when mistakes are made in matching specific consumer credit information (known in the industry as tradeline data) with a consumer's credit file.[31] The result is a so-called mixed file, where data about one consumer is mistakenly attributed to—and ends up in the credit file of—one or more other consumers with similar names. A 2012 FTC study found that roughly 35 percent of consumers saying they found an error on their credit reports also said the item or account in question did not belong to them.[32]

Among those consumers who have collection account disputes, the incidence of mixed files is even higher, with over 80 percent saying the collection item did not belong to them.[33]

Errors in credit reports have a wide range of causes and can be introduced by both CRAs and data furnishers. Some types of errors are introduced into individual files or small groups of files, while others have systemic or technological causes and can affect thousands or even millions of files. Several error types are related and can compound—for example, an error such as a misspelled name or an incorrect address can lead to a mixed file.

The CFPB highlighted a variety of reasons for matching errors in another report on the credit reporting system published in 2012. Matching errors can happen as a result of insufficient identifying information from data furnishers, changes to marital status, or two people being related, sharing an address, or

---

[31] Ibid.
[32] Ibid.
[33] Ibid.

having similar names.[34] Name changes in particular often lead to the creation of mixed files, the CFPB report notes.[35]

All types of errors can significantly affect a consumer's credit score, their ability to verify their identity with the CRAs, and their access to affordable credit, employment opportunities, and auto and homeowners insurance.

Other Error Sources: Data Furnishers and Debt Collectors

While a consumer may be the one taking out a loan, it is the furnishers—lenders, banks, and debt collectors—that are responsible for reporting information about the consumer's account to the credit bureaus. In this way, furnishers are a critical node in the credit reporting system: Any mistakes made at the furnisher level affect the data held by the bureaus and any subsequent decisions based on the credit reports they hold.[36]

Some furnisher errors are caused by outdated software or flaws in administrative procedures. In November 2017, the CFPB issued a consent order against Conduent Business Services, formerly known as Xerox, for software errors that led to incorrect information on over 1 million consumers being furnished to the credit bureaus.[37] The CFPB alleged that Xerox had been using unreleased, modified loan servicing software that incorrectly reported consumer accounts containing errors to the credit bureaus.[38] As this example demonstrates, mistakes do not necessarily happen at the account level. Errors in software can have a broad impact, in this case affecting over 1 million consumers.

In some cases a furnisher's internal procedures—or lack thereof—may cause inaccuracies. In a 2015 enforcement action against used auto dealer CarHop, the CFPB alleged that Universal Acceptance Corp., the entity furnishing data on behalf of CarHop, lacked any written procedures for accurately reporting consumer data.[39] As the CFPB alleged, Universal

---

34 CFPB, *Key Dimensions* 24.

35 Ibid.

36 CFPB, *Key Dimensions* 19: https://files.consumerfinance.gov/f/201212_cfpb_credit-reporting-white-paper.pdf.

37 CFPB, *CFPB Fines Xerox Business Services $1.1 Million for Incorrect Consumer Information Sent to Credit Reporting Agencies*: https://www.consumerfinance.gov/about-us/newsroom/cfpb-fines-xerox-business-services-11-million-incorrect-consumer-information-sent-credit-reporting-agencies/.

38 Xerox consented to the issuance of the consent order but did not admit or deny any of the CFPB's findings of fact.

39 CFPB, *CFPB Orders CarHop to Pay $6.4 Million Penalty for Jeopardizing Consumers' Credit* (2015): https://www.consumerfinance.gov/about-us/newsroom/cfpb-orders-carhop-to-pay-6-4-million-penalty-for-jeopardizing-consumers-credit/.

Acceptance "had no written policies and procedures regarding the accuracy and integrity of the consumer information it furnished until early August 2013. The policies it adopted that month were not reasonable or appropriate to the nature, size, complexity, and scope of the company's activities."[40] Where having consistent rules and procedures for handling consumer data mattered the most, the rules were not written down, were not sufficient, or simply did not exist, according to the CFPB.[41]

Another example involves a 2018 enforcement action against State Farm Bank, in which the CFPB alleged that State Farm violated the FCRA multiple times "by obtaining consumer reports without a permissible purpose; furnishing to credit-reporting agencies (CRAs) information about consumers' credit that the bank knew or had reasonable cause to believe was inaccurate; failing to promptly update or correct information furnished to CRAs; furnishing information to CRAs without providing notice that the information was disputed by the consumer; and failing to establish and implement reasonable written policies and procedures regarding the accuracy and integrity of information provided to CRAs."[42]

Debt collectors also furnish consumer credit information, and mistakes on their part can also be damaging to consumers. In a 2015 CFPB enforcement action against EOS CCA, a debt-collection firm based in Massachusetts, EOS was alleged to have purchased a portfolio of consumer debt, did not verify its information, and proceeded to collect on the portfolio.[43] Errors were allegedly so significant that the accuracy of the entire portfolio was ultimately disputed. In this way, consumers who are hounded by debt collectors for debts they do not owe can be doubly harmed: They need to not only stop the collection process but also repair the errors on their credit report.[44]

As these examples demonstrate, it is not enough to have rules in place. Meaningful enforcement of the FCRA and a close watch over both furnishers and CRAs are key to preventing mistakes that can affect millions of consumers. In order to prevent upstream mistakes that affect the bureaus,

---

[40] Ibid.

[41] As part of the consent order, Universal Acceptance Corp. did not admit or deny any of the CFPB's findings.

[42] CFPB, *Bureau of Consumer Financial Protection Settles with State Farm Bank* (2018): https://www.consumerfinance.gov/about-us/newsroom/bureau-consumer-financial-protection-settles-state-farm-bank/; State Farm consented to CFPB's issuance of the consent order but did not admit or deny any of its findings.

[43] CFPB, *CFPB Takes Action Against Debt Collector for Pursuing Disputed and Unverified Cellphone Debts* (2015): https://www.consumerfinance.gov/about-us/newsroom/cfpb-takes-action-against-debt-collector-for-pursuing-disputed-and-unverified-cellphone-debts/.

[44] EOS CCA did not admit or deny any of the CFPB's findings as part of the consent order.

lenders, and consumers, furnishing standards under the FCRA must be fully enforced and the CRAs must ensure that the information being fed into their records is accurate.

The Dispute Process

In order to dispute an alleged credit report error, a consumer must file a dispute with the CRAs. The major CRAs maintain a software system, called e-Oscar, that classifies each dispute with a code[45] and transmits the dispute data—including any supporting documentation provided by consumers—to furnishers.[46] While e-Oscar has been improved over time, consumer complaints related to the CRAs' investigations into problems on consumers' credit reports remain high—in 2020, 24 percent of all closed complaints to the CFPB about consumer or credit reporting were about disputes.[47]

One persistent consumer complaint is that furnishers do not always address the documentation supplied by consumers in support of their dispute. The e-Oscar system requires that the CRAs forward any supporting documents provided by the consumer to the appropriate data furnisher. But some furnishers neglect or refuse to open the supporting documentation, relying instead on their own data and the limited information provided by e-Oscar.[48]

Another common complaint is that credit bureaus often accept the results of furnisher investigations without scrutiny, essentially "parroting" the decision made by the furnisher. Failing to genuinely consider the validity of the furnisher's findings undermines the integrity of the dispute process.[49]

Additionally, consumers may not always get back the complete results of investigations regarding their dispute. In 2017, the CFPB found that at least one consumer reporting company did not provide the results of dispute investigations in consumer dispute notices. Instead, consumers were told that their dispute investigation was complete.[50]

---

[45] National Consumer Law Center (NCLC), *Automated Injustice Redux: Ten Years after a Key Report, Consumers Are Still Frustrated Trying to Fix Credit Reporting Errors* 6 (2019): https://www.nclc.org/images/pdf/credit_reports/automated-injustice-redux.pdf.

[46] Ibid.

[47] In 2020, the CFPB received 66,900 closed complaints regarding dispute investigations and 280,822 closed complaints regarding consumer or credit reporting. *See:* CFPB, *Consumer Annual Report.*

[48] NCLC, *Automated Injustice Redux* 6.

[49] Ibid.

[50] CFPB, *Supervisory Highlights Consumer Reporting Edition* (2017): https://files.consumerfinance.gov/f/documents/201703_cfpb_Supervisory-Highlights-Consumer-Reporting-Special-Edition.pdf.

Methodology

On Feb. 1, 2021, Consumer Reports launched the survey project Credit Checkup. Consumers were asked to take advantage of free weekly access to their credit reports from the major CRAs and to report on their experiences to Consumer Reports through a short questionnaire. The goal of this project was to obtain a better understanding of consumers' perceptions of their own credit reports. Although industry group Consumer Data Industry Association told CR that it disputes CR's methodology, the findings are consistent with previous research discussed in this paper.[51]

As described below, the project was voluntary and therefore not representative of the country as a whole. In fact, the participants were largely white, with only small percentages of individuals who identify as being of another race or ethnicity. Given that previous studies have shown that credit reporting errors can be worse for individuals of color,[52] these findings may understate the overall rate of problems that consumers find when checking their credit.

Survey Design

The survey asked questions regarding consumers' understanding of their reports, whether they had found errors, and the ease or difficulty of accessing their reports. This survey began Feb. 1, 2021 and ended April 1, 2021. More than 7,000 consumers participated in the project, with 5,858 completing the survey.[53] Responses were collected through a 14-question SurveyMonkey questionnaire. Consumer Reports made consumers aware of the survey through several promotional efforts—more on that below—and participation was voluntary.

---

[51] When asked about CR's findings, Francis Creighton—president and CEO of the Consumer Data Industry Association, the trade association that represents the credit bureaus—challenged the results. "We strongly caution against drawing conclusions from non-empirical surveys of consumers, such as this," Creighton says. "The credit reporting industry takes data accuracy extremely seriously, and improvements to the system cannot be achieved by relying on questionable and skewed data studies." He also says that "CDIA and our members are proud of our high-accuracy rates" and that "we are committed to continually improving the accuracy of credit reports." *See* Consumer Reports, *More Than a Third of Consumers Discovered Errors in Their Credit Reports, CR Study Finds:* https://www.consumerreports.org/credit-scores-reports/consumers-found-errors-in-their-credit-reports-a69 96937910/.

[52] Consumer Reports, *American Experiences Survey: January 2021 Results - Credit Report Errors, Video Doorbells, and Product Safety Recalls* (January 2021).

[53] The remaining respondents began but did not complete the survey.

Questions 1 through 13 were multiple choice; they can be found in the Appendix. Question 14 was a free-response question in which consumers were asked, "Is there anything else you would like to tell us about your experience checking your credit report?" Consumers were free to write anything and, in fact, addressed a wide variety of concerns.

Survey Promotion

The survey was the focus of a promotional campaign coordinated by Consumer Reports and partnering organizations. This campaign included social media promotion by both CR and the other organizations, as well as a series of panel discussions with consumer experts experienced in the credit reporting advocacy space. The priority goals of the campaign were to educate consumers about credit reporting, encourage them to take advantage of the CRAs temporarily offering free weekly access to credit reports, and ask them to participate in the survey. A majority of the survey participants checked their credit reports within a day of completing the survey, but some had already independently checked their reports and were allowed to participate in the survey if they reported having checked their reports within the previous month. Partnering organizations included Americans for Financial Reform, Consumer Action, National Association of Consumer Advocates, National Consumer Law Center, and U.S. PIRG.

Key Findings

The thousands of consumers who checked their credit reports and filled out our survey provided us with a picture of a credit reporting system that is rife with errors, is difficult to access and navigate, and can trap people into paying for services that they neither want nor need.

The consumers who provided us with written responses expressed deep frustration with a system that has an enormous impact on their lives but that they cannot control. As one wrote:

> TransUnion and Equifax make it difficult to find your free credit freeze functionality. And Equifax required me to get my free credit report via snail mail instead of online. In other words, they just do whatever they can to fool or persuade you to subscribe to their vastly overpriced services instead of allowing you to easily access the information that you're supposed to get for free. Considering their poor record on accuracy and security, these bureaus

should be forced to meet a much higher standard. Our financial lives depend on how these bureaus handle our information. And they are fumbling the ball left and right.

Credit Reports Contain Inaccuracies

More than one-third (34 percent) of the individuals who completed CR's Credit Checkup survey reported that they found at least one error on their report, with 29 percent reporting that they found errors in personal information and 11 percent finding account information errors.

Among those who found errors in their personal information, the most common were errors in address information, which can cause difficulty for the consumer when verifying their identity with the CRAs or during employment and tenant screenings.

Among those who found errors in account information, 41 percent saw accounts they didn't recognize. Others found debt reported to collections that they didn't recognize, one or more payments reported late that they recalled having made on time, and missed payments that they knew they had made.

In addition, legislation was enacted during the COVID-19 crisis to protect consumers with accounts that are in forbearance—in which a borrower is given the option of postponing or reducing payments on a loan for an established period of time—or accounts that have other accommodations. The law requires that accounts be frozen at their pre-accommodation status so that the borrower's credit score is not harmed because of the accommodation, as long as the consumer complies with the accommodation agreement. Of the individuals who told CR that they have an account in forbearance, 15 percent told us that their account was not being reported as "current."

Errors in Personal Information

Consumers who completed the Credit Checkup survey provided Consumer Reports with additional information about the types of errors they found in their reports. They noted bad addresses, extra addresses, and missing information that should have been included:

> Experian did not have my current address, for more than one year, or phone number. They omitted that I had lived in my current address previously for two years, more recently than a St. Louis address they listed. They listed our previous address, a five-plex in which we occupied two units, three times and characterized it as both a multifamily and an apartment complex. They listed an apartment in St. Louis that I did not live in.

Another consumer found multiple strange errors regarding their address:

> I found all sorts of combinations of details. There were five addresses listed—all pointing to my actual address—but each was slightly different from the others.

One consumer found an inconsistency between the Experian credit report accessed through AnnualCreditReport.com and the report accessed directly through Experian's site:

> The AnnualCreditReport.com report from Experian listed an additional address unknown to me. However, upon pulling an actual credit report with my FICO score from Experian, the unknown address was not listed.

Errors in Account Information

Consumers reported to CR concerns about inaccurate account information in their reports. As one wrote:

> I found a charge account that I did not recognize. It had been closed in 2017. It did not say closed at customer's request, which I always specify. I called TD Credit but they were unable to find me in their system. They said to talk to TransUnion for details. TransUnion told me to call them. The account is called "Shopper's Charge" followed by some numbers. Since I was part of the [Equifax] breach, I have to wonder if my information was used to open this account. We pay cash for cars and have not financed any large items. The account was only open for about 2 years. It does not have any adverse reporting associated with it. But I wish I could find out what it was all about.

Difficulties Accessing Credit Reports

Ten percent of consumers who completed the survey found accessing their credit reports "difficult" or "very difficult."[54] Of particular note is that consumers gave accounts of being locked out of their credit reports because of identity verification questions that they could not answer. Consumers were then told to verify their identity through the mail, a process that significantly delays access to credit reports. One consumer told us:

> I tried at first at AnnualCreditReport.com to get Experian, Equifax, and TransUnion all at once; after about 20 minutes I finally got an error message

[54] 6.50% of respondents expressed that accessing their credit report was "difficult," and 3.81% expressed that it was "very difficult."

> generated by Equifax, so I started over, this time only Experian; that came up OK; then I tried TransUnion; after 15 minutes I received a message that TransUnion couldn't confirm my identity and so I would have to call them; I didn't try again with Equifax.

Another consumer expressed suspicion that, because the identity verification questions contained information that matched a family member whose name is similar to theirs, their report probably contained bad or incorrect information. But because they couldn't answer the questions, they were unable to access their report to figure that out:

> The reason I only got the TransUnion credit report was because Experian wouldn't let me go forward and Equifax had security questions that didn't match me (although they matched my daughter who has the same first initial and last name). So Equifax has errors—but I can't get in to fix them!

Consumers also told CR that the security questions asked were very specific, often pertaining to details regarding credit accounts used years ago, posing problems for recollection. As one consumer noted, the Equifax "verification questions they asked relied on me remembering what account I might have opened four to 10 years ago, which I really can't do." Another consumer told CR they were tripped up by a question about a decade-old loan:

> The questions they ask to verify your identity are difficult even when it is really me. For example, they asked who the lender was on a mortgage refi I did 10 years ago, and refused my request for an online credit report because I had forgotten the lender name. I had to mail in a request, which I have done.

These complaints reveal that it is not always simple for consumers to check their credit online. The CRAs operate with the assumption that their information is correct, when too often it historically has not been, and use that information to verify identity. If a report has errors, and the identity verification system relies on those errors, consumers will be locked out of their reports. One consumer understood this problem and its implications, telling CR:

> I tried to get the other two credit agency reports, but after answering the security questions, I was told they could not provide the document online and I would have to mail a request. I tried to access the form to print out, and it would not work. So I could not access the other two credit agency reports

> online today. This concerns me, as the security questions were all 'no' answers. So there might be something on them that is inaccurate that they're asking me to verify. Which of course I can't. So I will try again tomorrow or so to try to access the other two.

Yet another consumer expressed concern that if they cannot verify their identity online, they are asked to do so by sending information through physical mail, which they did not trust:

> Yes—I tried to view all three credit reports, but Equifax would not let me view it online—it requires me to fill out a form and send (via the MAIL!!) photocopies of two forms of sensitive identifying information, such as Social Security card and driver's license! That is both frustrating and very risky.

Surprise Charges

Despite the legal requirement that consumers have access to credit reports free of charge, some consumers reported to CR that they were marketed to during the process of accessing their report, and some told us that they found they had been charged money as they went through the process to access their reports. As one consumer wrote, "The system seems rigged to try to sell you more services and make it overly difficult to get your credit report."

One consumer reported that they were able to avoid the charges by clicking past offers for paid services:

> Without a reason, it threw up a window to charge me for services starting at $1 to try it out, then more (I assume) to continue with upgraded reporting. It was confusing, since I knew they were supposed to offer it free. I discarded that window to find that I could finally print my report free.

Another consumer reported that they were unwittingly being charged for services they did not sign up for:

> Yes!!! TransUnion charged $25 to my AmEx card for 'membership' when I applied for the 'free credit report.' I called. Refund arrived via an AmEx email two days later. I believe Experian is trying to do the same thing, but as usual, one cannot reach the dispute center by phone. I will continue trying.

Another consumer shared that they were being charged for monthly services they did not sign up for:

> After entering a bunch of personal information, Experian said, 'Report unavailable online' and wanted me to send a letter with copies of documents (driver's license, Social Security number, etc.); Equifax said an error had occurred and they couldn't complete my request at this time; TransUnion ran me through an exhausting series of questions, sales offers, and ridiculous permutations until I was able to get a credit report and score displayed. Then I found that they had signed me up for a monthly service and charged my credit card $27 and change for the first month, to be charged monthly. I immediately canceled the 'subscription,' and had to call the helpline to get this charge removed from my card.

Other Frustrations and Confusion

Problems with Disputes

The Consumer Reports survey did not specifically ask about consumer experiences in disputing errors on their reports. Nevertheless, some consumers shared their frustrations with the dispute process and reported problems they had in disputing errors. One noted that he had tried to dispute bad information but couldn't get it removed:

> An account which never was mine is still on my credit report. That account was established in 2013 and closed in 2015, and years ago I contacted the credit report companies to remove that entire account from my record. That account is noted as closed, but still appears on my report. It was not removed.

And one consumer told CR that they could not dispute a problem that they found:

> I was concerned that a name was listed that I've never used, but was not allowed to dispute it on my credit report, as well as an address in a town I've never lived in, but was not allowed to dispute.

Combinations of Problems

Some consumers experienced just about every problem all at once. Problems in credit reporting are not mutually exclusive.

As shown below, consumers can easily experience the failures of the credit reporting system on multiple levels:

> Is this different from my credit score? I didn't get my credit score. When I tried, TransUnion wanted me to fill out a separate form, and it looked like the company wanted to charge me. Also, TransUnion had an address at which I have never lived. I filled out a dispute, but I was never asked for any details. The information used to verify my identification was for an ex-brother-in-law (ex for nearly 21 years) and someone I've never heard of. Also, it had as my only place of employment a place I worked at in 1988. Should I be concerned about this?

Marketplace and Policy Recommendations

A mix of marketplace and policy changes can improve the credit reporting system so that it works better for consumers. Consumer Reports recommends four broad categories of changes for policymakers and CRAs to implement.

Strengthen Accuracy Requirements for Credit Reports and Improve Enforcement of Existing Laws

Credit bureaus, as well as the lenders and debt collectors that furnish information to them, should be held responsible for maintaining the accuracy of consumers' credit reports.[55]

- CRAs and data furnishers should be required to match first name, last name, date of birth, and all nine digits of Social Security numbers when placing information on consumers' reports.[56]
- Furnishers and CRAs should be required to retain documents relating to an account for as long as the relevant information appears on the

---

[55] Consumer Reports has supported federal legislation requiring CRAs to better monitor furnishers for high error rates and to use stricter matching criteria: https://ourfinancialsecurity.org/wp-content/uploads/2020/01/2020.1.27-House-floor-credit-reporting-bill-su pport-letter.pdf; *See e.g.,* H.R. 3621 (116th Congress) - Comprehensive CREDIT Act of 2020.

[56] Consumer Reports has supported federal legislation requiring CRAs to match all nine digits of a consumer's social security number when placing information on credit reports: https://www.nclc.org/images/pdf/credit_reports/support-for-protecting-credit-score-2020.pdf; *See* e.g., H.R. 5332 (116th Congress) - Protecting Your Credit Score Act of 2020.

credit report, and should be required to delete information from a credit report if they cannot provide the documentation to back it up.

- Debt collectors should be required to document and maintain an itemized record of the total principal, interest, fees, and other charges that have been added to the debt, and the name of the original creditor when suing over a debt. Selling or collecting debt that is more than seven years old, which is too old to be reported on a credit report under the FCRA, should be made illegal.
- The dispute process must be improved so that it is responsive to consumers and thorough in its fact finding. Furnishers should not be allowed to dismiss a dispute without considering new information that is relevant to the complaint submitted by the consumer. The CRAs should not have the last word if consumers disagree with the results of a dispute.[57]
- The CFPB should require the CRAs to better monitor furnishers for high error rates.

Provide Consumers Control over Their Own Credit Information

Key to improving the accuracy of the credit reporting system is making sure consumers are appropriately informed about their credit records, are able to monitor their credit report without cost, and have control over when and how their credit information is used.

- Consumers should be able to access their credit reports and scores securely and free of charge at any time.[58]
- Consumers should not be harassed with advertisements for paid services while checking their free reports.
- Credit reports should be frozen by default, so potential lenders can access credit information only if a consumer grants them access.[59]

---

[57] Consumer Reports has supported federal legislation establishing consumers' right to appeal the results of dispute investigations. *See* e.g., H.R. 3621 (116th Congress) - Comprehensive CREDIT Act of 2020.

[58] Consumer Reports has supported federal legislation that allows consumers to check their credit reports and scores from the CRAs for free an unlimited number of times. *See* e.g., H.R. 5332 (116th Congress) - the Protecting Your Credit Score Act.

[59] Consumer Reports has supported federal legislation that requires consumers' credit to be frozen by default. *See* e.g., S. 1343 (117th Congress) - Consumer Credit Control Act of 2021.

- Consumers should be able to access their credit reports on a secure portal site where they can directly compare their reports, freeze and unfreeze their credit, and easily file disputes to correct errors.[60]

Redesign the Identity Verification System

The identity verification system used by Equifax, Experian, and TransUnion should be redesigned so that consumers are not locked out of their credit reports if they cannot answer a question based on inaccurate information. Should this happen, consumers should be given a method faster and more secure than physical mail to verify their identity. Consumers should not be blindsided by questions they cannot answer when trying to access their credit reports.

Rein in the Role of Credit Reports in Consumers' Lives

Even if credit reports were consistently accurate, there would be many strong arguments for restricting their use to their original purpose of measuring creditworthiness. CR has long documented the problems with using credit scores as a rating factor for auto insurance, for instance. A 2015 study found that a single driver who had a good credit score paid $68 to $526 more per year, on average, than similar drivers with the highest credit score, depending on the state they lived in.[61] These scores are not relevant to determining driver risk, and should not be used for that purpose.[62] Given the thoroughly documented inaccuracies of the system, it is simply unconscionable to use credit reports for other purposes, thereby extending the potential damage of such errors.

---

60 Consumer Reports has supported federal legislation that establishes a secure portal site where consumers are able to securely access their credit reports and scores from the CRAs for free, file disputes, and place security freezes. *See* e.g., H.R. 5332 (116th Congress) - the Protecting Your Credit Score Act.

61 CONSUMER REPORTS, *The Truth About Car Insurance*, Sept. 2015: http://www.consumerreports.org/cro/car-insurance/auto-insurance-special-report/index.htm.

62 Consumer Reports has supported federal and state legislation that restricts the use of credit reports in auto insurance pricing. *See* e.g., New Jersey A1657 (2020) Prohibits use of education, occupation, and credit score as rating factors in automobile insurance underwriting; HR 1756 (116th Congress) - Preventing Credit Score Discrimination in Auto Insurance Act.

Appendix: Complete Results from Consumer Reports' Credit Checkup Survey

The survey questions and descriptive statistics for 13 of the 14 questions are presented below. The final question of the survey was a free-response question asking consumers to tell CR anything they would like to about their experience checking their credit reports.

Credit Report Check Survey Tabs (Non-Representative Convenience Sample)	
When did you last check your credit report?	Percentage
Today	66
This week	18
This month	16
Base: All respondents. Note: Participants could also answer "This Year," "Never," or "Can't Recall." Those who did were redirected to check their credit report. They had to answer this question again before proceeding with the survey.	*5,839*
Which credit bureau(s) did you get your credit report from?	Percentage
Experian	59
TransUnion	57
Equifax	43
Unsure	3
Base: All respondents.	*5,858*
Did you use AnnualCreditReport.com to access your credit report(s)?	Percentage
Yes	73
No	24
Can't remember	3
Base: All respondents. Note: AnnualCreditReport.com was where Consumer Reports sent survey-takers who had not recently checked their credit reports.	*5,849*
Now we want to ask you about what you found on your credit report. Credit reports contain several types of data; personal information, such as your name and address; and information about any time you've borrowed money, including credit cards, auto loans, and, in some cases, other types of debt that have gone to collections, such as medical bills. We want to ask you about both in separate questions.	
Did you find any personal information on your credit report(s), such as misspellings or names or addresses that you don't recognize?	Percentage
Yes	29
No	71
Base: All respondents.	*5,821*

(Continued)

If you found incorrect personal information on your credit report, which types of errors did you find? Check all that apply.	Percentage
Wrong address (address you do not recognize, etc.)	56
Your name misspelled	33
Wrong name (a name that is not yours)	17
Other (please specify)	37
Base: Respondents who found incorrect personal information on their credit report.	*1,739*
Did you find information on your credit report(s) related to debts that you believe is incorrect? This can include payments that are noted as late when you know you made them on time, or an account that you don't recognize, such as a credit card that you don't have.	Percentage
Yes	11
No	89
Base: All respondents.	*5,821*
If you found an error on your report regarding a debt, what kind of error was it? Check all that apply.	Percentage
An account that I don't recognize	41
A debt reported to collections that I don't recognize	26
One or more payments reported late that I made on time	23
A missed payment that I know I made	12
Other (please specify)	33
Base: Respondents who found an error related to a debt on their credit report.	*695*
Combined: Any error on credit report (personal information and/or debt-related)	Percentage
No errors	66
Any error	34
Base: All respondents.	*5,858*
Some borrowers have an agreement with the lender, sometimes called a forbearance agreement, that allows them to skip payments on some of their debts, such as mortgages, credit cards, and student loans. These agreements can be made under various circumstances, but for many people, they have happened by arrangement or even automatically during the pandemic (such as for federal student loans). Do you have an account where you have an agreement with the lender that allows you to skip making payments?	Percentage
Yes	5
No	86
Unsure	8
Base: All respondents.	*5,835*

If you have an account for which you are being allowed to miss payments, is that account(s) being reported as "current" on your credit reports?	Percentage
Yes	75
No	15
Unsure	10
Base: Respondents who said "yes" when asked whether they have a forbearance agreement.	308

How easy or difficult was it to access your credit reports?	Percentage
Very easy	40
Easy	35
Not easy or difficult	14
Difficult	7
Very difficult	4
Base: All respondents.	*5,848*

How easy or difficult was it to read and understand what you saw on your credit report?	Percentage
Very easy	26
Easy	43
Not easy or difficult	23
Difficult	6
Very difficult	2
Base: All respondents.	*5,827*

Race/ethnicity (respondents could select all that apply)	Percentage
White	86
Black	3
Asian	2
Latinx	2
Biracial/multiracial	1
Native American	1
Pacific Islander	<1
Prefer not to say	6
Base: All respondents.	*5,858*

Written Statement of Jeremie Greer, Co-founder and Co-Executive Director of Liberation in a Generation

Introduction

Chairwoman Waters, Ranking Member McHenry, and members of the committee, thank you for holding today's important hearing and for the opportunity to address the biases and flaws of our current credit reporting system. My name is Jeremie Greer, and I am the Co-founder and Co-executive Director of Liberation in a Generation, a national racial justice and movement support organization working to build the power of people of color to totally transform the economy. We do this by both championing transformative policy solutions and by bringing together leaders of color across the country to undo what we call the Oppression Economy, where racism is not only profitable but also fuels a cycle that suppresses the economic vitality of people of color. In its place, we also aim to build what we call a Liberation Economy where all people of color have their basic needs met, are safe from harm, are valued, and belong.

The Role of the Credit Reporting System in Determining Our Place in the Economy

It is within this Oppression Economy that we find credit reporting agencies such as Experian, TransUnion, Equifax, and others, who have anointed themselves gatekeepers with the power to determine who can and cannot access the financial products, services, and capital necessary to navigate the economy. In doing so, these and other institutions have essentially created a dual financial system. On one side of this system is a wealth-building track—with products and services that include affordable mortgages, prime lines of credit, and low-cost credit cards— which make it possible for consumers to build long-term financial security. On the other side of this system is a predatory track—with products and services that include subprime mortgages, payday loans, check cashers, and auto title lenders—which largely excludes people from building wealth or strips them of the little bit of wealth they may own.

At the core of determining which side of our dual financial system a consumer may find themselves in are the scores and reports credit reporting agencies generate. Unfortunately, our history of credit discrimination, the preference of our current credit reporting system for mainstream financial products, and its unfair handling of alternative data has placed millions of Black, Latinx, low and moderate-income Asians, and Indigenous people on that predatory track I spoke of, relegated to live on the fringes of our credit system or to be ignored entirely. To this point, according to a study by the Consumer Financial Protection Bureau (CFPB), about 15 percent of Black and Latinx consumers are considered "credit invisible," meaning they have no credit record at all, while about 13 percent of these consumers are deemed to have "thin" or "unscorable" credit files.[63] Overall, the Bureau estimates that 45 million consumers have either no credit records or have unscorable credit files, meaning that a considerable portion of the population is locked out from accessing safe and affordable financial services that can help them build financial security and long-term wealth. To put the cost of this exclusion into perspective, the Credit Builders Alliance estimates that consumers with low or nonexistent credit scores could pay $200,000 more for lending products and services throughout a lifetime.[64]

As alarming as this is, the cost of exclusion extends far beyond these financial ramifications. Today, what started as a tool to measure a consumer's creditworthiness is now used as a tool to judge a range of other things—including whether someone can be employed, can rent a home, can access electricity and heat, or even be able to purchase health insurance.[65] Many of these other judgments are facilitated through specific products developed and sold by Experian, TransUnion, and Equifax, which have all shown to have issues with managing and furnishing information that makes it possible for us to transact in the mainstream economy.

Our Credit Scoring System Reinforces and Exacerbates Racial Inequities

While numerous issues plague our current credit reporting system, a fundamental problem that concerns us is that the scores themselves and the process by which they are created are racially biased. For example, while the intended goal of these scores is to allow financial institutions to make an objective decision about an individual's creditworthiness, evidence suggests that there is a connection between an individual's income and their score. Such a correlation is particularly alarming, considering households of color earn far less income than white households.

---

[63] Kenneth P. Brevoort, et al., "Data Point: Credit Invisibles," Consumer Financial Protection Bureau, 2015, http://files.consumerfinance.gov/f/201505_cfpb_data-point-credit-invisibles.pdf.

[64] David Newville, Anju Chopra, et al., "Alternative Data Reporting Helps Families Build Credit & Wealth," Prosperity Now, 2017, https://prosperitynow.org/files/resources/Alternative%20Data%20Fact%20File_September%202017.pdf.

[65] Jennifer Brown, "Unscoreable: How The Credit Reporting Agencies Exclude Latinos, Younger Consumers, Low-Income Consumers, and Immigrants," UnidosUS, 2019, https://financialservices.house.gov/uploadedfiles/hhrg-116-ba00-wstate-brownj-20190226.pdf.

According to the Federal Reserve's 2019 Survey of Consumer Finances, median Black and Latinx households earn about $41,000, while median white households earn about $70,000. In examining recent studies of credit score data by Experian[66] and WalletHub,[67] such income levels would place the typical Black and Latinx household within an average credit score range of about 643-681, which are considered "bad" and "fair" credit scores ranges, respectively. By comparison, the typical white household would be within an average credit score range of 700-737, which is considered a "good" credit score range. Similar patterns emerge when looking at neighborhoods: according to a 2017 Urban Institute study of 60 major US cities, the median credit score in predominantly white areas was 697, compared to 621 for nonwhite areas.[68] A 2012 CFPB study showed similar trends, finding that among the 200,000 credit files the agency had analyzed, the median FICO score within high-minority zip codes was far lower than the median FICO score observed within low-minority zip codes.[69] Overall, numerous studies show consumers of color consistently have lower credit scores than white consumers.[70]

In part, these disparities can be attributed to our nation's long history of systematically denying communities of color access to affordable credit while simultaneously steering these communities to wealth-stripping financial products. Over the course of generations, these discriminatory actions have served to suppress the wealth-building potential of communities of color and fuel a racial wealth gap that today sees Black and Latinx households owning just 6% of the nation's wealth,[71] despite making up about 30% of the

---

[66] Matt Tatham, "Can You Make Minimum Wage and Still Have a Maximum Credit Score?," Experian, 2018, https://www.experian.com/blogs/ask-experian/can-you-make-minimum-wage-and-still-have-a-maximum-credit-score/.

[67] Bianca Peter, "What Is the Average Credit Score in America?," WalletHub, 2020, https://wallethub.com/edu/cs/average-credit-scores/25578#credit-score-by-income.

[68] Caroline Ratcliffe, Steven Brown, "Credit scores perpetuate racial disparities, even in America's most prosperous cities," Urban Institute, 2017, https://www.urban.org/urban-wire/credit-scores-perpetuate-racial-disparities-even-americas-most-prosperous-cities.

[69] "Analysis of Differences between Consumer- and Creditor-Purchased Credit Scores," Consumer Financial Protection Bureau, 2012, https://files.consumerfinance.gov/f/201209_Analysis_Differences_Consumer_Credit.pdf.

[70] Lisa Rice, Deidre Swesnik, "Discriminatory Effects of Credit Scoring on Communities of Color," Suffolk University Law Review, 2013, https://cpb-us-e1.wpmucdn.com/sites.suffolk.edu/dist/3/1172/files/2014/01/Rice-Swesnik_Lead.pdf.

[71] "Distribution of Household Wealth in the U.S. since 1989," Board of Governors of the Federal Reserve System, 2020, https://www.federalreserve.gov/releases/z1/dataviz/dfa/distribute/chart/#quarter:124;series:Net%20worth;demographic:race;popu lation:all;units:shares.

population. To put this dynamic into perspective, the following are a few examples that have contributed to this racial wealth gap:

- Post-civil war Black sharecroppers being provided with short-term predatory credit that left many vulnerable to falling victim to a cycle of perpetual economic insecurity.[72]
- Mid-20th century would-be homebuyers of color systematically denied, or "redlined," from accessing mainstream housing credit,[73] which left many vulnerable to the predatory practice of "contracts for deed." Eventually, this practice would strip billions in wealth from Black communities throughout the country who wanted nothing more than to secure their share of the American Dream.[74]
- The intentional targeting of communities of color by subprime mortgage lenders in the run-up to the 2008 Housing Crisis. As the committee knows, this steering and targeting not only led Black and Latinx homeowners to disproportionately lose their homes during the housing crisis,[75] but also wiped away more than half the median household wealth held by these communities in the process.[76]

Today, these historical racial economic injustices and inequities are further reinforced by the ways our current credit reporting system goes about calculating scores.[77] Overall, though it is illegal to use race (and other

---

72 Charles Lewis Nier III, "The Shadow of Credit: The Historical Origins of Racial Predatory Lending and its Impact upon African American Wealth Accumulation," *University of Pennsylvania Journal of Law and Social Change*, 2007, https://www.law.upenn.edu/journals/jlasc/articles/volume11/issue2/Nier11U.Pa.J.L.%26Soc.Change131(2007).pdf.

73 According to an analysis by George Lipsitz, a Professor of Black Studies and Sociology at the University of California, Santa Barbara, 98% of all government-backed mortgages issued between 1934 and 1968 went to White homebuyers.

74 Natalie Moore, "Contract Buying Robbed Black Families In Chicago Of Billions," *NPR*, 2019, https://www.npr.org/local/309/2019/05/30/728122642/contract-buying-robbed-black-families-in-chicago-of-billions#:~:text=Black%20families%20in%20Chicago%20 lost,a%20new%20report%20released%20Thursday.&text=Meanwhile%2C%20the%20contract%20seller%20held,and%20could%20evict%20the%20buyer.

75 Debbie Gruenstein Bocian, et al., "Foreclosures by Race and Ethnicity: The Demographics of a Crisis," for Responsible Lending, 2010, https://www.responsiblelending.org/mortgage-lending/research-analysis/foreclosures-by-race-and-ethnicity.pdf.

76 "Survey of Consumer Finances, 1989 - 2019," Board of Governors of the Federal Reserve System, 2020, https://www.federalreserve.gov/econres/scf/dataviz/scf/chart/#series:Net_Worth;demographic:racecl4;population:all;units:media n.

77 Lisa Rice, Deidre Swesnik, "Discriminatory Effects of Credit Scoring on Communities of Color," Suffolk University Law Review, 2013, https://cpb-us-e1.wpmucdn.com/sites.suffolk.edu/dist/3/1172/files/2014/01/Rice-Swesnik_Lead.pdf.

protected class statuses) in determining credit risk, each of the five FICO score calculation categories—payment history, amounts owed, length of credit history, new credit, types of credit used—can have particularly unequal and discriminatory effects on consumers of color.[78] Take, for example, length of credit history, a category that accounts for 15% of our FICO credit scores and presumably improves your score the longer you have a credit account open and active. As with the other FICO score calculation categories, the issue with this category is that you need credit to get credit, which places communities of color at an unfair disadvantage because of our history of racial economic exclusion.

Unlike the typical white household, the typical household of color often lacks the wealth to help ensure that their children can enter the credit system as early as possible, whether that be by helping their child open a credit card in their name during their college years or by co-signing a loan to finance a car, or even simply by not passing down debt.[79] Together, these and other actions taken by families with more significant economic resources can help to ensure that the next generation can begin their adult lives firmly within the wealth-building track I spoke of earlier. Sadly, research from the CFPB shows that the reality of being credit invisible or having unscorable credit files, and thus living within the predatory track of our dual financial system, begins at an early age in the lives of Black and Latinx consumers and persists over time.[80]

Beyond the ways the system goes about calculating our scores, historical racial economic disadvantages are also further reinforced by the kinds of data our current credit reporting system prefers. For example, when it comes to factoring in on-time payments, our current system favors mortgages and credit card payments over alternative data sources and credit products, like rental and cell phone payments. Considering that people of color are far less likely to own their homes or have access to a credit card,[81] the current system effectively overlooks many within the community solely because their monthly expenses do not go towards paying down a more traditional credit

---

[78] Ibid.

[79] Natalie Campisi, "From Inherent Racial Bias to Incorrect Data—The Problems With Current Credit Scoring Models," Forbes, 2021, https://www.forbes.com/advisor/credit-cards/from-inherent-racial-bias-to-incorrect-data-the-problems-with-current-credit-scoring-models/.

[80] Kenneth P. Brevoort, et al., "Data Point: Credit Invisibles," Consumer Financial Protection Bureau, 2015, http://files.consumerfinance.gov/f/201505_cfpb_data-point-credit-invisibles.pdf.

[81] Tamara E. Holmes, "Credit card race, age, gender statistics," creditcards.com, 2019, https://www.creditcards.com/credit-card-news/race-age-gender-statistics/.

product. At the same time that the current system does not fully capture the financial lives of consumers of color, it also penalizes consumers for holding "bad" debt, such as payday loans, unpaid student loan debt, unpaid utilities, and court fines and fees. Even worse, the system also penalizes consumers for actions outside of their control, such as a sudden job loss and holding debt that has no bearing on a person's creditworthiness, such as medical debt. Disproportionately, these kinds of debts are held by people of color.

Racial Implications of the Credit Reporting System Are Amplified Further by High Errors

In addition to the disparate effects and outcomes I highlighted, another major problem with our current credit reporting system is that the data used to generate these assessments is often inaccurate. To this point, a comprehensive and congressionally mandated study by the Federal Trade Commission (FTC) in 2013 found that 26 percent of consumers had identified errors in one of their three credit reports and that for five percent of consumers, these errors could lead to paying more for auto loans and insurance.[82] Two years later, some of the same consumers the FTC engaged in 2013 continued to express that some of the disputed information on their files remained inaccurate.[83] In other words, the sensitive consumer data that these companies collect to generate their scores, and then sells to other financial institutions to determine a consumer's "worthiness," not only has enormous consequences for where consumers are placed within our financial system but is also marred with issues that can significantly cost consumers. Yet, despite this, little has changed in the years since the FTC studies were published as a Consumer Reports survey fielded earlier this year found that more than a third of respondents (34%) had at least one error on their credit report, with 29 percent

---

[82] Jon Leibowitz et al., "Report to Congress Under Section 319 of the Fair and Accurate Credit Transactions Act of 2003," Federal Trade Commission, 2012, https://www.ftc.gov/sites/default/files/documents/reports/section-319-fair-and-accurate-credit-transactions-act-2003-fifth-interim-federal-trade-commission/130211factareport.pdf.

[83] "FTC Issues Follow-Up Study on Credit Report Accuracy," Federal Trade Commission, 2015, https://www.ftc.gov/news-events/press-releases/2015/01/ftc-issues-follow-study-credit-report-accuracy.

finding errors related to personal information, such as incorrect address information, and 11 percent finding errors related to account information.[84]

Adding to these issues, while federal agencies like the CFPB have made it easier for consumers to have the information and resources necessary to dispute inaccurate information on their credit reports,[85] consumers continue to find it incredibly difficult to navigate our credit reporting system. To this point, according to the Bureau's most recent Consumer Response annual report, out of the 542,300 consumer complaints the agency received last year, nearly 60 percent (319,300) were related to credit or consumer reporting, with almost 70 percent of those complaints (191,300) related to incorrect information on credit reports.[86] These indifferences related to data accuracy and consumer's wellbeing are symbolic of the systemic issues that have long afflicted our credit reporting system broadly and the big three credit reporting agencies specifically. Put simply, our current credit reporting system does not serve consumers particularly well.

Much of these issues are a byproduct of our private credit reporting system and the monetization of our data. Similar to the problems that have surfaced around Big Tech firms of today, credit reporting agencies like Experian, TransUnion, and Equifax were among some of the first commercial big data firms to methodically turn our personal, economic data into a multi-billion-dollar product, whose consequences can determine how we show up in the economy and the kinds of lives we can lead in it. And just like today's Big Tech firms, the many issues raised before the committee today and previously—from inaccurate data, to the carelessness when handling our data (best exemplified by the 2017 Equifax data breach), to the difficulty so many have in navigating error disputes, to the lack of innovation, accountability, and transparency— stem from the fact that the actual end-user of these scores is not the consumer, but rather financial institutions.[87] As private, publicly traded companies and venture-backed firms, the primary focus of the credit reporting

---

84 Syed Ejaz, "A Broken System: How The Credit Reporting System Fails Consumers And What To Do About It," Consumer Reports, 2021, https://advocacy.consumerreports.org/research/a-broken-system-how-the-credit-reporting-system-fails-consumers-and-what-to-do-about-it/.

85 "How do I dispute an error on my credit report?" Consumer Financial Protection Bureau, 2019 (updated), https://www.consumerfinance.gov/ask-cfpb/how-do-i-dispute-an-error-on-my-credit-report-en-314/.

86 "Consumer Response Annual Report," Consumer Financial Protection Bureau, 2021, https://files.consumerfinance.gov/f/documents/cfpb_2020-consumer-response-annual-report_03-2021.pdf.

87 Penelope Wang, "Why It's Still So Hard to Fix Credit Report Errors," Consumer Reports, 2020, https://www.consumerreports.org/credit-scores-reports/why-its-still-hard-to-fix-credit-report-errors/.

industry is creating value for their shareholders and investors, rather than doing what is best for the consumer whose data generates that value. As a result, this has tilted the incentives within the system towards volume and profit and away from accuracy, privacy protections, and customer service.[88]

Conclusion

Ultimately, to begin ending the dual financial system that allows some of us to build wealth and others to be largely excluded from doing so, we need to reform the current credit reporting system in fundamental ways. It is for this reason that we support Congresswoman Pressley's Comprehensive CREDIT (Credit Reporting Enhancement, Disclosure, Innovation, and Transparency) Act and Congressman Gottheimer's Protecting Your Credit Score Act, which put forward several needed reforms to bring greater transparency and accountability to Experian, TransUnion, and Equifax, and the credit reporting system writ large.

In particular, we are encouraged by the fact that the Comprehensive CREDIT Act would begin to reduce the broad gatekeeper powers credit reporting agencies have by significantly limiting the use of credit checks for hiring and employment purposes, while the Protecting Your Credit Score Act would institute several essential changes to not only provide consumers with greater protections but also greater access and control over their data. In addition, we are also encouraged that the committee is considering a proposal like the National Credit Reporting Agency Act, which by creating a public credit reporting option would not only begin to provide the public with the kind of competition, innovation, and accountability that has been missing in the current system but can also lead to the kind of system that can finally break down the walls of the dual financial system that exist today.

Considering the lack of accountability and general regard for consumers in the current system, and the impact that the various biases within the system have on consumers of color, we believe that consumers need a more robust system that works in their best interest. We look forward to supporting efforts that would move us in this direction and thank you for the opportunity to share our perspective with the committee today. I look forward to your questions and further discussing ways to overhaul our credit reporting system.

---

[88] Ibid.

Written Statement of Daniel J. Quan, Adjunct Scholar, Center for Monetary and Financial Alternatives, Cato Institute

Introduction

Chairwoman Waters, Ranking Member McHenry, and distinguished members of the Committee on Financial Services, my name is Dan Quan, and I am an adjunct scholar at the Cato Institute's Center for Monetary and Financial Alternatives. I am also a co-founder and General Partner of Nevcaut Ventures, a venture capital fund that invests in financial technology (FinTech) startups. In addition, I provide advisory services through my own firm, Banks Street Advisory, and as a Senior Advisor with McKinsey. Previously, I was Senior Advisor to the Director at the Consumer Financial Protection Bureau (CFPB) and led its FinTech initiative, Project Catalyst.

I am honored to take part in today's hearing entitled, "A Biased, Broken System: Examining Proposals to Overhaul Credit Reporting to Achieve Equity." My testimony will focus on the public credit bureau proposal that was first developed by the think tank Dēmos[89] and later endorsed by then-presidential candidate Joe Biden.[90]

The Credit Reporting Industry

At $14.6 trillion,[91] the consumer credit market in the United States is the largest and most competitive in the world. This vibrant credit market depends on a functioning credit reporting industry that is mostly made up of three national credit reporting agencies, Equifax, Experian, and TransUnion. TransUnion alone maintains 3.1 billion tradelines, processes more than 2

---

[89] See Amy Traub. "Establish a Public Credit Registry." *Dēmos*, April 3, 2019. Available at https://www.demos.org/sites/default/files/2019-03/Credit%20Report_Full.pdf.

[90] See "Biden-Sanders Unity Task Force Recommendations." July 8, 2020. Available at https://joebiden.com/wp-content/uploads/2020/08/UNITY-TASK-FORCE-RECOMMENDATIONS.pdf.

[91] See "Quarterly Report on Household Debt and Credit, 2021: Q1." Center for Microeconomic Data, Federal Reserve Bank of New York, May 21, 2021. Available at https://www.newyorkfed.org/medialibrary/interactives/householdcredit/data/pdf/hhdc_2021q1.pdf.

billion credit updates monthly, and matches these to more than 236 million active credit consumer profiles in the United States.[92]

The credit reporting agencies have been the subject of serious criticisms, most of which concern three areas:

1. *Accuracy*. A number of studies and surveys have indicated that credit reports have accuracy issues. The most comprehensive and authoritative study conducted by the Federal Trade Commission (FTC) shows that almost one in four consumers have an error on their credit reports that could affect their credit score, and 5% of consumers had errors that could result in less favorable credit terms.[93]
2. *Security*. American consumers can not be assured that their sensitive personal information is safe and secure. The Equifax data breach in 2017 that exposed the personal information of 147 million American consumers is one of the largest in recent history. Still, credit bureaus are not subject to any federal supervision on data security.
3. *Equity*. Forty-five million Americans are excluded from the mainstream credit system according to a CFPB study published in 2015.[94] Black, Hispanic, and low-income consumers are disproportionately credit invisible or unscorable.[95]

Public Credit Bureau: An Unworkable Solution

In response to these concerns, the Biden campaign, drawing on a proposal by Dēmos, a think tank based in New York City, endorsed the idea of a public credit bureau to supplement or even replace the private credit reporting agencies. The Dēmos proposal calls for:

---

[92] Data supplied by TransUnion.

[93] See "Report to Congress Under Section 319 of the Fair and Accurate Credit Transactions Act of 2003." *Federal Trade Commission*, December 2012. Available at https://www.ftc.gov/sites/default/files/documents/reports/section-319-fair-and-accurate-credit-transactions-act-2003-fifth-interim-federal-trade-commission/130211factareport.pdf.

[94] See "Data Point: Credit Invisibles." *Consumer Financial Protection Bureau*, May 2015. Available at https://files.consumerfinance.gov/f/201505_cfpb_data-point-credit-invisibles.pdf.

[95] See "Who Are the Credit Invisibles?" *Consumer Financial Protection Bureau,* December 2016. Available at https://files.consumerfinance.gov/f/documents/201612_cfpb_credit_invisible_policy_report.pdf.

1. Establishing a public credit bureau within the CFPB.
2. A 7-year transition period within which credit data will be furnished to the public bureau. During this time, private credit bureaus are required to provide their (historical) credit data to the public credit bureau. At the end of the transition period, lenders are only allowed to use data from the public credit bureau. The private credit bureaus known today will essentially cease to exist.[96]
3. Credit information can only be used for lending. The use of credit information for employment, housing, and insurance will be prohibited.[97]
4. The public credit bureau will develop new algorithms that minimize disparate racial impact by including non-traditional data sources such as rental history and utility bills.

The Dēmos proposal's policy goals are to *"improve equity, transparency, accuracy, accountability, appropriateness, security and public awareness of credit information."*[98]

These are certainly laudable goals. However, I believe that they can best be achieved by retaining and improving upon the existing, private sector credit reporting industry than by establishing a public credit bureau.

First, improving equity in credit access is best achieved by private sector innovations. The proposed bureau is supposed to achieve more equitable credit access by taking advantage of "new algorithms" that will consider new data sources such as rental history and bill payment. However, it is doubtful that by doing so the bureau will improve upon what the existing system is capable of achieving. This is so in part because the algorithms in question are not so new.

The so-called "new algorithms" have been developed by for-profit companies to tackle the credit access challenge without any government interventions.[99] With the advancement of open banking and the underlying

---

[96] Note the Biden-Sanders Unity Task Force Recommendations do not explicitly prohibit lenders from using private credit bureaus.

[97] Note the Biden-Sanders Unity Task Force Recommendations still allow the use of credit information for federal hiring.

[98] See Amy Traub. "Establish a Public Credit Registry." *Dēmos*, April 3, 2019. Available at https://www.demos.org/sites/default/files/2019-03/Credit%20Report_Full.pdf.

[99] There was a failed attempt to solve this problem by creating a credit reporting agency that collects rent and bill payment data in the hope of helping consumers build credit. See Ylan Q. Mui. "Official Joined Consumer Regulator After Watching Breakdown of Credit Company." *The Washington Post*, July 20, 2011. Available at https://www.washingtonpost.com/

financial infrastructure built by data aggregators, consumers now have the ability to permit third-parties to access their financial data housed within financial institutions. Riding this wave of innovation, Experian, FICO, and Finicity partnered to create Experian Boost and Ultra FICO. Both programs operate on an opt-in basis and are entirely free of charge. They allow consumers to use their on-time bill payment history and streaming subscriptions to increase their FICO scores. With the consumer's explicit consent, the payment data flows directly from the consumer's checking account to Experian and is incorporated in the "new algorithm" developed by FICO. According to Experian, users can boost their credit score by an average of 12 points, and to date, credit scores have been collectively increased by more than 69 million points.[100]

The FICO score is important, but it is not the only metric lenders use to assess credit risk. A growing number of lenders, most of them venture-backed, see the promise of using on-time payment history data in credit decisioning and have developed cash flow based credit underwriting models (i.e., another "new algorithm") to lend to consumes who lack a credit history. In fact, such "new algorithms" received the attention of 5 federal banking regulators, which issued a joint statement affirming the benefits and promise of the use of cash flow data.[101]

Many technology-driven companies are already innovating to serve the need of the 45 million consumers who have been traditionally left behind. The public credit bureau will not add any value to the emerging market-based solutions. Nor is there any good reason to suppose that the bureau would have the know-how and experience to develop better solutions.

Second, transparency is a real issue that requires a different kind of policy intervention. The Dēmos proposal argues that existing credit algorithms are opaque and lack useful information for consumers to improve credit. This is a fair criticism, but creating a public credit bureau that provides free credit reports and scores will not solve the problem.

Today consumers who have an internet connection or a smart phone can obtain free credit reports and credit scores relatively easily. However, most of

business/economy/official-joined-consumer-regulator-after-watching-breakdown-of-credit-company/2011/04/17/gIQAJV1rPI_story.html.

[100] See https://www.experian.com/consumer-products/score-boost.html.

[101] See "Interagency Statement on the Use of Alternative Data in Credit Underwriting." Board of Governors of the Federal Reserve System, Consumer Financial Protection Bureau, Federal Deposit Insurance Corporation, National Credit Union Administration, Office of the Comptroller of the Currency, December 3, 2019. Available at https://files.consumerfinance.gov/f/documents/cfpb_interagency-statement_alternative-data.pdf.

them (myself included) still have a hard time understanding why their credit applications are rejected by lenders.

Ultimately it is lenders (not credit bureaus) that are responsible for the issues in transparency. Lenders are required under the Equal Credit Opportunity Act (ECOA) and the Fair Credit Reporting Act (FCRA) to issue adverse action notices to consumers whose credit applications are declined. Those notices must explain why adverse actions were taken. The intention of such notices is to provide transparency to the credit underwriting process so that consumers may improve their odds of getting approved in the future. Unfortunately, almost every lender simply complies for the sake of complying by issuing adverse action notices that contain cryptic reason codes that most consumers do not understand. This is a long-standing issue. The CFPB hosted an adverse action notice tech sprint last October[102] in an attempt to use its persuasion power to nudge the industry to come up with more consumer-friendly solutions, and this is where the focus should be.

Third, the public credit bureau will not necessarily improve data accuracy. The Dēmos proposal recommends that data furnishers be held accountable for providing accurate information to the public credit bureau. At the same time, the public credit bureau will use "the most robust methods available to ensure that credit information is accurate and to avoid mixed files (cases where one person's credit accounts are mixed into someone else's file)."[103]

If consumers are to achieve financial freedom, their credit files must contain accurate information. But steps have already been taken toward this end. Improving credit report accuracy has been one of the CFPB's top policy priorities.[104] Since 2012, it has been supervising the credit reporting bureaus for accuracy[105] while holding data furnishers accountable for their failure to supply accurate information to them.[106] Although we do not yet know just how

---

[102] See "Tech Sprint on Electronic Disclosures of Adverse Action Notices." Available at https://www.consumerfinance.gov/rules-policy/innovation/cfpb-tech-sprints/electronic-disclosures-tech-sprint/.

[103] See Amy Traub. "Establish a Public Credit Registry." *Dēmos*, April 3, 2019. Available at https://www.demos.org/sites/default/files/2019-03/Credit%20Report_Full.pdf.

[104] See Richard Cordray. "Prepared Remarks of CFPB Director Richard Cordray at the Consumer Advisory Board Meeting." *Consumer Financial Protection Bureau*, March 2, 2017. Available at https://www.consumerfinance.gov/about-us/newsroom/prepared-remarks-cfpb-director-richard-cordray-consumer-advisory-board-meeting-march-2017/.

[105] See "Supervisory Highlights Consumer Reporting Special Edition" *Consumer Financial Protection Bureau*, March 2017. Available at https://files.consumerfinance.gov/f/documents/201703_cfpb_Supervisory-Highlights-Consumer-Reporting-Special-Edition.pdf.

[106] See Chi Chi Wu, Michael Best, and Sarah Bolling Mancini. "Automated Injustice Redux: Ten Years after a Key Report, Consumers Are Still Frustrated Trying to Fix Credit Reporting

successful its efforts have been—the last FTC accuracy study was conducted a decade ago—it behooves policymakers to request a new study to determine what those efforts have accomplished before considering any radical policy reform.

Furthermore, assuming that consumers' credit reports still contain many errors today, it isn't clear how a public credit bureau would succeed in reducing the same errors that affect its own reporting. For the 7-year transition period it would inherit the same errors in files transferred to it from the private credit bureaus. And thereafter it would continue to receive files from the same error-prone sources the private bureaus rely upon.

Fourth, accountability can be achieved without establishing the public credit bureau. The Dēmos proposal correctly states that consumers have a right to dispute errors in their credit files. Although there are deep disagreements about the dispute process,[107] both H. R. 3621 and H. R. 5332 contain proposals to improve it. The merits of those proposals can be debated, but fundamentally, it is possible to improve the dispute process in the existing system.

Fifth, appropriateness can be achieved without the public credit bureau. The Dēmos proposal would allow credit information to be used in lending only.[108] However, the FTC in 2007 conducted a study that shows credit-based insurance scores are "effective predictors of risk under automobile policies."[109] There can be a healthy policy debate (and the commission of new studies if needed) about whether credit reports can be used for employment,

---

Errors." *National Consumer Law Center*, February 2019. Available at https://www.nclc.org/images/pdf/credit_reports/automated-injustice-redux.pdf.

[107] Credit bureaus blame credit repair firms for abusing the system while consumer groups criticize credit bureaus for "gross inadequacies in dispute processes." See Rebecca E. Kuehn. "Statement of Rebecca E. Kuehn Partner, Hudson Cook, LLP On Behalf of the Consumer Data Industry Association Subcommittee on Oversight & Investigations Committee on Financial Services United States House of Representatives Hearing on Consumer Credit Reporting: Assessing Accuracy and Compliance." May 26, 2021. Available at https://financialservices.house.gov/uploadedfiles/hhrg-117-ba09-wstate-kuehnr-20210526.pdf; See Chi Chi Wu, Michael Best, and Sarah Bolling Mancini. "Automated Injustice Redux: Ten Years after a Key Report, Consumers Are Still Frustrated Trying to Fix Credit Reporting Errors." *National Consumer Law Center*, February 2019. Available at https://www.nclc.org/images/pdf/credit_reports/automated-injustice-redux.pdf.

[108] The Biden-Sanders Unity Task Force recommendation would allow the use of credit information in federal hiring.

[109] See "Credit-Based Insurance Scores: Impacts on Consumers of Automobile Insurance: A Report to Congress By the Federal Trade Commission." *Federal Trade Commission,* July 2007. Available at https://www.ftc.gov/reports/credit-based-insurance-scores-impacts-consumers-automobile-insurance-report-congress-federal.

insurance, or other purposes. Congress and states can pass laws to expand or limit the use of credit reports and the private sector will simply comply.

Sixth, it is not clear why proponents of a public credit bureau think it would be more secure than the private sector. While the Equifax data breach is surely damaging, one should not forget the consequences from the 2015 data breach at the Office of Personnel Management that exposed sensitive information of more than 22 million federal employees.[110] There is no safe haven in today's networked world. What is urgently needed is enhanced data security supervision rather than a public credit bureau.

Seventh, substantial public awareness and credit education has already been effectively achieved without a public credit bureau. While there is surely room for improvement, public awareness of credit reports has significantly increased as consumers can obtain free credit reports and scores via many channels.[111] Today, consumers can receive free updated credit reports and scores as frequently as every week. This is a significant improvement from the early days when consumers had to proactively request free credit reports via the arcane and clunky annualcreditreport.com every 12 months.

I have so far demonstrated that all the policy goals in the public credit bureau proposal can be as effectively achieved via innovation and by reforming the existing credit reporting industry. There are also significant negative consequences of establishing a public credit bureau that make the proposal undesirable.

Intrusion of Privacy

The public credit bureau may pose a significant threat to consumers' privacy. From the moment consumers make their first credit transaction, the federal government would monitor every credit account applied for, every account opened and closed, every payment made (on time or late), every lender from which money was borrowed, where the consumer has lived, and even who they have worked for. Putting so much sensitive personal information in the hands of the government, especially when consumers have no way of opting

---

110 See Patricia Zengerle, Megan Cassella. "Millions more Americans hit by government personnel data hack." *Reuters*, July 9, 2015. Available at https://www.reuters.com/article/us-cybersecurity-usa/millions-more-americans-hit-by-government-personnel-data-hack-idUSKCN0PJ2M420150709.

111 See "Minutes for Academic Research Council Meeting." *Consumer Financial Protection Bureau*, November 20, 2020. Available at https://files.consumerfinance.gov/f/documents/November_20th_ARC_Summary_FINAL.pdf.

out, should be a concern big enough to override any potential merits of the public credit bureau.

Huge Taxpayer Cost and Waste

The cost of setting up and running the public credit bureau needs to be seriously considered. For FY 2020, the CFPB had a workforce of 1,503 employees[112] and an operating budget of $580 million.[113] TransUnion, the smallest of the three national credit bureaus, employed 8,200 people worldwide and had an annual operating cost of $2.1 billion in 2020.[114] Of course those are not apples-to-apples comparisons, but they give us a sense of how much the federal government needs to be expanded to run the public credit bureau.

Anti-Competition and Stifling Innovation

The public credit bureau will crowd out private investment in the credit reporting industry. Funded by tax revenue, the public credit bureau will ultimately monopolize credit reporting. If members of this Committee are already concerned about the lack of competition among the three national credit bureaus today, the situation will be far worse once the public credit bureau becomes the sole place for lenders to turn to. The budding and promising innovation in expanding credit access will cease to exist.

Policy Recommendations

The credit reporting industry has a number of health issues that merit appropriate legislative and regulatory interventions. Here is some food for thought.

---

[112] See "Office of Minority and Women Inclusion Annual Report to Congress." *Consumer Financial Protection Bureau*, March 2021. Available at https://files.consumerfinance.gov/f/documents/cfpb_2020-omwi-annual-report_2021-03.pdf.

[113] See "Fiscal Year 2020: Annual Performance Plan and Report, and Budget Overview." *Consumer Financial Protection Bureau*, February 2020. Available at https://files.consumerfinance.gov/f/documents/cfpb_performance-plan-and-report_fy20.pdf.

[114] See "2020 Form 10-K." *TransUnion*, February 2021. Available at https://investors.transunion.com/~/media/Files/T/Transunion-IR/reports-and-presentations/transunion-q4-2020-form-10-K.pdf.

Refreshing the Accuracy Study

There has not been a rigorous accuracy study since the FTC conducted one 10 years ago. Many changes have taken place in the past 10 years, including the increased regulatory scrutiny on accuracy and the substantial growth in consumer awareness thanks to the proliferation of free credit reports and scores.[115] The CFPB has indicated that it is exploring a new accuracy study,[116] and it has garnered support from both the industry and consumer advocates. However, it has yet to conduct the study. Members of this Committee should insist on the completion of this study.

Supervising Data Security

The Equifax breach took place 5 years after the CFPB began to examine credit bureaus. However, the CFPB was never given the authority to oversee data security and as a result it was not able to assess the adequacy of Equifax's information security. There needs to be federal supervision of data security. When it comes to data security, credit bureaus should be held to the same standard as financial institutions. Congress needs to act quickly before the next breach hits.

Reforming the Dispute Process

It is vitally important that consumers have accurate information in their credit files. Inaccurate information and derogatory information are not the same, even though the inaccurate information that consumers try to get rid of during the dispute process is almost always derogatory. Derogatory information, if accurate, is equally valuable in helping lenders assess creditworthiness. There are already a number of proposals and I think they all merit serious considerations. I would like to offer two high-level suggestions. First, the dispute process should be made easy for consumers. A frictionless dispute process can yield high success rates and reduction in errors. Innovation can play an important role here.

---

[115] See "Minutes for Academic Research Council Meeting." *Consumer Financial Protection Bureau*, November 20, 2020. Available at https://files.consumerfinance.gov/f/documents/November_20th_ARC_Summary_FINAL.pdf.

[116] See "Director Kraninger's Remarks During the November 2020 Academic Research Council Meeting." *Consumer Financial Protection Bureau*, November 23, 2020. Available at https://www.consumerfinance.gov/about-us/newsroom/director-kraningers-remarks-november-2020-academic-research-council-meeting/.

Second, consumers should be able to directly dispute with data furnishers and have the updates reflected in all bureau reports. Errors in furnishing and reporting lags are often times the source of inaccuracy in credit files.

Protecting Consumers's Data Rights under DFA Section 1033

Congress can pass legislation to improve accuracy, transparency, and security in credit reporting, but it would not be able to effectively bring credit invisible consumers into the credit system. Competition and innovation remain the best means to achieving equity in credit access. Much of the encouraging innovation in improving credit access discussed earlier in my testimony depends on the reliable access to consumers' financial data housed within and controlled by financial institutions.

Section 1033 of the Dodd Frank Act requires financial institutions to allow third parties that are permissioned by consumers to access their financial records. This is called open banking or open finance. Consumers' data is no longer compiled, furnished, and sold without their own consent. Instead, the consumer decides who can access their own financial records, for what purposes, and for how long. While much progress has been made, "many large financial institutions, which hold the majority of consumers' data, have too often resisted the intent of Section 1033 by creating obstacles to easy data access."[117]

It has been more than 10 years since the Dodd Frank Act was enacted and 5 years since the CFPB first studied consumers' data access rights. Now is the time for the CFPB to fulfill its mandate and write a pro-consumer, pro-competition, and pro-innovation rule. The rule should root out existing anticompetitive practices by requiring complete access to consumers' financial data and explicit and transparent consumer consent and control.

Conclusion

The public credit bureau solution would be overkill for the long standing issues with the credit reporting industry. The solution is not only likely to fail to achieve the goals it sets out to reach, but it will also create a massive

---

[117] See Letter to Acting Director David Uejio from 18 progressive groups. May 27, 2021. Available at https://www.economicliberties.us/wp-content/uploads/2021/05/CFPB-Letter_5.27.pdf.

bureaucracy that wastes public funds, intrudes on privacy, and stifles innovation.

There is no need to tear down the entire system. With appropriate legislative and regulatory interventions and a conducive environment to foster innovation, Congress, regulators, consumer groups, and the private sector can work together to reduce racial disparities in credit, improve accuracy, and protect consumers' sensitive data.

Thank you for the opportunity to provide this information, and I welcome any questions that you may have.

Written Statement of Amy M. Traub, Associate Director of Policy and Research, Dēmos

Thank you, Chairwoman Waters, Ranking Member McHenry, and Members of the Committee for the opportunity to testify today.

My name is Amy Traub and I am Associate Director of Policy and Research at Dēmos. Dēmos is a dynamic think tank that powers the movement for a just, inclusive, multiracial democracy and economy. One of our core principles is economic democracy: The idea that "we the people" must be able to exercise real power over the economic decisions that shape our lives. We focus on Black and brown communities that have been largely excluded from economic decision-making. Economic exclusion is particularly clear in the case of the nation's credit reporting system.

In my testimony this morning, I will make the case that credit reporting is part of our nation's infrastructure, necessary to full economic participation and thriving for people and families nationwide. I'll share evidence of the systemic racial inequity in credit reporting and will show that the many failures of the system arise from the structure of the industry—and thus require structural change. Finally, I'll argue that publicly controlled credit reporting offers the best opportunity to rebuild the system and ensure that it operates in the public interest and promotes racial equity.

Dēmos welcomes the introduction of the National Credit Reporting Agency Act, which would shift power to consumers by enabling them—for the first time—to opt out of the flawed private credit reporting system and to choose a fairer public option. We look forward to working with the Committee to further strengthen this bill. We also support the Comprehensive CREDIT

Act and urge Congress to enact this legislation, which would directly reform private credit reporting.

Credit Reports and Scores Determine Access to Economic Opportunity

Credit reports and scores play a large role in determining Americans' access to economic security and opportunity: A consumer's creditworthiness as evaluated by the credit reporting industry determines how much she will have to pay each month in interest on credit cards and other debt, and whether she can buy a car, be approved for a mortgage, rent an apartment, get a loan to start a business, or even secure employment. Consumers cannot opt out of having personal data about their borrowing and payment activities collected and evaluated unless they are willing to exclude themselves from the mainstream of economic activity. At the same time, the financial, real estate, auto sales, and a wide range of other industries rely on the credit reporting system to assess consumer risk.

The credit reporting system is a gatekeeper to a broad range of economic opportunities for consumers and commercial opportunity for businesses. Legal scholar and former Dēmos President K. Sabeel Rahman defines infrastructure as encompassing "goods and services, which together operate at scale, enable widespread downstream uses, and thus serve as foundational necessities for economic and social life."[118] Viewed through this lens, consumer credit and credit reporting are core parts of our nation's financial infrastructure. Yet this privately controlled infrastructure is failing consumers.

The Credit Reporting System is Failing American Consumers

My fellow witnesses will detail the ways that our biased, broken credit reporting system is failing American consumers. They will describe the outrageous inaccuracy of credit reports;[119] the nightmare process of getting

---

[118] K. Sabeel Rahman, "Infrastructural Regulation and the New Utilities," *Yale Journal on Regulation*, Vol. 35, 2018, https://digitalcommons.law.yale.edu/cgi/viewcontent.cgi?article=1529&context=yjreg.

[119] *Report to Congress Under Section 319 of the Fair and Accurate Credit Transactions Act of 2003*, Federal Trade Commission, 2012, https://www.ftc.gov/sites/default/files/documents/

errors corrected;[120] and the failure to invest in security for our most personal financial information—a failure that has resulted in massive data breaches.[121] They will document the traps credit reporting companies use to lure consumers into paying for what is, by law, a free credit report[122] and will show how personal credit information is being used for purposes far beyond the original context of consumer lending.[123] It is clear why credit reporting is consistently among the greatest sources of complaints to the Consumer Financial Protection Bureau.[124]

All of these failures of credit reporting must be addressed, but the most devastating failure is the way that credit reporting reproduces and spreads racial inequality, hindering efforts to achieve a truly equitable economy. Although credit scores never formally take race into account, they draw on data about personal borrowing and payment history that is profoundly shaped by generations of discriminatory public policies and corporate practices that limited access to wealth for Black and Latinx families.[125] Discrimination in employment, lending, education, and housing have produced significant racial disparities in credit history so that today, credit scores and other lending algorithms disproportionately represent Black and Latinx loan consumers as "riskier" than white consumers.[126]

---

reports/section-319-fairand-accurate-credit-transactions-act-2003-fifth-interim-federal-trade-commission/130211factareport.pdf.

[120] Chi Chi Wu, Michael Best, and Sarah Bolling Mancini, *Automated Injustice Redux*, National Consumer Law Center, February 2019, https://www.nclc.org/images/pdf/credit_reports/automated-injustice-redux.pdf.

[121] *Bad Credit: Uncovering Equifax's Failure to Protect Americans' Personal Information*, Office of Senator Elizabeth Warren, February 2018, https://www.warren.senate.gov/files/documents/2018_2_7_%20Equifax_Report.pdf.

[122] Syed Ejaz, "A Broken System," *Consumer Reports*, June 2021, https://advocacy.consumerreports.org/wp-content/uploads/2021/06/A-Broken-System-How-the-Credit-Reporting-System-Fails-Consumers-and-What-to-Do-About-It.pdf.

[123] Shawn Fremstad and Amy Traub, *Discrediting America*, Dēmos, June 2011, https://www.Dēmos.org/sites/default/files/publications/Discrediting_America_Dēmos.pdf.

[124] Ed Mierzwinski, Mike Litt, and Gideon Weissman, *Analysis: CFPB Complaints Surge During Pandemic, Led By Credit Report Complaints*, U.S. PIRG, 2020, https://uspirg.org/sites/pirg/files/reports/Pandemic%20CFPB%20Complaints%20Report%20Analysis_0.pdf.

[125] Amy Traub, *Establish a Public Credit Registry*, Dēmos, 2019, https://www.Dēmos.org/sites/default/files/2019-03/Credit%20Report_Full.pdf.

[126] *Past Imperfect: How Credit Scores and Other Analytics "Bake In" and Perpetuate Past Discrimination*, National Consumer Law Center, 2016, https://www.nclc.org/images/pdf/credit_discrimination/Past_Imperfect050616.pdf; Megan Leonhardt, "Black and Hispanic Americans Often Have Lower Credit Scores," *CNBC*, January 28 2021, https://www.cnbc.com/2021/01/28/black-and-hispanic-americans-often-have-lower-credit-scores.html.

One recent study finds that 1 in 3 Black consumers has a FICO credit score below 620, twice the rate of white consumers.[127] Meanwhile, a majority of white consumers have a FICO score above 700, compared to just 20 percent of Black consumers.[128] Black and Latinx consumers are also more likely than white consumers to be "credit invisible" or lacking in documented credit history.[129] As a result, whenever credit data is used in decision-making it multiplies inequality. Transforming credit reporting is far from the only step needed to address racial economic inequity, but it is one powerful tool to disrupt the cycle of disadvantage.

The Credit Reporting System is Public Infrastructure, Yet Is Dominated by Private Interests

Although the vast majority of American consumers rely on credit reporting to access economic opportunity, the credit reports of more than 200 million Americans are controlled by just 3 private companies: Equifax, Experian, and TransUnion. As private corporations, the aim of the credit reporting agencies is to generate profit, which they do by extracting, packaging, and selling data about consumers' personal borrowing and payment activity. Since consumers are not the customers of the private credit reporting agencies, they have no market mechanism to demand accountability or fairness: Consumers cannot opt out of the system or choose to work with a competing company. In effect, by controlling credit data, the 3 credit reporting agencies have consumers at their mercy—they have arbitrary, unaccountable power over our financial destinies.

The oligopolistic structure of the credit reporting industry is the reason it is biased, broken, and failing American consumers. The many problems we will discuss today—from the high error rate to the dismal reality that credit reporting reproduces and spreads patterns of racial inequality—all stem from the fact that credit reporting is part of our public infrastructure that is under a stranglehold by 3 private companies. Congress can and should continue to

[127] Jung Hyun Choi et al., *Explaining the Black-White Homeownership Gap*, Urban Institute, 2019, https://www.urban.org/sites/default/files/publication/101160/explaining_the_black-white_homeownership_gap_a_closer_look_at_disparities_across_local_markets_0.pdf.

[128] Choi et al.

[129] Kenneth Brevoort, Philipp Grimm, and Michelle Kambara, *Data Point: Credit Invisibles*, Consumer Financial Protection Bureau Office of Research, 2015, https://files.consumerfinance.gov/f/201505_cfpb_data-point-credit-invisibles.pdf.

regulate the industry: The Comprehensive CREDIT Act is a powerful bill that addresses many of the harmful outcomes of the system and Dēmos supports this legislation. Yet without tackling the flawed structure of the industry itself, Congress and regulatory agencies will always be playing a game of catch up with a private industry that has no built-in incentives for accountability to the consumers whose financial fate it shapes. This is why Dēmos has proposed a public credit registry with the public interest at its core. I will briefly describe Dēmos' concept for the public credit registry.

A Public Credit Registry Is Needed to Serve the Public Interest

Dēmos has proposed establishing a public credit registry housed in the Consumer Financial Protection Bureau.[130] Under our plan, the publicly run credit registry would gradually replace the current for-profit corporate system and is designed to address the structural flaw in the credit reporting industry. By design, the public credit registry will be responsive to consumer needs and equity concerns rather than the corporate bottom line. The public credit registry will develop algorithms that diminish the impact of past discrimination, deliver transparent credit scoring, provide greater data security, and offer a publicly accountable way to resolve disputes. The use of credit information for non-lending purposes, such as employment, housing, and insurance, will be curtailed.

I will describe how the public credit registry will improve equity, transparency, accuracy, accountability, appropriateness, security, and public understanding of credit information compared to the current private system.

- *Equity:* The public credit registry will seek public input to develop new algorithms for predicting creditworthiness with a goal of minimizing disparate racial impact. New credit reporting algorithms could draw on alternative data sources (beyond lending), when these data have been shown to be predictive and to minimize racial disparities. Data sources could include allowing consumers to opt into reporting bank account cashflow data, rental payments, or utility data in order to have a more full and fully representative credit file. It is important that these data sources be opt-in rather than mandatory

[130] Amy Traub, *Establish a Public Credit Registry*.

because of equity considerations relating to each source of data.[131] In addition to drawing on new data sources, the public credit registry will research proposals to exclude certain adverse credit data from credit reports and scores, for example, medical debt or payment delinquencies on predatory loans. The public credit registry will reduce the amount of time that adverse credit information remains on a credit report from 7 years to 4 years.

- *Transparency:* The algorithms used to determine creditworthiness will be publicly available with clear explanations of what consumers can do to improve their credit. Whereas the algorithms that determine credit scores are currently trade secrets owned by private companies, public access to algorithms will enable consumers to understand exactly how actions like paying a bill late or taking out a loan will affect consequential determinations about their financial futures. This transparency shifts power from secretive companies to consumers themselves. Credit reports and scores, which are entirely based on data about consumers' own behavior, will be free to consumers at any time.
- *Accuracy:* Lenders and other companies that furnish consumer credit data to the public credit registry will be held accountable for providing accurate information. The CFPB will impose fines on companies found to consistently furnish inaccurate or incomplete information. At the same time, the public credit registry will use the most robust methods available to ensure that credit information is accurate, including matching information to a consumer based on the full name of the consumer plus either the consumer's full date of birth or the consumer's Social Security Number or Individual Taxpayer Identification Number.
- *Accountability:* Consumers will have a right to dispute inaccurate information on their credit report and will be provided free copies of any documents used by the public credit registry to ascertain the accuracy of a disputed item. Consumers will have the right to appeal the results of a dispute and provide additional evidence. As a last resort, consumers will have the right to sue the public credit registry for a failure to fulfill its responsibilities.

---

[131] *Comments in Response to Request for Information Regarding Use of Alternative Data and Modeling Techniques in the Credit Process*, National Consumer Law Center et al., 2017, https://www.nclc.org/images/pdf/credit_reports/comments-alt-data-may2017.pdf.

- *Appropriateness:* The public credit registry will limit the use of credit information, preventing misuse in areas beyond the original purpose of lending. Credit information will only be provided for lending purposes, not employment, housing, or insurance. The federal government may not use credit information to make decisions about immigration status or for any purpose other than lending. Credit information will not be shared with any other government agency.
- *Security:* While no electronic data is 100 percent secure, the public credit registry's ultimate accountability to American consumers will provide a greater incentive to enhance data security compared to the private credit reporting agencies, which so far have faced minimal consequences for even the most severe data breaches.[132] Americans already trust their government with extensive personal financial information through the Internal Revenue Service, which has a strong record of data security. As an additional safeguard against fraud and identity theft, all personal credit information will be frozen by default, meaning that prospective lenders will be unable to access consumer credit data without prior authorization from a consumer. There will be no charge to consumers for removing credit freezes or placing new ones on their credit information.
- *Public awareness:* The public credit registry will fulfill the CFPB's mission of educating consumers about credit products and how to develop and maintain a good credit score. The public credit registry will also provide free or low-cost credit counseling and credit rehabilitation services, through contracts with licensed non-profit organizations that already provide these services.

The Transition to a Public Credit Registry

According to Dēmos' proposal, the public credit registry will be established as a function of the Consumer Financial Protection Bureau. Over a period of 7 years, all consumer credit reporting will shift from the private credit reporting agencies (CRAs) to the public credit registry. The 7-year transition period allows the public credit registry to amass sufficient data on consumers to fully replace the private, for-profit CRAs. As soon as the public credit

---

[132] Mike Litt and Ethan Lutz, *Equifax Breach: One Year Later,* U.S. PIRG Education Fund, 2018, https://uspirg.org/reports/usp/equifax-breach-one-year-later.

registry is launched, any furnisher of data that currently reports to any private CRA will also be required to report data to the public agency. Consumers will be able to immediately opt out of having their credit data furnished to private CRAs. Private CRAs and furnishers of credit data will be required to report the age of all accounts to the public credit registry, so that the positive credit history of long-time payers can be reflected in the public registry's records. During the transition period, prospective lenders seeking credit information could continue to consider data from the private CRAs in making lending decisions, but lenders would not be permitted to discriminate against prospective borrowers who have opted out of reporting to the private CRAs. After the public credit registry has collected consumer credit data for 7 years, lenders will only be permitted to consider data from the public credit registry to make lending decisions—lenders will no longer be allowed to consider data from private CRAs or any other private source.

Many countries in Asia and Europe have public credit registries, although these are primarily oriented toward ensuring the stability of lenders, not the benefit of consumers. The United States will be a pioneer in establishing a consumer-oriented public credit registry that also benefits lenders through its greater accuracy, predictiveness, and public perceptions of fairness.

Dēmos Welcomes the Introduction of the National Credit Reporting Agency Act

The National Credit Reporting Agency Act creates a public credit registry as an alternative, rather than a replacement, for the corporate-dominated credit reporting system. A public option for credit reporting has the potential to shift power to consumers by enabling them—for the first time—to opt out of the flawed private credit reporting system and to choose a public system with strong mechanisms to promote equity, transparency, accuracy, and accountability.

We particularly value this bill's creation of an advisory committee on new credit scoring models. The committee would bring together a wide range of stakeholders in the credit reporting system, including consumer advocates, academics, lenders and other members of industry, as well as consumers who are directly affected by credit reporting errors, predatory lending, and other harms of the current system, to evaluate proposals for new credit scoring models, with the aim of both maximizing predictiveness in loan repayment and minimizing disparate impact by race, gender, disability or other protected categories. Building on the input of the advisory committee and following public hearings, the public credit registry would adopt a new credit scoring model, publicly available on the agency website, along with plain-language explanations of what factors contribute to improved or impaired credit and what consumers can do to improve their credit.

The National Credit Reporting Agency Act works best as an adjunct to the Comprehensive CREDIT Act, whose reforms of the private credit reporting system—including improving the dispute process, guaranteeing free credit scores, and banning the inappropriate use of credit information for employment purposes—would remain critically important as long as the private system continues to exist.

In Conclusion

The credit reporting system is part of our nation's financial infrastructure, necessary to Americans' financial flourishing, yet this critical system is failing consumers and is one of many economic and political systems putting Black and brown consumers at a disadvantage. What's more, the many failures of the credit reporting system arise from the structure of the industry, where the 3 corporations that dominate the industry have no business incentive for accountability to the consumers whose financial fate they profoundly influence.

Dēmos strongly supports the Comprehensive CREDIT Act, which would address many of the worst outcomes of the broken system. Yet this legislation does not change the underlying incentive structure of the industry, which is inimical to the interests of consumers. This is why Dēmos has proposed a public credit registry with the public interest at its core. We welcome the introduction of the National Credit Reporting Agency Act and look forward to working with the Committee to further strengthen and improve this bill.

Thank you and I look forward to your questions.

Written Statement of Chi Chi Wu, Staff Attorney, National Consumer Law Center

Introduction and Summary

Chairwoman Waters, Ranking Member McHenry, and Members of the Committee, thank you for inviting me to testify today regarding consumer credit reporting and the need for reform. I offer my testimony here on behalf of the low-income clients of the National Consumer Law Center.[133] NCLC has long advocated for stronger laws and regulation to ensure accuracy and fairness in the U.S. credit reporting system and to reform the Big Three credit bureaus (Equifax, Experian and TransUnion), known as the nationwide consumer reporting agencies under the Fair Credit Reporting Act (FCRA) and colloquially as "credit bureaus."

Throughout the decades, NCLC has documented the many problems and abuses of the credit reporting system. Over and over again, we have described and provided evidence of:

- The systemic errors in credit reporting, which are a result of deliberate decisions and longstanding failures of the credit bureaus, and lead to unacceptable error rates;
- The kafka-esque automated dispute system used by the credit bureaus;
- The need to mitigate the punitive impact of a system that treats consumers who have fallen on hard times as irresponsible deadbeats;
- Systemic racial disparities in credit scoring;
- The unfair impact of medical debt on credit reports; and
- The problems with use of credit reports for employment purposes.[134]

---

[133] The National Consumer Law Center is a nonprofit organization specializing in consumer issues on behalf of low-income people. We work with thousands of legal services, government and private attorneys, as well as community groups and organizations, from all states who represent low-income and elderly individuals on consumer issues. As a result of our daily contact with these advocates, we have seen many examples of the damage wrought by abuses from credit bureaus from every part of the nation. It is from this vantage point that we supply these comments. *Fair Credit Reporting* (9th ed. 2017) is one of the twenty-one practice treatises that NCLC publishes and annually supplements. This testimony was written by Chi Chi Wu, with editorial review by Carolyn Carter and assistance from Leonard Bennett, Sylvia Goldsmith, Matthew Osborne, Joanne Faulkner and other consumer attorneys.

[134] *See, e.g.,* Who's Keeping Score? Holding Credit Bureaus Accountable and Repairing a Broken System: Hearing: Before the H. Comm. on Fin. Servs., 116th Congr. (2019); An

Just last month, NCLC again provided testimony on the failures of the credit bureaus in an Oversight and Investigations Subcommittee hearing entitled "Consumer Credit Reporting: Assessing Accuracy and Compliance"[135]

All of the problems and failures with our consumer credit reporting system stem from two fundamental facts:

1. Credit bureaus are entirely private companies that are publicly traded, which means their highest duty is to shareholder profit, not the public good or the American consumer.
2. The paying clients of credit bureaus are not consumers, but the creditors and debt collectors who furnish or use the information contained in the credit bureaus' databases.

The fact that these are private, profit-seeking companies explains why the credit bureaus are constantly expanding their products into uses, such as employment, insurance, and tenant screening, that ultimately harm Americans and contribute to the massive inequality in our nation. The fact that their customers are creditors and other users of information explains the unacceptable error rates and bias against consumers who complain about errors.

These two factors are why it's time for a new paradigm for credit reporting, a public credit registry. While public agencies are not perfect, at least they would not have profit-making as their top priority. They would be responsive to public pressure and government oversight. They could also be charged with developing credit scoring models to reduce the yawning racial and economic inequality in this country.

A public credit registry would also respond to the Supreme Court's decision just this past Friday in *TransUnion v. Ramirez*, – S.Ct. – , 2021 WL 2599472 (U.S. June 25, 2021), which seriously impairs the ability of consumers to seek relief for inaccuracies under the FCRA. If consumers are not able to obtain legal redress for FCRA violations, a key means of

---

Overview of the Credit Reporting System: Hearing Before the Subcomm. on Fin. Inst. and Consumer Credit of the H. Comm. on Fin. Servs., 113th Congr. (2014) (testimony of Chi Chi Wu); Use of Credit Information beyond Lending: Issues and Reform Proposals: Hearing Before the Subcomm. on Fin. Inst. and Consumer Credit of the H. Comm. on Fin. Servs., 113th Congr. (2010) (testimony of Chi Chi Wu).

[135] Consumer Credit Reporting: Assessing Accuracy and Compliance: Hearing Before the Subcomm. on Oversight and Investigations of the H. Fin. Serv. Comm., 117th Congr. (2021) (testimony of Chi Chi Wu).

enforcement disappears, making the broken credit reporting system much, much harder to fix. A public credit registry would replace or provide an alternative to this broken system.

Enough is enough. The American consumer deserves better. It is time for a fundamental and wholesale reform of the credit bureaus, in fact such reform is long overdue.

Financial Reputations at Stake

Credit reports and credit scores play a crucial role in consumers' lives, and their importance has only grown in recent years. Of course, credit reports and scores can determine a consumer's ability to obtain credit and the amount they have to pay for it, which affects their ability to purchase a home – the pathway to establishing middle class wealth for most consumers. But even for renters, 90% of landlords use credit reports and scores,[136] which means a bad score could shut out a renter out of apartments in a decent school district or even permanent housing. An article in the New York Times Magazine last month documented how much a bad credit score can hurt the ability of many Americans to simply find a stable roof over their heads:

> Without any say in the matter, Americans are now labeled with a new layer of identity: a three-digit judgment of economic worthiness. "It's a number that went from being nonexistent to being a gatekeeper to getting housing," says Lisa Servon of the University of Pennsylvania, the author of "The Unbanking of America." The $14.4 billion credit-reporting industry in the United States — the consumer-credit subset of that market is dominated by the big three: Experian, TransUnion and Equifax — quietly assumed a new yet profound role in the American class system to the extent it influenced who could live where and who received a second chance after financial disaster.
>
> * * *
>
> All this financial surveillance of America's poor has helped lead to the creation of a permanent credit underclass. A survey conducted in the fall of 2018 in Norcross, Ga., a city of about 17,000 outside Atlanta, concluded that

136 Transunion SmartMove, TransUnion Independent Landlord Survey Insights, Aug. 7, 2017, https://www.mysmartmove.com/SmartMove/blog/landlord-rental-market-survey-insights-infographic.page.

> nine of the city's 14 hotels, motels and extended stays had become "primarily residential facilities." When the respondents — 70 percent of whom were Black — were asked to name the biggest barrier to more permanent housing, one person after another cited bad credit. "They are trapped by the credit bureaus," says Malik Watkins, an affordable-housing researcher at the Carl Vinson Institute of Government at the University of Georgia, who was an author of the survey. In Gwinnett County Public Schools, the largest school system in Georgia, 91 bus stops at hotels, motels or extended stays pick up nearly 600 students.[137]

In addition, credit reports and scores can affect whether and at what price Americans can obtain insurance and hence their ability to own a car. Nearly one-third of employers use credit reports, affecting a consumer's ability to find a job. Even hospitals have been known to pull a credit report before offering medical services[138] and the Department of Homeland Security had included a credit score check in its now-vacated Public Charge Rule.[139] It's essentially the report card for a consumer's financial life.

Yet for such an important record, credit reports and scores suffer from profound problems and abuses. For one thing, credit reports are still too full of errors - parents and students would never accept report cards so full of mistakes and inaccuracies. Or put another way – these credit histories are our financial reputations. To quote Shakespeare, "Who steals my purse steals trash" but "he that filches from me my good name ... makes me poor indeed."[140]

Credit bureaus constantly filch the good name of American consumers with errors and inaccuracies. The often-cited 2012 Federal Trade Commission (FTC) study on credit reporting errors found that 1 in 5 consumers (or over 20%) have verified errors in their credit reports, and 1 in 20 consumers (or 5%) have errors so serious that they would be denied credit or need to pay

---

[137] Mya Frazier, When No Landlord Will Rent to You, Where Do You Go?, N.Y. Times, May 23, 2021, https://www.nytimes.com/2021/05/20/magazine/extended-stay-hotels.html?referringSource=articleShare.

[138] PJ Randhawa & Erin Richey, KSDK News, Nov. 21, 2020, Why some hospitals run credit checks on patients, https://www.ksdk.com/article/news/investigations/hospitals-want-your-credit-score-for-what/63-b360768d-a138-40f6-b572-e3fa0bc95526.

[139] Inadmissibility on Public Charge Grounds, 84 Fed. Reg. 41,292, 41,503 (final rule Aug. 14, 2019). Regarding the current status of the rule, *see* USCIS, Public Charge Letter to Interagency Partner, April 12, 2021, https://www.uscis.gov/sites/default/files/document/notices/SOPDD-Letter-to-USCIS-Interagency-Partners-on-Public-Charge.pdf.

[140] Shakespeare, Othello, Act III, scene 3.

more for it.[141] With an estimated 208 million Americans in the credit reporting system,[142] this means that 42 million consumers have errors in their credit reports, and 10 million have errors that can be life altering.

The credit reporting industry has attempted to rebut these FTC statistics by, among other things, claiming that the problems with errors have been fixed in the intervening years since 2012.[143] Yet just this month, we have a study from Consumer Reports authored by fellow witness Syed Ejaz in which, out of nearly 6,000 consumers, 34% found at least one error in their credit reports, 29% found errors in their personal information, and 11% found errors related to their account information.[144]

Moreover, another indication that the massive accuracy problems in credit reporting have not been resolved is the dramatic explosion of complaints last year to the Consumer Financial Protection Bureau (CFPB) about credit reporting. In 2020, the CFPB received over 319,000 complaints about credit or consumer reporting, over twice as many as in 2019 and constituting 59% of the overall complaints received by the CFPB last year.[145] Since the CFPB started accepting complaints about credit reporting in December 2011, there have been over 700,000 such complaints.[146] And in 2021, there were already over 90,000 credit reporting complaints in the first four months, constituting 59% of complaints to CPFB in the first third of the year.[147]

This level of errors and inaccuracy is unacceptable for an industry so important to the financial lives of Americans. We would not be satisfied with the 5% serious error rate reported by the FTC for other critical industries –

---

[141] Federal Trade Comm'n Report to Congress Under Section 319 of the Fair and Accurate Credit Transactions Act of 2003 (Dec. 2012).

[142] Kenneth Brevoort, Philipp Grimm & Michelle Kambara, CFPB Office of Research, CFPB Data Point: Credit Invisibles 12 (May 2015), http://files.consumerfinance.gov/f/201505_cfpb_data-point-credit-invisibles.pdf.

[143] Terry Clemans, FTC/CFPB Consumer Reporting Accuracy Workshop Report, National Mortgage Professional, https://nationalmortgageprofessional.com/news/74194/ftccfpb-consumer-reporting-accuracy-workshop-report, Mar. 19, 2020 (NCAP "made further changes that have increased the accuracy of consumer credit reports. NCAP eliminated areas that were problematic, and created new ways to improve other long time challenges").

[144] Syed Ejaz, Consumer Reports, A Broken System – How the Credit Reporting System Fails Consumers and What to Do About It, June 10, 2021, https://advocacy.consumerreports.org/wp-content/uploads/2021/06/A-Broken-System-How-the-Credit-Reporting-System-Fails-Consumers-and-What-to-Do-About-It.pdf.

[145] Consumer Financial Protection Bureau, Consumer Response Annual Report January 1 – December 31, 2020 (March 2020), at 9, https://files.consumerfinance.gov/f/documents/cfpb_2020-consumer-response-annual-report_03-2021.pdf.

[146] Data generated from CFPB Consumer Complaints Database, https://www.consumerfinance.gov/data-research/consumer-complaints/search/ (viewed May 22, 2021).

[147] *Id.*

imagine if 5% of automobiles spontaneously exploded or 5% of airplanes fell out of the sky? Yet after decades of advocacy, legal changes, regulation, and enforcement, we are still faced with a fundamentally flawed credit reporting system. As the CFPB has noted, "experience indicates that [the credit bureaus] lack incentives and under-invest in accuracy."[148]

A Half Century Battle for Fair Treatment

In 2020, we celebrated the 50th Anniversary of the Fair Credit Reporting Act. This means that the problems and abuses of credit bureaus have been the subject of attention and reform for over half a century. Despite this, the situation has only gotten worse as credit reports remain full of flaws but are used by more and more businesses to deny consumers the necessities of life. In fact, with the Supreme Court's decision last Friday in *TransUnion v Ramirez*, – S.Ct. – , 2021 WL 2599472 (U.S. June 25, 2021), discussed in Section D below, we fear that the credit bureaus' culture of impunity will worsen as the Court has made it that much more difficult for consumers to seek justice for credit reporting errors.

The following are some of the key types of errors in credit reports, including examples from legal cases, media articles, and the CFPB complaint narratives. Additional examples are available in Appendix A to my testimony from last month before the Oversight and Investigations Subcommittee.[149]

Mixed Files

In 1968, Senator William Proxmire, often considered the father of the FCRA, noted: "There are many varieties of inaccurate information, but I shall mention only two. One is the case of mistaken identity, where two individuals with the same names are confused, and the deserving individual is denied credit because of something done by the other person."[150] Fifty years later, this type of error- the mixed file - still harms too many consumers. Mixed files are caused by insufficient and overly loose matching criteria, in particularly the

---

[148] Consumer Financial Protection Bureau, Supervisory Highlights Consumer Reporting Special Edition, Winter 2017, at 21, https://files.consumerfinance.gov/f/documents/201703_cfpb_Supervisory-Highlights-Consumer-Reporting-Special-Edition.pdf.

[149] Consumer Credit Reporting: Assessing Accuracy and Compliance: Hearing Before the Subcomm. on Oversight and Investigations of the H. Fin. Serv. Comm., 117th Congr. (2021) (testimony of Chi Chi Wu).

[150] 114 Cong. Rec. 24,903 (1968).

practice of matching data based on only 7 out of 9 digits of a Social Security number.

In May 2015, the credit bureaus entered into a settlement with over 30 Attorneys General agreeing to a number of reforms, including establishing minimum standards for matching criteria and providing for escalated handling for mixed file disputes.[151] Yet six years later, consumers are still facing problems from mixed files.

> *Twin trouble*
> Just last month, Verge news writer Mitchell Clark wrote an extensive article about how his file at the credit bureaus has been consistently mixed with his twin sister Alita:
>
> Sometimes they associate her name with my social security number, sometimes it's the other way around — and sometimes we both show up under the same SSN.... Over and over, Alita and I have been rejected for credit cards, despite both having good credit. I was rejected for a car loan by a bank that I've used for years — despite having enough cash to immediately pay off the loan. Neither of us has had issues with getting access to housing, but it's hard to feel sure it won't happen in the future. The problem isn't banks or lenders but the credit system itself, a vast and invisible information network with little incentive to correct even the simplest of problems.[152]

The credit reporting errors at issue in *TransUnion v. Ramirez* are also an example of a mixed file error of an even more egregious type, when credit bureaus match consumers to records based on only their names and no other identifiers. As the majority opinion in *TransUnion v. Ramirez* recounted:

> Beginning in 2002, TransUnion introduced an add-on product called OFAC Name Screen Alert. .... OFAC maintains a list of "specially designated nationals" who threaten America's national security. Individuals on the OFAC list are terrorists, drug traffickers, or other serious criminals....

---

[151] Assurance of Voluntary Compliance/Assurance of Voluntary Discontinuance, In the Matter of Equifax Info. Serv. L.L.C., Experian Info. Sols., Inc., and TransUnion L.L.C., § IV (E)(5) and (F)(7) (May 20, 2015), https://www.ohioattorneygeneral.gov/Files/Briefing-Room/News-Releases/Consumer-Protection/2015-05-20-CRAs-AVC.aspx.

[152] Mitchell Clark, Credit agencies can't tell my sister and me apart, The Verge, May 12, 2021, https://www.theverge.com/22421193/credit-reporting-infrastructure-errors-experian-equifax-transunion.

When this litigation arose, Name Screen worked in the following way: When a business opted into the Name Screen service, TransUnion would conduct its ordinary credit check of the consumer, and it would also use third-party software to compare the consumer's name against the OFAC list. If the consumer's first and last name matched the first and last name of an individual on OFAC's list, then TransUnion would place an alert on the credit report indicating that the consumer's name was a "potential match" to a name on the OFAC list. TransUnion did not compare any data other than first and last names. Unsurprisingly, TransUnion's Name Screen product generated many false positives. Thousands of law-abiding Americans happen to share a first and last name with one of the terrorists, drug traffickers, or serious criminals on OFAC's list of specially designated nationals.

Sergio Ramirez learned the hard way that he is one such individual. On February 27, 2011, Ramirez visited a Nissan dealership in Dublin, California, seeking to buy a Nissan Maxima. Ramirez was accompanied by his wife and his father-in-law. After Ramirez and his wife selected a color and negotiated a price, the dealership ran a credit check on both Ramirez and his wife. Ramirez's credit report, produced by TransUnion, contained the following alert: "***OFAC ADVISOR ALERT - INPUT NAME MATCHES NAME ON THE OFAC DATABASE." App. 84. A Nissan salesman told Ramirez that Nissan would not sell the car to him because his name was on a " 'terrorist list.' " Id., at 333. Ramirez's wife had to purchase the car in her own name.

TransUnion LLC v. Ramirez, – S.Ct. – , 2021 WL 2599472, at *4 (U.S. June 25, 2021)

Identity Theft

Credit bureaus and furnishers both bear a share of the blame for the fallout from identity theft. The credit bureaus' loose matching procedures contribute to the problem of identity theft, and their data breaches give thieves the tools needed to commit fraud. When consumers try to fix the aftereffects of identity theft, furnishers often fail to believe them and the credit bureaus take the furnishers' side. Furnishers often require police reports, even though practitioners report that many police departments are unwilling to provide them and the FTC has stated that its Identity Theft Affidavit is sufficient to dispute accounts resulting from identity theft.[153] In fact, some practitioners

[153] Seena Gressin, Federal Trade Commission, Most ID theft victims don't need a police report, Apr. 27. 2017, https://www.consumer.ftc.gov/blog/2017/04/most-id-theft-victims-dont-need-

report that furnishers are insisting on a criminal prosecution before they will treat a fraud account as identity theft, which can be an almost impossible bar. Other practitioners report that credit bureaus will not treat a police report as valid if it does not contain a police officer's signature or an official police department seal, or both, even though many police departments will only provide a computer-generated report with the officer's name printed.

> *Not a Best Buy*
> Thomas Kemlage is a prominent dentist in his 50s. In the Fall of 2019, Dr. Kemlage discovered a $1,700 charge for electronics purchases at Best Buy on his JPMorgan Chase card. He immediately reported the fraudulent charges to Chase, which instructed him to file a police report, which he did on December 6, 2019. The police actually investigated and "determined from Best Buy surveillance video that 'the purchase at Best Buy was made by someone other than me.'" Yet not only did Chase refuse to remove the charge, it reported his account as over 180 days past due and charged off, seriously harming his credit record. Dr. Kemlage disputed this reporting and requested a fraud block, as was his right under the FCRA. All three credit bureaus refused to apply a fraud block. Experian's stated reason for this denial was that "[t]he identity theft report that you provided to us does not meet the guidelines established by the federal Fair Credit Reporting Act for the following reason(s): The report does not reference identity theft" – despite the fact that both the police report as well as an FTC Identity Theft Affidavit that Dr. Kemlage submitted described the identity theft at issue.[154]

Additional examples from the CFPB Complaint Database of the credit bureaus and furnishers refusing to believe identity theft victims and refusing to remove fraudulent accounts from the victims' credit report are included in Appendix A to my testimony from last month.[155]

Being Declared Dead

In one of the worst types of credit reporting errors, consumers are labeled as "deceased" when they are alive and breathing. Another reform required by the 2015 AG settlement was to identify ways to "preventing inaccurate reporting

---

police-report. "In most cases, you can use your Identity Theft Report in place of a police report to clear your account and credit records of transactions that resulted from the identity theft").

154 Complaint, Kemlage v. Equifax Info. Serv., LLC, Cause No. 4:21-cv-00469 (Apr. 22, 2021).

155 Consumer Credit Reporting: Assessing Accuracy and Compliance: Hearing Before the Subcomm. on Oversight and Investigations of the H. Fin. Serv. Comm., 117th Congr. (2021) (testimony of Chi Chi Wu).

of Disputed Deceased Indicators."[156] Six years later, consumers are still facing the terrible burden of being falsely declared dead.

Being declared dead leads to a broken heart

In January 2017, James Rennick applied for a home-equity loan in order to renovate his house. His wife of five decades, Angela, was dying of lung, kidney, bone and brain cancer and Rennick wanted to make renovations to ease her last days and to cover burial costs. But Rennick was unable to get a loan because Equifax and Experian had declared him dead. Rennick's credit history information was mixed up with that of another man, an unrelated James Palmer. As a result, not only was he unable to accommodate his dying wife, Rennick himself "died of a broken heart" according to his daughter. Both Rennick and his wife had to be cremated "because there wasn't enough money for the more expensive option of burial."[157]

Furnisher Errors

Errors in credit reports can often be caused by furnishers. Common errors include attributing an account or debt to the wrong consumer, incorrectly recording a payment history, or failing to properly report a bankruptcy or loan modification. Debt collectors are a frequent source of errors.[158]

Debts of the father[159]

Medical bills are the most common type of debt collection item on credit reports. In some cases, they might not even be reported for the correct patient. For example, in March 2018, debt collection agency AR Resources (ARR) reported 19 medical bills of 83-year old Francisco Perez Gonzalez on the credit report of his son, Francisco J. Perez Ramones. ARR refused to correct this error despite the son disputing these debts around 30 times.

---

[156] Assurance of Voluntary Compliance/Assurance of Voluntary Discontinuance, In the Matter of Equifax Info. Serv. L.L.C., Experian Info. Sols., Inc., and TransUnion L.L.C., § IV(F)(2)(A) (May 20, 2015), https://www.ohioattorneygeneral.gov/Files/Briefing-Room/News-Releases/Consumer-Protection/2015-05-20-CRAs-AVC.aspx.

[157] Andrew Keshner, This woman says Equifax mixed up her father's credit report and 'destroyed' his life — and now she hopes to convince a jury, Marketwatch, Oct. 29, 2019, https://www.marketwatch.com/story/this-woman-says-equifax-mixed-up-her-fathers-credit-report-and-destroyed-his-life-now-she-hopes-to-convince-a-jury-2019-10-25. *See also* Malverty v. Equifax Information Services, LLC, 407 F.Supp.3d 1257 (2019).

[158] The CFPB found that debt collectors are responsible for 40% of disputes to the credit bureaus even though they only supply 13% of the accounts to credit reports. CFPB, Key Dimensions and Processes in the U.S. Credit Reporting System: A review of how the nation's largest credit bureaus manage consumer data 14, 29 (2012), https://files.consumerfinance.gov/f/201212_cfpb_credit-reporting-white-paper.pdf.

[159] Perez Ramones v. Experian Info. Sols., LLC, 2021 WL 1839535 (S.D. Fla. May 7, 2021).

These disputes noted that the son and father had different names and dates of birth, yet ARR refused to correct the information. The credit bureaus simply accepted ARR's response despite clear evidence that the debt collector had tagged the wrong consumer. Furthermore, this collector seems to have questionable dispute investigation policies – one of its investigators stated in a deposition that "she wouldn't 'delete an account just because the last name is different' because that is inconsistent with ARR's policies."[160]

CARES Act Violations

The Coronavirus Aid, Relief, and Economic Security (CARES) Act provides credit reporting protections if a creditor approves a consumer for an "accommodation," *i.e.*, a forbearance, payment deferral, loan modification, or other relief granted to a consumer affected by the COVID-19 pandemic.[161] If the creditor granted an accommodation and the consumer was current at the time, the CARES Act requires the account to be reported as current so long as the consumer complies with the accommodation agreement. If the consumer was already delinquent when they received the accommodation, but complies with the accommodation agreement, the creditor must report the same delinquency status during the accommodation period.[162] This past year, a common furnisher error was failing to properly follow the credit reporting requirements of the CARES Act.

Violation of CARES Act After Loan Transfer (Texas)

I'm currently on a forbearance plan until XX/XX/XXXX and I've been on one since XX/XX/XXXX of last year due to Covid. I filed applied for a forbearance plan with LoanCare and per the terms of the plan if my loan was current prior to entering the forbearance that's how it would be reported. Until XX/XX/XXXX XXXX was reporting my [sic] correctly to the credit bureaus then suddenly after selling my loan they reported me late and closed my account. This needs to be corrected ASAP! My loan was current before and according to the plan so why am I being reported late now when it was being reported Pay as agreed until now.

CFPB Complaint No. 4311035, filed April 20, 2021

---

160 *Id.* at *5.

161 Pub. L. No. 116-136, § 4021 (Mar. 27, 2020).

162 *Id.*

Reforms Are Long Overdue

The types of errors documented above have been harming and abusing consumers for over 50 years. It is well past time for major structural changes to the credit reporting industry, which should include:

- *A public credit registry.* A public credit registry would alleviate errors because it would not have incentives to engage in practices, such as overly inclusive matching criteria, that favor creditors but harm consumers. It would also be more responsive to fixing systematic errors such as the decades-old glitch that leads to living consumers being marked as deceased. At a minimum, there should be a public credit registry as an option where the consumer makes the choice of whether to use it or a private credit bureau. Thus, we would support a bill such as the draft National Credit Reporting Agency Act of 2021.
- *Stricter matching criteria.* Congress should require the credit bureaus to use stricter matching criteria, including matching information based on all nine digits of the consumer's Social Security number (SSN) or eight digits plus full name and address. At a minimum, the CFPB should be required to engage in a rulemaking to impose stricter requirements and generally establishing minimum procedures to ensure "maximum possible accuracy." Stricter matching criteria would partially address the negative fallout of the *TransUnion v. Ramirez* decision, since the abuses of TransUnion falsely tagging consumers as potential terrorists and drug dealers stemmed from poor matching practices.

A Broken Dispute System

One of the key tools in the FCRA to combat inaccuracies is the consumer's right to dispute errors and the credit bureaus' obligation to conduct a reasonable investigation. Yet the FCRA-mandated dispute system has been a travesty of justice for decades, as documented by NCLC's 2009 report *Automated Injustice: How a Mechanized Dispute System Frustrates Consumers Seeking to Fix Errors in their Credit Reports*. The report documented how the credit bureaus' entire role in dispute "investigation" was to convey disputes to furnishers through the highly automated e-OSCAR system. This system primarily uses shorthand two- or three-digit codes, with, in a minority of instances, up to just a line or two of text. The credit bureaus used the same four or five codes over 80% of the time. Workers did not examine documents, contact consumers by phone or email, or exercise any form of human discretion in resolving a dispute.

In preparation for a February 2019 credit reporting hearing before this Committee, we released a 10-year update entitled *Automated Injustice Redux: Ten Years after a Key Report, Consumers Are Still Frustrated Trying to Fix Credit Reporting Errors*. This updated report documented how, despite a decade of attempts at reform, credit bureaus and furnishers continue to have serious problems in ensuring the accuracy of credit reports, and the dispute process remains ineffective and biased. *Automated Justice Redux* contains story after story from lawsuits and the CFPB Complaint Database to illustrate the frustrations and harms caused to consumers from these problems.

Both the 2009 report and the 2019 update describe how credit bureaus are universally biased in favor of furnishers and against consumers in disputes. In a practice known as "parroting," credit bureaus blindly adopt the response of the furnisher without performing any independent review. The credit bureaus' practice is akin to a referee who always rules for one team. In 2017, the CFPB characterized parroting as a violation when it stated in a Supervisory Highlights report that it had cited the credit bureaus for "fail[ing] to review and consider the attached documentation and relied entirely on the furnisher to investigate the dispute."[163] Despite this CFPB pronouncement, the credit bureaus continue to engage in the practice.

Indeed, the credit bureaus' failure to conduct any meaningful investigation of disputes has only gotten worse, as they have pushed, often successfully, their argument that they are not required to resolve "legal" disputes. Starting in 2010 with the case *Carvalho v. Equifax Info. Servs., LLC*,[164] the credit bureaus as well as furnishers have aggressively pushed this theory with success, much to the detriment of consumers. The scope of what credit bureaus and furnishers claim to be a legal dispute has broadened to

---

[163] CFPB, Supervisory Highlights Consumer Reporting Special Edition, Winter 2017, https://files.consumerfinance.gov/f/documents/201703_cfpb_Supervisory-Highlights-Consumer-Reporting-Special-Edition.pdf, at 10-11.

[164] 629 F.3d 876 (9th Cir. 2010).

include issues such as forgery,[165] mixed files,[166] and identity theft.[167] The credit bureaus and furnishers are using the "legal dispute" argument to gut the investigation requirements of the FCRA, and avoid any legal responsibility for their failures.

Recently, the CFPB has finally pushed back against this issue, decrying in an amicus brief the "formalistic distinction between factual and legal questions" because "[s]uch a distinction is inconsistent with the text and purpose of FCRA."[168]

It is way past time to fix the broken, Kafka-esqe credit reporting dispute system. Reforms must include:

- *Right of appeal.* Congress should establish a right for consumers to appeal when they disagree about the results of a dispute. The appeal could either be to an independent unit in the credit bureau or to a regulator, such as the CFPB or FTC. If the unit is housed within a credit bureau, the unit must have direct and unfettered authority to make independent decisions and not be subject to any restrictions or incentives to process disputes quickly or in favor of furnishers.
- *Sufficient resources and independent review.* Congress should clarify that the credit bureaus must devote sufficient resources and conduct independent analyses in disputes.

We note these reforms were included in the Comprehensive CREDIT (Credit Reporting Enhancement, Disclosure, Innovation, and Transparency) Act of 2020, which the House of Representatives passed in January 2020 and which we strongly supported.[169] These reforms were also included in the

---

[165] Uppal v. Wells Fargo Bank, N, 2020 WL 6150923 (M.D. Fla. Oct. 20, 2020) (dismissing claim where plaintiff alleged forgery of documents as a legal dispute).

[166] Thompson v. Trans Union Data Sol., 2021 WL 1923409, at *3 (N.D. Ill. May 13, 2021) (denying dismissal; Chase argued it was a legal dispute where the consumer "states that he did not authorize the credit card and did not know anything about it).

[167] Perez Ramones v. Experian Info. Sols., LLC, 2021 WL 1839535, at *5 (S.D. Fla. May 7, 2021)("the Court finds unavailing the Defendant's argument that it was not required to determine whether the Plaintiff "legally owed the debts" being reported.... the Plaintiff's thirty disputes that the debts at issue were not his is not akin to a legal challenge").

[168] Brief of Amicus Curiae Consumer Financial Protection Bureau, Gross v. CitiMortgage, Inc., 9th Circuit No. 2017160, https://files.consumerfinance.gov/f/documents/cfpb_amicus-brief_gross-v-citimortgage_2021-14.pdf. Gross v. CitiMortgage involved furnisher dispute investigations the rationale would apply to credit bureaus as well.

[169] *See* Letter supporting HR 3755, The Comprehensive Consumer Credit Reporting Reform Act of 2017, https://nclc.org/images/pdf/credit_reports/letter-ccra-waters-2017.pdf.

Protecting Your Credit Score Act, which the House passed in June 2020 and we also supported. We would again support the Comprehensive CREDIT Act and the Protecting Your Credit Score Act in 2021.

The Urgent Need for Injunctive Relief under the FCRA to Restore Consumer's Ability to Seek Justice Under the Act

This past Friday, the Supreme Court dealt an enormous blow to the ability of consumers to protect themselves and their financial reputations under the FCRA. In *TransUnion v. Ramirez*, – S.Ct. – , 2021 WL 2599472 (U.S. June 25, 2021), the Court held that in order to bring a legal action in federal court to enforce our rights under the Act, it's not enough to have an error in a credit report. It's not enough to have an outrageously egregious error, such as a false accusation that the consumer is a potential terrorist or drug dealer. It's not even enough to show that the error was systematic and deliberate, affecting thousands of innocent consumers. None of these evils is enough, according to a majority of the Supreme Court, to establish "concrete injury" under Article III of the Constitution. As Justice Thomas wrote in his dissent:

> [O]ne need only tap into common sense to know that receiving a letter identifying you as a potential drug trafficker or terrorist is harmful. All the more so when the information comes in the context of a credit report, the entire purpose of which is to demonstrate that a person can be trusted.
>
> And if this sort of confusing and frustrating communication is insufficient to establish a real injury, one wonders what could rise to that level. If, instead of falsely identifying Ramirez as a potential drug trafficker or terrorist, TransUnion had flagged him as a "potential" child molester, would that alone still be insufficient to open the courthouse doors? What about falsely labeling a person a racist? Including a slur on the report? Or what about openly reducing a person's credit score by several points because of his race? If none of these constitutes an injury in fact, how can that possibly square with our past cases ...
>
> TransUnion LLC v. Ramirez, – S.Ct. – , 2021 WL 2599472, at *23 (U.S. June 25, 2021)

Instead of concluding - as the vast majority of Americans would - that being falsely accused of being a terrorist or drug dealer is enough to cause injury in fact, the Supreme Court required that the error must be disclosed to a third party in order to have "standing" under Article III of the Constitution. In other words, a consumer who spots a blatant, offensive error in their credit report needs to wait until a creditor, employer, or landlord sees that error – needs to wait to have their reputation besmirched and ruined in the eyes of a complete stranger - before they have the ability to seek redress in federal court. They can attempt to submit a dispute under the FCRA, but if the Kafka-esque, broken dispute system described above does not fix the dispute, they could be rendered unable to do anything about it but must wait for the opprobrium of having a stranger judge them based on false information.

The Supreme Court's decision was based on a Constitutional issue, but Congress is not powerless to act to restore the rights of consumers to seek protection under the FCRA. In fact, the majority opinion by Justice Kavanaugh provides a blueprint for fixing this terrible situation – by establishing the right of consumers to seek injunctive relief under the Act. The majority opinion states:

> To support its statement that a material risk of future harm can satisfy the concrete-harm requirement, *Spokeo* cited this Court's decision in *Clapper*. But importantly, *Clapper* involved a suit for injunctive relief. As this Court has recognized, *a person exposed to a risk of future harm may pursue forward-looking, injunctive relief to prevent the harm from occurring, at least so long as the risk of harm is sufficiently imminent and substantial.*
>
> TransUnion LLC v. Ramirez, – S.Ct. –, 2021 WL 2599472, at *12 (U.S. June 25, 2021) (emphasis added)

Thus, Congress can restore the ability of consumers to seek justice by allowing them to ask a court to "fix that report." That's all it takes. And, it's a provision that is already in both the Comprehensive CREDIT Act and the Protecting Your Credit Score Act. By establishing the right to injunctive relief under the FCRA, Congress can legislatively reverse the terrible decision in *TransUnion v. Ramirez* and provide fairness and justice to consumers wrongfully defamed by credit bureaus.

- *Injunctive relief for consumers.* Congress should restore the ability of consumers to seek a judicial remedy for credit reporting errors without needing to suffer the embarrassment and shame of a third party viewing the error. Congress can do so by giving consumers the right to seek injunctive relief under the FCRA.

The Vicious Cycle Effect of Using the Past to Shape the Future

Credit reporting and scoring penalizes consumers who have fallen on hard times through no fault of their own, such as from illness, job loss, third-party fraud, or natural disasters, treating them as irresponsible deadbeats. The most recent examples, of course, are workers who were financially burdened by the massive economic dislocation caused by the COVID-19 pandemic.

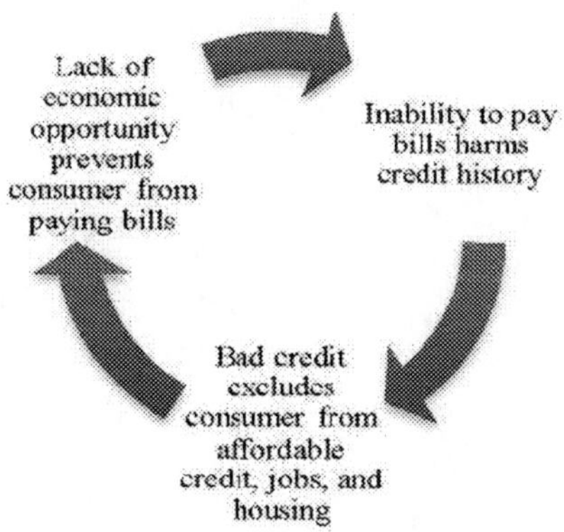

Credit scores assume that delinquencies caused by, for example, a 50% reduction in income because a hospitality worker's hours were reduced due to COVID-19 should be treated the same as a default due to poor financial management by the consumer. Yet these are two fundamentally different circumstances, and likely two very different consumers.

More problematically, consumers who have had the bad luck of being affected by illness, disaster, or other extraordinary life events could have their economic lives significantly impaired for seven years (or ten years, in the case of bankruptcies). The credit reporting damage from the life event may shut them out of affordable credit markets, and could cause them to be denied jobs or housing, or to pay hundreds of dollars more in auto insurance premiums. The cumulative impact of these financial calamities could strand a consumer economically for years after the event itself, which in turn makes it more difficult for them to pay their bills and repair their credit standing. This creates a vicious cycle in a consumer's economic life. These issues are discussed in depth in our report, *Solving the Credit Conundrum: Helping Consumers' Credit Records Impaired by the Foreclosure Crisis and Great Recession* (2013).

We need a better way to judge consumers. We need a system that can distinguish between consumers who are truly irresponsible and those who simply fell on hard times. We need a system that can take into account extraordinary life events.

Part of the solution is to require the credit bureaus be more precise and distinguish between consumers who have an extraordinary life event versus those who are truly irresponsible. Some proposals to do so would be:

- *Protect economic victims of COVID-19.* Establish a moratorium on negative credit and consumer reporting for events that occurred during the COVID-19 pandemic period and for other significant disasters.
- *Help victims of abusive lending practices.* Consumers are unfairly penalized when they have been the victim of abusive practices, such as predatory mortgages or student loans resulting from for-profit school fraud. Adverse information related to these abuses should be removed from credit reports.
- *Limit reporting of medical debt.* Medical debt is one of the most unfair forms of negative information in credit reports, as discussed in Section I below, and the reforms discussed in that section would alleviate some of the harm for consumers who have experienced financial distress from illness and high healthcare bills.
- *Limit non-credit uses of credit reports and scores.* The harm from negative credit reporting would be reduced by prohibiting non-credit uses of credit information. As discussed in Section G, there is no good evidence for the use of credit reports in employment, and its use in rental housing and insurance is also highly problematic.[170]
- *Shorter time limits for negative information.* The FCRA should be amended to shorten the time periods for negative information to four years (seven years for bankruptcies). This would lessen the amount of time that adverse information can harm consumers. There is

[170] For a discussion of why the use of credit scores in insurance is unfair, *see* Stephen Brobeck, et al., Consumer Federation of America, The Use of Credit Scores by Auto Insurers: Adverse Impacts on Low-and Moderate-Income Drivers (Dec. 2013), https://consumerfed.org/pdfs/useofcreditscoresbyautoinsurers_dec2013_cfa.pdf.

> nothing special about the current seven-year time limit for negative information under the FCRA. It is certainly not universal. For example, the time limit for negative information in Sweden – a country that is as economically vibrant and prosperous as the United States if not more so – is three years.[171]

Most of these reforms were included in the Comprehensive CREDIT Act introduced in the last session of Congress, which we supported. The first item, a moratorium on negative credit reporting during the COVID-19 period, was included as Section 110401 of the HEROES Act, H.R. 6800, by the House of Representatives during the 116th Congress.

Racial Disparities in Credit Reporting Reinforce Inequality

The vicious cycle effect of using the past to judge the future is also responsible for the stunning racial disparities in credit scores. Study after study has found that Black and Latinx communities have lower credit scores as a group than whites. A list of older studies is available in our policy brief, *Past Imperfect: How credit scores and other analytics "bake in" past discrimination and perpetuate it* (2016). A more recent report found that over 50 percent of white households had a FICO credit score above 700, compared with only 20.6 percent of Black households.[172] Members of the Committee can check out statistics for their own states and counties using the Urban Institute's Credit Health app: https://apps.urban.org/features/credit-health-during-pandemic/.

Communities of color have lower credit scores as a group because credit histories starkly reflect the racial economic divide and wealth gap in this country. Communities of color have less income than white Americans, but it is the disparity in assets that is most stunning: the typical Black family has

[171] Marieke Bos and Leonard Nakamura, Federal Reserve Bank of Philadelphia, Working Paper No. 12-19/R, Should Defaults Be Forgotten? Evidence from Quasi-Experimental Variation in Removal of Negative Consumer Credit Information, Apr. 2013, at 1, www.philadelphiafed.org/research-and-data/publications/working-papers/2012/wp12-29R.pdf.

[172] Jung Hyun Choi, et al., Urban Inst., Explaining the Black-White Homeownership Gap: A Closer Look at Disparities across Local Markets (Nov. 2019), https://www.urban.org/research/publication/explaining-black-white-homeownership-gap-closer-look-disparities-across-local-markets, at 8.

one-eighth (or less than 13%) of the wealth of a typical white family; Latinx families have one-fifth (20%) of the wealth of white families.[173]

The racial wealth gap, in turn, is due to both current discrimination and decades of intentional systematic discrimination. Housing discrimination, in particular, is responsible for much of the racial wealth gap as it deprived Black communities of the ability to accumulate wealth through homeownership.[174] Current discrimination also has an impact on family financial situations. For example, a recent study found that a history of incarceration heavily impacts the credit scores of both the incarcerated individuals and their families,[175] and it's been well-established that Black communities are disproportionately targeted by the criminal justice system.[176] Black communities also bear the bulk of financial burdens when municipalities make heavy-handed use of criminal fees and fines to obtain revenue.[177]

With far less wealth to draw on, Black consumers – and the friends and family to whom they might turn – are far less able to cushion the blow of financial calamities, such as the COVID-19 economic crisis. It's not surprising for credit scores to reflect the racial disparities in the economic conditions of Black and white communities. As a *measurement tool*, they work well, in that they reveal the entrenched inequality that current and historical discrimination has engendered. The problem is when credit scores are used as a *decision making* tool without consideration of these disparities. Using tools that "bake in" racial disparities results in perpetuating and reinforcing these same disparities, creating the vicious cycle.

The solutions necessary to stop this vicious cycle go beyond the credit reporting system. Racial equity requires measures such as restorative justice

---

173 Neil Bhutta, Andrew C. Chang, Lisa J. Dettling, and Joanne W. Hsu, Federal Reserve, Disparities in Wealth by Race and Ethnicity in the 2019 Survey of Consumer Finances, FED Notes, September 28, 2020, https://www.federalreserve.gov/econres/notes/feds-notes/disparities-in-wealth-by-race-and-ethnicity-in-the-2019-survey-of-consumer-finances-20200928.htm.

174 See Richard Rothstein, The Color of Law: A Forgotten History of How Our Government Segregated America. Liveright Publishing Corporation, 2017 (documenting decades of intentional housing discrimination, including redlining by government agencies).

175 Mónica García-Pérez, Sarah Gaither, William Darity Jr., Samuel DuBois Cook Center on Social Equity, Duke University, Baltimore Study: Credit Scores, March 2020, https://equitablegrowth.org/working-papers/baltimore-study-credit-scores/.

176 Michelle Alexander, The New Jim Crow: Mass Incarceration in the Age of Colorblindness, New Press, 2010.

177 Fines and Fees Justice Center, Racial Disparities, https://finesandfeesjusticecenter.org/tag/racial-disparities/ (viewed June 24, 2020)(links to multiple studies discussing racial disparities in criminal fines and fees).

efforts in lending and homeownership programs. But some credit reporting measures that could help achieve racial justice include:

- *Limit non-credit uses of credit reports and scores.* Severely restrict the use of credit reporting information in employment and rental housing, and ban it for insurance.
- *Carefully test alternative data:* As discussed below, alternative data and scores can be a promising, but carry risks. Even the more promising forms of alternative data, such as bank account data, will still exhibit some racial disparities given the unequal economic positions of Black and white households, but may be an improvement from traditional credit scores as a "less discriminatory alternative."
- *Develop a scoring model with fewer racial disparities.* As part of a public credit registry, the registry should have as an explicit mission to develop a credit scoring model that actively takes past and present discrimination into account and is intentionally designed to reduce racial disparities.

Alternative Data: Proceed with Caution

There has been a great deal of attention focused on another perplexing problem of the credit reporting system - "credit invisibility." According to the CFPB, 26 million Americans (or about 1 in 10) do not have a credit history, and another 18 million are unscorable because their histories are too scant ("thin") or old.[178] The CFPB also found that Black, Latinx, and low-income consumers are more likely to have no credit history or to be unscorable.

Policymakers, advocates, and the credit industry have all promoted alternative sources of data as the solution to credit invisibility. While there is promise in some forms of alternative data, there are also significant risks. In a hearing in the Oversight and Investigations Subcommittee last month,[179] the credit bureaus aggressively advocated for policies that would help them include more alternative data in their files, claimed it would address the problems of credit reporting including racial disparities.

---

[178] Consumer Financial Protection Bureau, Data Point: Credit Invisibles, May 2015, http://files.consumerfinance.gov/f/201505_cfpb_data-point-credit-invisibles.pdf.

[179] Consumer Credit Reporting: Assessing Accuracy and Compliance: Hearing Before the Subcomm. on Oversight and Investigations of the H. Fin. Serv. Comm., 117th Congr. (2021).

However, feeding more data to the credit bureaus is not the solution. Feeding them more data only increases the oligopoly power of these three companies, giving them even more power over our information and our financial lives. Moreover, alternative data is not a panacea for the problems in credit reporting. There are also tens of millions of consumers with poor credit scores and histories, disproportionately Black and Latinx.[180] A bad credit history is more harmful than no credit history, and alternative data will not eliminate racial disparities in credit scores.

As with so many aspects of credit and financial services, "the devil is in the details" when it comes to alternative data. The manner in which alternative data is used is important. Using alternative data to create special scores that are separate from credit bureau-based scores is preferable, such as UltraFICO or FICO XD. In contrast, wholesale addition of the same data to traditional credit reports could damage consumers who already have a thick file and credit score. Also, it is absolutely critical that efforts to use alternative data be voluntary opt-in, with knowing consumer consent, to increase the control that consumers – not private companies – have over our own information.

The other critical issue is that the type of data matters. Some data shows promise, other data is a mixed bag, and some data is harmful enough that it should not be used.

- *Bank account transaction/cashflow data looks promising but carries risks.* Bank account transaction data appears to be the most promising form of alternative data. First, it incorporates an analysis of ability to repay, since it includes both income and expense information. Second, it may avoid the need to rely on long historical timeframes and thus not consider negative marks from economic hardships from many months ago. Also, it might be able to show when there has been a healthy sustained recovery from an extraordinary life event such as a job loss or illness due to COVID-19. Research by FinRegLab indicates that cash-flow data holds promise for helping borrowers

180 According to the Urban Institute's Credit Health app, 22% of adults with credit files had a subprime credit score in October 2020, which would be nearly 46 million Americans. Urban Institute, Credit Health during the COVID-19 Pandemic, Feb 25, 2021, https://apps.urban.org/features/credit-health-during-pandemic/.

who might otherwise face constraints on their ability to access credit.[181]

However, bank account transaction data raises security and privacy issues, as it could be used in ways consumers do not expect or misused to ensure ability to collect, not ability to repay. It should only be used when the consumer has knowingly and actively consented to its use, and it must be protected from access by collectors and others who would use it against consumers.[182]

- *Gas and electric utility data would likely be harmful.* Most gas and electric companies currently only report accounts on traditional credit reports when they are very seriously delinquent. "Full file" monthly reporting of gas and electric bill payment data has the potential to give millions of low-income consumers bad or worse credit scores by adding payments that are only 30 or 60 days late. Reporting of late payments could also undermine state consumer protections, such as prohibitions against wintertime shut offs for vulnerable consumers, including the elderly.

  For these reasons, NCLC and several dozen other consumer and utility rights groups have consistently opposed the "Credit Access and Inclusion Act."[183] We also oppose that bill because it would preempt state consumer protection laws protecting the privacy of utility customers and hinder states from regulating tenant screening agencies.
- *Rental data could be promising but carries risks.* Pilot projects using rental data have had promising results, especially those that do not report 30- or 60-day late payments. However, the COVID-19 pandemic has complicated efforts to use rental payment data, given that millions of tenants are behind in their rent obligations and at risk of eviction.
- *Subprime credit information would hurt consumers.* Payday loans and other forms of subprime credit are often not reported on traditional

---

[181] FinRegLab, The Use of Cash-Flow Data in Underwriting Credit: Empirical Research Findings, July 2019, https://finreglab.org/wp-content/uploads/2019/07/FRL_Research-Report_Final.pdf.

[182] For more details about our concerns regarding the use of bank account data, *see* NCLC et al., Comments to the CFPB in Response to the ANPR Regarding Consumer Access to Financial Records Under Section 1033 of the Dodd-Frank Act, Feb. 4, 2021, https://www.nclc.org/issues/credit-reports.html.

[183] Consumer groups' opposition letter to H.R. 435, Credit Access and Inclusion Act, Dec. 8, 2017, https://nclc.org/images/pdf/legislation/letter-oppose-hr435-hfsc.pdf.

credit reports. Adding these types of credit could damage the credit records of these borrowers. High-cost credit is often designed to lead to a cycle of debt, and even merely using a subprime form of credit can negatively affect a credit score.

- *Telecommunications data – the jury's still out.* Unlike regulated electric and gas service, telecom (cell phone, Internet, and cable) industries have fewer consumer protections that could be undermined by monthly reporting. Outstanding questions include the level of accuracy of the data and the impact on consumers who dispute their bills because of issues such as cramming and questionable surcharges.

The Unfinished Business of the Equifax Data Breach

It's been over three and a half years since the Equifax data breach became public. It was arguably the worst data breach in American history, not only because it affected 148 million Americans or one in two American adults, but it also involved some of the most critical personal information we have – SSNs (which are the golden keys for identity thieves), dates of birth, and in some cases drivers' license numbers. And despite much outrage and extensive media coverage, American consumers are still nowhere close to being safe in the aftermath.

Notwithstanding numerous hearings in both the House and the Senate, the only measure taken by Congress was to include a provision in the Economic Growth, Regulatory Relief, and Consumer Protection Act (EGRRCPA) of 2018 providing free security freezes[184] – something that state legislatures were already well on their way to doing. And the federal security freeze came at the high cost of preempting those state laws, some of which were more protective of consumers in that they applied freezes to employment and tenant screening use of credit reports.

Congress must do better. It should:

- *Give the CFPB clear supervision authority* under the Gramm Leach-Bliley Act and the FCRA over data security at the credit bureaus. The CFPB should be given this authority so that it has a clear mandate to supervise the credit bureaus regarding this area.

---

[184] Pub. L. No. 115-174,§ 301(a), codified at 15 U.S.C. § 1681c-1(i).

- *Impose significant and hefty penalties* when the negligence of the credit bureaus leads to data breaches.
- *Freeze credit reports by default* to prevent identity theft and give consumers more control over their credit reports. The switch for access to our credit reports should automatically be set to "off." We as American consumers should get to decide when to turn it "on." And in the process of turning the switch on, credit bureaus and other CRAs should be required to verify the identity of the consumer to make sure it is really that person.[185]

Medical Debt Unfairly Penalizes Consumers

As the COVID-19 pandemic has starkly shown, expenses for life-saving or medically necessary care are often unexpected, and can throw a family into an immediate financial crisis.[186] This crisis is compounded when families cannot pay for these surprise expenses and the debt is reported to credit bureaus. The impact of medical debt on credit reports is nothing short of stunning. The CFPB found that medical debt represents 58% of all third-party debt collection entries that appear on credit reports,[187] and nearly one in five credit reports contains a medical debt item.[188] Moreover, there is strong evidence that medical debt items are not an accurate reflection of the creditworthiness of the consumer.[189]

---

[185] Note that there has been a bill introduced in the Senate during this Congress to establish a credit freeze by default. S.1343 - Consumer Credit Control Act of 2021 (117 Congr.)(Sen. Reed).

[186] *See, e.g.,* Sarah Kliff, Covid Killed His Father. Then Came $1 Million in Medical Bills, N.Y. Times, May 21, 2021, https://www.nytimes.com/2021/05/21/upshot/covid-bills-financial-long-haulers.html; Sarah Kliff, A $22,368 Bill That Dodged and Weaved to Find a Gap in America's Health System, N.Y. Times, Marc. 10, 2021, https://www.nytimes.com/2021/03/10/upshot/covid-bill-health-gap.html.

[187] Consumer Fin. Prot. Bureau, Market Snapshot: Third-Party Debt Collections Tradeline Reporting, July 2019 ("More than half (58 percent) of total third-party debt collections tradelines were for medical debt alone"), https://files.consumerfinance.gov/f/documents/201907_cfpb_third-party-debt-collections_report.pdf#page=13.

[188] Consumer Fin. Prot. Bureau, Consumer Credit Reports: A Study of Medical and Non-Medical Collections (Dec. 11, 2014), https://files.consumerfinance.gov/f/201412_cfpb_reports_consumer-credit-medical-and-non-medical-collections.pdf.

[189] Consumer Fin. Prot. Bureau, Data Point: Medical Debt and Credit Scores (May 2014), https://files.consumerfinance.gov/f/201405_cfpb_report_data-point_medical-debt-credit-scores.pdf. (finding that that medical debt unfairly penalizes a consumer's credit score by 10 points, and for a medical debt collection item that is subsequently paid, by up to 22 points). *See also* Consumer Fin. Prot. Bureau, Consumer Credit Reports: A Study of Medical and Non-

In response to this study and other evidence, both FICO and VantageScore developed scoring models that reduced the impact of medical debt. But these changes do help not mortgage applicants, because Fannie Mae and Freddie Mac do not use these models right now, despite working on this issue for many years[190] and even a statutory provision requiring updated scoring models.[191]

A more effective solution than changing scoring models would be to prohibit the reporting of medical debt for medically necessary services and to delay the reporting of other medical debt for one year to give consumers time to resolve complex, confusing medical billing issues. Both of these solutions were included in the Comprehensive CREDIT Act that the House passed in January 2020, as well as H.R. 2547, the Comprehensive Debt Collection Improvement Act, passed by the House this year, both of which we strongly supported.

Use of Credit Reports in Employment Is Unreasonable and Discriminatory

The use of credit reports in employment is a practice that is harmful and unfair to American workers. Despite many good reasons to avoid engaging in this practice, nearly one-third of employers (31%) do so today.[192] This appears to be a decrease from the 47% of employers who checked credit reports in 2012[193] but a significant increase from only 19% in 1996.[194]

Medical Collections 7, 28 (Dec. 11, 2014), https://files.consumerfinance.gov/f/201412_cfpb_reports_consumer-credit-medical-and-non-medical-collections.pdf. (consumers whose credit reports show only collection items consisting of medical bills are more reliable payers, owe less, and have more available credit).

190 Samantha Fields and Amy Scott, More people could qualify for mortgages under new rule, NPR Marketplace, Aug. 14, 2019, https://www.marketplace.org/2019/08/14/more-people-could-qualify-for-mortgages-under-new-rule/.

191 Economic Growth, Regulatory Relief, and Consumer Protection Act (EGRRCPA) of 2018, Pub. L. No. 115-174,§ 310.

192 National Association of Professional Background Screeners, How Human Resource Professionals View the Usage and Effectiveness of Background Screening Methods, 2108, at 10, https://pubs.thepbsa.org/pub.cfm?id=9E5ED85F-C257-C289-9E8E-A7C7A8C58D00.

193 Society for Human Resource Management, Background Checking—The Use of Credit Background Checks in Hiring Decisions, July 19, 2012, at https://www.shrm.org/hr-today/trends-and-forecasting/research-and-surveys/pages/creditbackgroundchecks.aspx.

194 Matt Fellowes, *Credit Scores, Reports, and Getting Ahead in America*, Brookings Institution, May 2006 at n.3 (citing 1996 data from the Society for Human Resource Management).

The use of credit reports in employment should be severely restricted for the following reasons.

- *Credit checks create a fundamental "Catch-22" for job applicants.* A simple reason to oppose the use of credit history for job applications is the sheer absurdity of the practice. Simply put, workers who lose their jobs are likely fall behind on paying their bills due to lack of income. If credit reports are used against them, these workers now find themselves shut out of the job market because they're behind on their bills. This leads to a financial death spiral: the worse the impact of unemployment on their debts, the harder it is to get a job to pay them off.
- *The use of credit checks in hiring discriminates against Black and Latinx job applicants.* As discussed in Section E, study after study has documented how, as a group, Black and Latinx consumers have lower credit scores than whites. Since credit scores are a translation of the information in credit reports, that means these groups fare worse when their credit reports are considered in employment.
- *Credit history does not predict job performance.* Credit reports were designed to predict the likelihood that consumers will miss a payment on a loan, not whether they will steal or behave irresponsibly in the workplace. The overwhelming weight of evidence is that people with impaired credit histories are ***not*** more likely to be bad employees or to steal from their employers. As a Stanford professor who reviewed several relevant studies for her PhD thesis concluded "existing research provides few convincing correlations between personal financial data and employee behavior."[195]
- *As discussed in Section A, credit reports suffer from unacceptable rates of inaccuracy, especially for a purpose as important as use in employment.*

---

[195] Barbara Kiviat, The art of deciding with data: evidence from how employers translate credit reports into hiring decisions, Socio-Economic Review, Volume 17, Issue 2, April 2019, Pages 283–309, https://doi.org/10.1093/ser/mwx030 (citing studies from Weaver (2015) finding no link between credit outcomes and productivity; Bryan and Palmer (2012) finding no consistent relationship between credit report data and job performance or termination and Bernerth *et al.* (2012) finding no correlation between credit scores and supervisors' reports of bad workplace behavior).

Fundamentally, the issue at stake is whether workers are fairly judged based on their ability to perform a job or whether they're discriminated against because of their credit history. Congress should ban the use of credit reports for employment purposes, with only very limited exceptions for a few specific job positions.

Conclusion

For 50 years, Congress, the FTC and now the CFPB, state legislatures and regulators, consumer advocates, private attorneys, and everyday Americans have battled a credit reporting industry that continues to abuse consumers with too many errors and a biased and dysfunctional dispute system. The same industry is shamelessly shilling its products for inappropriate and destructive uses such as rental housing and employment, contributing to one of the most appalling problems in this country – the massive economic and racial equality that threatens to tear this country apart.

Fifty years of abuse and dysfunction is enough.

It's time for a new paradigm for credit reporting, one that is responsive to consumers, to the American people and to the good of our country. It's time for a public credit registry, ideally exclusively as the only credit bureau. At a minimum, there should be a public credit registry as a public option where the consumer makes the choice of whether to use it or a private credit bureau.

Short of a public credit registry, or if it is a public option and private credit bureaus continue to exist, Congress should:

1. Reintroduce and pass a bill similar to the Comprehensive CREDIT Act, as well as a bill similar to the Protect Your Credit Score Act. Both bills were passed by the House of Representatives in the last Congress but not by the Senate. The bills included provisions such as:
   - Providing consumers with a right of appeal for credit reporting disputes;
   - Requiring stricter matching criteria or a CFPB rulemaking that imposes such criteria and establishes minimum procedures to ensure maximum possible accuracy;

- Clarifying that the credit bureaus must devote sufficient resources and conduct independent analyses in disputes;
- Providing consumers with a right to seek injunctive relief compelling credit bureaus to fix a credit report;
- Shortening the time that negative information can remain on a consumer report to four years (seven years for bankruptcies)
- Prohibiting the inclusion of medical collections on credit reports until after one year from the bill, and the inclusion of any debts for medically necessary services;
- Requiring the removal of adverse information resulting from predatory mortgages or private student loans resulting from for-profit school fraud; and
- Severely restricting the use of credit reports in employment and banning the use of credit reporting information in insurance.

2. Establish a moratorium on negative credit and consumer reporting for events that occurred during the COVID-19 pandemic period, similar to Section 110401 of the HEROES Act, H.R. 6800, passed by the House of Representatives during the 116th Congress.
3. With respect to data security for the credit bureaus, Congress should:
   - Give the CFPB clear supervision authority over data security at the credit bureaus;
   - Impose significant and hefty penalties when the negligence of credit bureaus leads to data breaches; and
   - Freeze credit reports by default to prevent identity theft and give consumers more control over their credit reports.

Written Statement of Brad Thaler, Vice President of Legislative Affairs, National Association of Federally-Insured Credit Unions

Dear Chairwoman Waters and Ranking Member McHenry:

I write to you today on behalf of the National Association of Federally-Insured Credit Unions (NAFCU) in conjunction with tomorrow's hearing, "A Biased, Broken System: Examining Proposals to Overhaul Credit Reporting to Achieve Equity." As you are aware, NAFCU advocates for all federally-insured not-for-profit credit unions that, in turn, serve nearly 125 million consumers with personal and small business financial service products.

NAFCU believes an accurate, fair, transparent, and equitable credit reporting system is imperative for both consumers and financial institutions, and we thank you for holding a hearing on this important topic.

The nation's credit reporting system is an important tool for financial institutions, such as credit unions, to responsibly lend to consumers while ensuring safety and soundness. As you consider proposals to reform the system, we urge you to reject efforts aimed at blanket suppression of adverse information in credit reports as this could lead to significant changes in how lenders use credit information to make loans and disrupt consumer access to credit. A better step would be to encourage efforts to allow credit reporting to reflect loans where payments are deferred or in forbearance, so these loans do not negatively affect a consumer's credit score.

An example of this approach is the relief in Section 4021 of the *Coronavirus Aid, Relief, and Economic Security Act* (CARES Act), which requires furnishers of information to credit reporting agencies (CRAs) to report an account current if an accommodation has been made during the pandemic. Accounts delinquent prior to the accommodation are reported as such unless the consumer brings the account current during the accommodation. This approach strikes a good balance by preserving the accuracy of credit reports while also protecting the credit profiles of consumers who receive payment relief due to the pandemic. Section 4021 is effective until 120 days after termination of the COVID-19 national emergency, hence consumers can avail themselves of this relief for the duration of the pandemic.

To that end, while we are supportive of the aim of Title III – Student Borrower Credit Improvement Act and Title IV – Credit Restoration for Victims of Predatory Activities and Unfair Consumer Reporting Practices of H.R. 4120, the *Comprehensive Credit Reporting Enhancement, Disclosure, Innovation, and Transparency Act* (Comprehensive CREDIT Act), to help students and consumers repair their credit, especially those who have been taken advantage of by predatory entities, we are concerned this legislation goes too far in suppressing adverse information and could diminish the accuracy of the credit reporting system. If lenders, such as credit unions, are unable to trust that credit reports are complete and accurate, they will have to devote more resources to investigating a borrower's credit history, increasing the cost of credit across the system, and reducing access to credit for historically marginalized communities. We ask that you instead consider an approach that utilizes coding of accounts, such as the approach by Section 4021 of the CARES Act noted above.

NAFCU recognizes that an effective dispute process by which consumers can rectify errors in their credit reports is essential to ensuring a fair and accurate credit reporting system. However, we are concerned about legislative approaches, such as in the *Protecting Your Credit Score Act* and Title I – Improvements to the Dispute Process of the Comprehensive CREDIT Act, that would require furnishers of information, such as credit unions, to review and consider new or additional information each time a consumer disputes the accuracy of information in their credit report. We have some concerns that this could result in predatory credit repair companies continually disputing accurate information, at great cost to financial institutions and consumers. Such continuous dispute opportunities could lead to situations where accurate "negative" information ends up being excluded from credit scores due to ongoing disputes. This will also leave less bandwidth for real disputes to be investigated.

Moreover, we have concerns about the expansion of private rights of action under the *Protecting Your Credit Score Act*, which could have a chilling effect on credit unions and other financial institutions that could see a rise in frivolous lawsuits that will take resources away from serving consumers. Allowing courts injunctive relief could also lead to situations where courts may interpret the *Fair Credit Reporting Act* (FCRA) differently than the Consumer Financial Protection Bureau (CFPB), leading to confusion amongst financial institutions on how to comply with the FCRA.

NAFCU is supportive of the *Protecting Your Credit Score Act's* efforts to hold CRAs accountable for their obligations under the *Gramm-Leach-Bliley Act* and to improve data security at the CRAs. We believe that there should be further examination as to whether the CFPB or the Federal Trade Commission (FTC) is best suited to establishing appropriate standards.

NAFCU and its member credit unions also support the use of alternative credit score models to enhance access to affordable credit for creditworthy borrowers who have historically been marginalized. Credit unions work hard to provide products and services for their members, particularly those in underserved communities, including rural areas. Alternative credit score models that do not penalize borrowers for a lack of traditional credit history and include other data sources to verify creditworthiness have the potential to increase access to credit for these communities especially, furthering financial inclusion. Section 501 of Title V – Clarity in Credit Score Formation of the Comprehensive CREDIT Act, which would require the CFPB to carry out a study to assess the impact of non-traditional data in credit reports, could be a good step to further examine the use and potential of these models.

Finally, we have serious concerns about proposals, such as the *National Credit Reporting Agency Act*, that would create a government-run credit bureau under the CFPB. NAFCU has concerns about the cost of establishing and running a government credit bureau, but more importantly, we think that such a system will not benefit consumers as much as improving upon the current private sector credit reporting industry. Furthermore, government retention of credit reporting information could erode consumer privacy, particularly if a single agency presented a data-rich target for criminals. We believe that consumers and lenders alike benefit from a robust, competitive, and innovative private sector credit reporting industry that is constantly evolving to consider new sources of data and increase the scope of the system to include underserved consumers. Replacing this system with a government-run credit bureau will stifle innovation and competition and have the unintended consequence of reducing access to credit.

We thank you for your leadership and appreciate the opportunity to share our thoughts on the importance of an accurate, fair, transparent, and equitable credit reporting system. We look forward to continuing to work with you on this important issue, as well as pandemic relief and economic recovery. Should you have any questions or require any additional information, please contact Sarah Jacobs, NAFCU's Associate Director of Legislative Affairs.

Written Statement of Marc H. Morial, President & CEO, National Urban League

National Urban League | *Empowering Communities. Changing Lives.*

June 29, 2021

The Honorable Maxine Waters
Chairwoman
Committee on Financial Services
United States House of Representatives
2129 Rayburn House Office Building
Washington, DC 20515

Dear Chairwoman Waters,

As President and CEO of the National Urban League, and on behalf of its 90 affiliates in 36 states and the District of Columbia, I'm writing to thank you and members of the committee for holding this hearing on

"A Biased, Broken System: Examining Proposals to Overhaul Credit Reporting to Achieve Equity." I appreciate the opportunity to provide our perspective on how best to improve credit scoring models in an effort to advance fair and equitable access to credit for traditionally underserved communities nationwide.

I proudly serve as the President & CEO of the National Urban League, the nation's largest civil rights and advocacy organization. The National Urban League has 91 affiliates across the U.S., who provide direct services to 2 million people annually. As a premier, HUD-approved, housing counseling agency, we operate housing programs at more than 40 of our affiliates nationwide. We know firsthand the impact that low credit scores have on prospective borrowers. Below, I offer solutions to help ensure creditworthy borrowers have access and reasonable pricing in the conventional loan market.

The mission of the Urban League is to enable African Americans and other underserved communities to secure economic self-reliance, parity, power, and civil rights. We help our constituents attain economic self-reliance through homeownership, job training, good jobs, entrepreneurship, and wealth accumulation. Our views and recommendations are based on decades of direct program experience in urban communities across the country and our historic role in documenting and fashioning remedies to address our nation's long and unfortunate history of discrimination against communities of color.

Credit scores can serve as an arbitrary barrier to the housing market because they do not provide a full picture of an applicant's ability to repay a loan. Reforms to the current credit scoring model are necessary to better account for new technological advances in the industry that address the shortcomings of the current model. As a general rule, the way in which creditworthiness is determined must account for the way in which consumer behavior in the 21st Century has changed. To that end, the use of additional sources of data that provide more insight into consumer financial behavior can help provide compensating factors for borrowers with low credit scores

Several advances have taken place in the credit scoring industry that help predict the risk of default of consumers. These advances such as the use of rental payments, cashflow data, as well as cell phone, cable, and utility payments have helped increase access to capital for many consumers who were traditionally frozen out of the market or were required to pay higher borrowing costs, including many borrowers of color. Unfortunately, these highly-predictive sources of data are excluded from current credit score models, with few exceptions.

While alternative data is often used in some automated underwriting processes, low credit scores generally bar many consumers from reaching the automated underwriting stage. As a result, many creditworthy borrowers are denied access to conventional loans in large part because the data does not reside at the nationwide consumer reporting agencies, Equifax, Experian, and Transunion (CRAs).

The National Urban League supports a new credit scoring model that better predicts risk through the use of these emerging scoring technologies. We applaud the committee for considering the use of new credit scoring models that leverage additional data that can be found outside of the primary CRAs in an effort to help expand access to fair and affordable credit. In our view, rental history alone can more accurately determine a borrower's financial readiness to own a home. As such, it should be included in the borrower's credit score. The CRAs must also lower the existing barriers to reporting while doing more to incentivize landlords to provide this information and protect consumer information.

Alternative credit scoring models use emerging scoring technologies and new data sources to accurately predict risk and can help more borrowers qualify for a conventional mortgage loan or qualify at better terms. The incorporation of these emerging scoring technologies into a new credit scoring model, to the extent that it's possible without having a disparate impact on applicants, would help the many creditworthy borrowers that are currently frozen out of the home mortgage market. Pilot programs can provide a responsible way to determine the impact of alternative sources of data in the origination process and should be used to validate a new credit scoring model.

Lastly, housing counseling should serve as a compensating factor for prospective borrowers with lower than average credit scores. Doing so would increase the number of responsible homeowners currently barred from the market due to unreasonably high credit score requirements. Empirical research demonstrates that homebuyers who work with housing counselors have better outcomes than those who navigate the housing market on their own. Data has long shown that face-to-face, pre-purchase education, and counseling services offered by many Urban League affiliates, can help reduce loan delinquencies by as much as 29 percent. Similar to private mortgage insurance, housing counseling should also be allowed to count as a credit enhancement factor, allowing borrowers who do not have the requisite credit score to access the traditional housing market.

Thank you for your consideration of the National Urban League's policy priorities. Should you have any further questions, please feel free to reach out to Julius Niyonsaba (*jniyonsaba@nul.org*) at the National Urban League's Washington Bureau.

Sincerely,

Marc H. Morial
President & CEO
National Urban League

Written Statement of UnidosUS

UNIDOSUS

STRONGER COMMUNITIES. STRONGER AMERICA.

A Biased, Broken System: Examining Proposals to Overhaul Credit Reporting to Achieve Equity

House Committee on Financial Services Hearing

Statement for the Hearing Record

July 14, 2021

UnidosUS, formerly the National Council of La Raza (NCLR), is the largest national Hispanic* civil rights and advocacy organization in the United States. For more than 50 years, we have worked to advance opportunities for low- and moderate-income (LMI) Latino families so that they can achieve economic stability and build wealth.

We appreciate the opportunity to submit this written statement for the record. This effort by the committee to understand barriers to an inclusive system of credit is critical.

UnidosUS, with our network of nearly 300 Affiliates—community-based organizations across the United States and Puerto Rico—provides education, health care, housing counseling, workforce development, and financial coaching programs to millions of citizens and immigrants in the United States annually. Furthermore, our network of community-based financial and housing counseling providers helps inform our understanding of Latinos' financial challenges and opportunities. The UnidosUS Wealth and Housing Alliance (UWHA) (formerly the National Homeownership Network, or NHN) is the nation's largest network of community-based organizations working to empower Latino wealth-building through homeownership.[1]

Moreover, for more than two decades, UnidosUS has published reports and testimony and engaged in advocacy on supporting strong fair housing and fair lending laws, increasing access to financial services for LMI individuals, and promoting homeownership in the Latino community. Additionally, UnidosUS conducts its own original community-based research on the experiences of LMI communities of color, including *Closing the Latina Wealth Gap: Building an Inclusive Economic Recovery after COVID* (2021); *The Future of Banking: Overcoming Barriers to Financial Inclusion for Communities of Color* (2019) (an update of *Banking in Color: New*

---

* The terms "Hispanic" and "Latino" are used interchangeably by the U.S. Census Bureau and throughout this document to refer to persons of Mexican, Puerto Rican, Cuban, Central and South American, Dominican, Spanish, and other Hispanic descent; they may be of any race.

Findings on Financial Access for Low- and Moderate-Income Communities (2014)); and *Small Dollars for Big Change: Immigrant Financial Inclusion and Access to Credit* (2017).

As we described in our landmark 2019 report, *The Future of Banking*, as it is currently structured the financial services industry makes financial inclusion—including access to credit and to useful and affordable financial products and services that meet people's needs—very difficult for LMI people of color. Financial exclusion, in turn, exacerbates other economic challenges such as low wages and unaffordable housing and creates additional barriers to economic inclusion and an equitable economic recovery.

Historically, these barriers compel LMI populations to rely on high-cost alternative financial services (AFS), which hold a virtual monopoly over the financial marketplace for people who are underbanked and unbanked. These services can leave households in self-perpetuating cycles of debt and financial ruin. Recently, such vulnerabilities—and the systemic inequities they reproduce—have only been worsened by the economic stresses of the pandemic, as described below.

In our previous expert testimony in 2019 before the Committee on Financial Services,[2] we focused on how the credit scoring system is systematically biased against low-income consumers, consumers of color, younger consumers, and immigrants. We also demonstrated how these structural barriers affect consumers and limit access to credit, in addition to affecting their ability to obtain employment, rent an apartment, turn on their utilities, or access health insurance. In short, the current credit scoring system affects almost every aspect of the personal financial life of everyday Americans, especially Latinos.

That testimony pointed out that, "Latinos have had longstanding challenges connecting to mainstream financial institutions and obtaining credit, similar to other communities of color. As the youngest and fastest-growing segment of the nation's population, Latinos' economic opportunities will have a significant role in shaping the nation's economic future. Increased credit scores and credit visibility are important components of ensuring that Latinos can unlock these opportunities."

Given these barriers, we concluded that the system needed reforms that would provide a truer picture of the ability of Latinos to use credit wisely: "For Latinos, who represent 18% of the population, it is important that our credit rating system serve them in a fair and inclusive manner. If we continue to rely on credit bureaus as gatekeepers who determine access to housing, employment, and health coverage, in addition to making lending decisions, the credit rating system will need to reflect a more accurate and transparent depiction of the credit-worthiness of these underserved populations."

Building on this work, our report, *The Future of Banking*,[3] found that both poor credit and credit invisibility are particular barriers among LMI consumers and communities of color: "Poor credit and the lack of established credit are significant barriers for LMI consumers attempting to access mainstream banking and/or credit products and services. Nearly 30% of consumers in low-income neighborhoods are credit invisible, meaning they have no record with the three nationwide credit reporting agencies—Experian, TransUnion, and Equifax. An additional 15% have records that are deemed 'unscorable' due to insufficient credit history. Black and Latino consumers are also more likely to be credit invisible or deemed unscorable than White consumers. In all, one in 10 U.S. adults (26 million people) are credit invisible, and an additional 19 million have unscorable credit files."

The report also described the possibilities and perils of the innovations in financial services (known as "fintech") and made several relevant recommendations regarding necessary reforms of the financial system, including:

- Development of a nationwide network of "navigators" to better help the underbanked and unbanked understand and use the options provided by the financial system
- A more inclusive credit rating system that includes additional metrics responsive to bills that lower-income consumers pay
- Measures to make more credit available for low- and moderate-income consumers

The Need for an Inclusive Economic Recovery from the Pandemic

The pandemic exacerbated preexisting racial-ethnic income and wealth disparities. To better understand the depths of the impact, we conducted a poll in February 2021,[4] which showed the following:

- As a result of COVID-19, Latinas are far more likely than other groups to find it difficult to afford necessities, such as food (36%).
- Latinas are in a poor position to withstand the economic impact of the pandemic, with 49% spending "most or all" of their life savings during the pandemic. This was more than double the rate for White women (24%) or White men (19%).
- One-quarter of Latinas have, during the pandemic, "gone into debt or maxed out a credit card" or "missed a car, student loan, or credit card payment."

Our 2021 report, *Closing the Latina Wealth Gap: Building an Inclusive Economic Recovery after COVID*,[5] described the financial challenges that Latinas face, noting that, "A major factor in driving the triple crisis is that most Latinas are 'low earners,' meaning in this report that they have a low income (making less than $25,000 annually) or a lower education level (completed a high school degree or less). Among Hispanic women, about four in 10 low earners (41%) report that the pandemic had a major effect on their personal finances, and they have not recovered financially. More than half of Latina low earners (54%) report that they spent most or all of their savings during the pandemic." The report also showed that, "During the pandemic, about four in 10 Hispanic women (42%) who are low earners report having received food donations and experienced difficulties affording basic necessities (40%). About one-quarter missed a car, student loan, or credit card payment (26%), while more than one in 10 (12%) had utilities shut down due to lack of payment."

Noting that "[m]ore than half of Hispanic renters are rent-burdened, paying more than 30% of their income to cover rent," the report also found that the pandemic particularly impacted Latinas and Hispanic men: "About one in five Latinas (19%) and Hispanic men (18%) missed at least one rent or mortgage payment during the pandemic. In comparison, 12% of White women and 10% of White men missed at least one payment. "

The study also found that medical debt among Latinos during the pandemic was a particular concern: "One year after the beginning of the pandemic, medical debt is one of the top financial concerns for Latinas, even more so than credit card debt, car loans, or home mortgages. More than half (54%) of Latinas—and six in 10 Hispanic men—are extremely or very concerned about medical debt."

At the same time, the report found that the opportunity for economic contribution and dynamism with Latinos is enormous: "Before the pandemic, most of the business growth in the United States was driven by the increase in Hispanic-owned businesses. Latina entrepreneurship was faster-growing than business ownership among Hispanic men.... Latinas are one of the fastest-growing segments of business owners in the United States, and about half believe that owning a business is a very important part of the American Dream."

Addressing barriers to credit is an essential part of our economic recovery as a nation and addressing the adverse racialized outcomes of our credit reporting system is a means to that end.

Specific Steps by Congress toward a More Inclusive Credit Economy Are Essential

The Congress should advance policies that increase the transparency of the credit rating process for consumers, improve consumers' equitable access to credit, and reduce financial exploitation of LMI consumers.

For example, in 2020 the House of Representatives passed the "Protecting Your Credit Score Act." To address errors on consumer reports, this bill would require credit reporting agencies and those institutions and businesses that provide them with consumer data to conduct basic identity verification. It also would create a secure online portal, empowering consumers to freeze their credit, file disputes, and check their credit reports for free.

The House also previously passed the "Comprehensive CREDIT Act," a measure that would give consumers a right of appeal in disputes and limit the use of credit reports for employment (other than in the context of national security or background checks, for example). It includes a number of additional consumer protections to address financial predation and unfair and inaccurate debt reporting, such as:

- Requiring removal of adverse information from fraudulent lending activity regarding private education loans and residential mortgage loans
- Expediting the removal of debt that is no longer owed
- Prohibiting the inclusion of an arrest that did not result in conviction
- Generally reducing the time period that adverse information stays on a credit report from seven years to four years
- Limiting the inclusion of certain medical debt

The bill also called on the Consumer Financial Protection Bureau (CFPB) to develop rules for fair credit reporting algorithms and provides a host of additional consumer protection measures, including rules to provide for access to consumer reporting information for non-native English speakers and those with disabilities and the registration of credit reporting agencies.

Both of these important bills have been reintroduced this session and deserve a fair hearing and full consideration in the Congress. It is clear that the credit system, meant to be an engine of economic recovery and empowerment for consumers, instead is too often an instrument of systemic exclusion, leaving those who might power our recovery at the mercy of high costs and fees and financial predation. Such proposals represent an important opportunity to power the American Dream with an inclusive recovery, and to empower those who have been the most essential—and have borne the greatest impact—during the pandemic with real economic possibility in the form of improved access to credit.

Notes

[1] UWHA develops effective programs that blend research, advocacy, and direct housing and financial counseling. UWHA is a HUD-approved housing counseling intermediary and trains hundreds of housing counselors emphasizing individual, culturally competent counseling. Established in 1997, UWHA includes 50 independent community-based organizations that support more than 60,000 families a year.

[2] Jennifer Brown, Esq., for UnidosUS, *Unscoreable: How the Credit Reporting Agencies Exclude Latinos, Younger Consumers, Low-Income Consumers, and Immigrants*, Committee on Financial Services, 116th Cong., 1st sess., February 26, 2019, http://publications.unidosus.org/bitstream/handle/123456789/1927/unidosus_testimony_22619.pdf?sequence=1&isAllowed=y.

[3] UnidosUS and PolicyLink. *The Future of Banking: Overcoming Barriers to Financial Inclusion for Communities of Color* (Washington, DC: UnidosUS, 2019).

[4] *Cited in* UnidosUS. *Closing the Latino Wealth Gap: Building an Inclusive Economic Recovery after COVID* (Washington, DC: UnidosUS, 2021), http://publications.unidosus.org/bitstream/handle/123456789/2150/unidosus_closingthelatinawealthgap.pdf?sequence=5.

[5] UnidosUS. *Closing the Latino Wealth Gap: Building an Inclusive Economic Recovery after COVID* (Washington, DC: UnidosUS, 2021), http://publications.unidosus.org/bitstream/handle/123456789/2150/unidosus_closingthelatinawealthgap.pdf?sequence=5.

Written Statement of Francis Creighton, President & CEO, Consumer Data Industry Association

CDIA

Consumer Data Industry Association
1090 Vermont Ave., NW, Suite 200
Washington, D.C. 20005-4905

P 202 371 0910

CDIAONLINE.ORG

June 29, 2021

The Honorable Maxine Waters, Chairwoman
The Honorable Patrick T. McHenry, Ranking Member
Committee on Financial Services
United States House of Representatives
Washington, DC 20515

Dear Chairwoman Waters and Ranking Member McHenry:

As you prepare for your hearing this morning on a government takeover of credit reporting and lending standards, we wanted to share a few thoughts on the folly of this idea. This bill will hurt consumers and create uncertainty and instability in the financial system at a time when consistency and prudent decision-making is critical as we rebound from the COVID-19 pandemic and work to promote access to credit for all Americans.

Shifting the lending system from risk-based pricing to race-based decision-making will lead to higher prices and a less fair system for everyone. Private sector competition, especially in the credit reporting ecosystem, inspires innovation. Through this competition, we have seen the rise of new data sources, trended data and dynamic scoring models, all created to help benefit consumers, especially un- and under-banked consumers. Replacing a competitive system with one dominated by a government-run credit bureau, will result in fewer incentives for further innovation, ultimately hurting consumers and increasing prices.

Private credit bureaus are answerable to consumers, courts, Congress and regulators—and for a good reason: to benefit consumers. Credit bureaus are subject to consumer protection laws including the Fair Credit Reporting Act, Gramm-Leach Bliley Act, the Equal Credit Opportunity Act, and are supervised and examined on their legal obligations. There are also and similar state laws that credit bureaus are subject to, many of which also regulate banks and other users of credit reports. The result is that consumers deal with a fair and just system that judges them on their own personal circumstances, regardless of gender, race, marital status or other similar factors. As the Federal Reserve found in a study on disparate impact in lending, there is "no evidence of disparate impact by race, ethnicity or gender" resulting from credit reporting. Government-determined credit models based on race will not meet these same high standards.

Global experience shows that private credit bureaus outperform government-run credit bureaus in access to private credit. Private credit reporting systems increase financial inclusion, create better opportunities for consumers to have greater access to credit, lower costs of credit and lead to more diversified products and services from lenders.

Giving the government massive amounts of private, sensitive, personal credit bureau data would be a huge risk to consumers' data security. A government operated credit bureau would not have the same regulatory and oversight structure credit bureaus face today (credit bureaus are supervised and examined on their cybersecurity practices by the CFPB). This vast expansion of government control would expose our most personal financial information to a bureaucracy that has shown it can't protect data (the OPM data breach in 2015, the Solar Winds breach and multiple national security breaches are just a few examples). Governments have proven repeatedly that they are not able to properly secure information, whether that be national security information, taxpayer data or its own employees' information.

The government-run credit bureau would be housed within the CFPB, meaning credit scoring would be controlled by political appointees—exposing the consumer credit market to political considerations and leaving consumers with higher prices and limited options for credit.

Supporters of this proposal have said that their goal is to eliminate risk-based pricing. But risk-based pricing has been a great success, especially for minority communities. A recent report showed that access to credit has improved across the United States over the past decade, with members of minority populations seeing more improvement than anywhere else. For example, from the years 1989-2019, the share of Black households who obtained a home loan grew 10.1%, the fastest group of any ethnic group in the country. This is the direct result of risk-based pricing practices that allows lenders to manage risk and make credit available.

Competition among credit bureaus spurs innovation and helps ensure accuracy in the system – a government monopoly on credit reporting would eliminate that. If a bank or other lender thinks there are problems with one credit bureau's data, in most cases they can stop using that bureau and use a different one. Likewise, the credit bureaus are constantly introducing new products and tools to give lenders better insights into their customers, competition that ultimately helps consumers. A government takeover of credit reporting would eliminate that.

Under a government-run credit bureau, consumers facing problems with their credit reports would now have to go to a government office and ask for the government to change their data. Consumer experience with the Social Security Administration, Internal Revenue Service or Department of Veterans' Affairs suggest that a government-run credit bureau would be a nightmare for consumers to deal with.

A government take-over of credit reporting and lending standards would hurt consumers, put the government in charge of credit allocation and will not advance the goal of racial equity. Instead, we will have a system that creates volatile and unstable lending environments, with inconsistent policies and credit decisions swinging back and forth from election to election, and fewer choices for consumers. We urge Members of the Committee to reject this and other ill-advised ideas.

To improve the credit reporting system, we should make some changes to bring more people in to the financial system. There is broad agreement that we should immediately pass legislation expanding the kinds of data reported to credit bureaus, in fact, bi-partisan legislation that would do just that has passed your Committee with strong, bipartisan votes. We hope the Committee in this Congress will finally pass bi-partisan legislation that will increase financial inclusion and allow it to become law.

Sincerely,

Francis Creighton

Francis Creighton
President & CEO

Written Statement of Jim Nussle, President & CEO, Credit Union National Association

Credit Union National Association
CUNA

Jim Nussle
President & CEO

Phone: 202-508-6745
jnussle@cuna.coop

99 M Street SE
Suite 300
Washington, DC 20003-3799

June 29, 2021

The Honorable Maxine Waters
Chairwoman
House Committee on Financial Services
U.S. House of Representatives
Washington, DC 20515

The Honorable Patrick McHenry
Ranking Member
House Committee on Financial Services
U.S. House of Representatives
Washington, DC 20515

Dear Chairwoman Waters and Ranking Member McHenry,

On behalf of the Credit Union National Association (CUNA), I am writing in regard to hearing entitled, "A Biased, Broken System: Examining Proposals to Overhaul Credit Reporting to Achieve Equity." CUNA represents America's credit unions and their more than 120 million members.

The credit reporting system plays a critical role in the financial lives of Americans as the data collected and maintained are influential metrics for many lending decisions. The Fair Credit Reporting Act (FCRA), which establishes the system's legal framework, was passed by Congress in 1970 to ensure the integrity of consumers' data maintained by the credit reporting agencies (CRAs). CUNA supports the purpose of the FCRA and its importance in ensuring consumers' financial information is handled and used in an appropriate and responsible manner.

Credit unions, as both users and furnishers of information to the CRAs, have a substantial interest in promoting the accuracy and quality of the data contained in the system. For that reason, credit unions take their compliance responsibilities seriously and strive to develop and implement sound credit reporting policies and procedures, train personnel on those policies and procedures, and promptly resolve any issues that may arise. This dedication to being responsible stewards of consumer information is why credit unions have a reputation as consumers' best option in the financial services marketplace.

Accurate and complete credit reports are essential to credit unions providing safe and affordable financial services to their members. Whereas credit unions' field of membership restrictions were originally designed as a mechanism for determining borrowers' credit worthiness, today credit unions and other financial institutions rely on credit reports and credit scores to assess credit worthiness and inform lending decisions. It is in the interest of all stakeholders in the lending process for borrowers' credit reports to be accurate and complete.

While we agree the current system is imperfect and the FCRA should be examined for necessary amendments and modernized to promote clarity and accountability, CUNA is concerned about the negative impact on consumers' access to credit that could result from well-intentioned but overly disruptive changes to the system. The bills being considered in today's hearing would make sweeping changes to the credit reporting framework, most notably establishing limits on the data contained in credit reports, creating a public credit reporting agency, substantially increasing the power and influence of the partisan Consumer Financial Protection Bureau (CFPB), and many others.

We caution Congress against taking these actions for a myriad of reasons. In particular, the FCRA has been an area of growing litigation risk over the past decade and the proposed legislation could further exacerbate the problem of frivolous suits. In the case of credit unions, frivolous litigation means that access to safe and affordable financial services becomes more expensive and potentially less available for credit union members.

Regarding the creation of a mandated consumer-facing online portal, we are concerned about the potential for significant cybersecurity risk to consumers, financial institutions, and companies. This would be an unnecessary risk given that consumers can dispute the accurateness of information on their credit reports with the credit reporting agency or with their creditor. The FCRA requires these disputes to be resolved in a timely manner and, if the disputed information is incorrect, the information in question is eliminated from the report. As such, consumers already wield significant tools to dispute information and correct errors without introducing a potential vulnerability to the system.

We are also concerned about the proposed creation of a public credit reporting agency within the CFPB. Such an agency would not only expand the influence of the Bureau within the lending ecosystem but also require considerable costs and many years to fully implement before providing a benefit to consumers – if any benefit at all. The money and time required to successfully launch such a massive undertaking would be better allocated towards prudent regulatory oversight, financial inclusion initiatives, and grant programs aimed at supporting rural and underserved communities and increasing access to credit.

Ultimately, there is no evidence to support the notion that a public credit reporting agency would be more transparent, innovative, or inclusive than the current private system. In fact, given the Executive Branch's firm control over the CFPB and its leadership, a public CRA could allow an administration to meddle in the nation's lending ecosystem to the detriment of fair and equitable access to credit. This type of heavy-handed government control could serve to undermine confidence in the integrity of the credit reporting system itself, which is an essential tool in the credit underwriting process. The foreseeable problems that could arise down the road from this proposed "solution" warrant a serious reconsideration of the legislation.

In the meantime, Congress and the regulatory agencies have already taken steps to encourage inclusion and increased access without stepping into the system as a de facto competitor. These steps have facilitated positive change in the system, such as the increased exploration of "alternative data" as a tool to expand access to credit. We encourage policymakers to put forward more ideas that would encourage rather than hinder such progress.

On behalf of America's credit unions and their more than 120 million members, thank you for the opportunity to share our views and look forward to working with you on these important issues.

Sincerely,

Jim Nussle
President & CEO

Written Statement of Thomas Aiello, Director of Federal Affairs, National Taxpayers Union

June 29, 2021

The Honorable Maxine Waters
Chairwoman
House Committee on Financial Services
Washington, DC 20515

The Honorable Patrick McHenry
Ranking Member
House Committee on Financial Services
Washington, DC 20515

Dear Chairwoman Waters, Ranking Member McHenry and Members of the Committee:

On behalf of the National Taxpayers Union, the nation's oldest taxpayer advocacy organization, I write to express our strong opposition to the three legislative proposals that will be considered at tomorrow's hearing entitled "A Biased, Broken System: Examining Proposals to Overhaul Credit Reporting to Achieve Equity." At this hearing, committee members will discuss a trio of schemes which will put the government before consumers, threaten the accuracy of credit reporting, and restrict the availability of credit for lower-income Americans. These proposals are structurally flawed and deserve no support. It is our hope that you stand with taxpayers and consumers by rejecting these dangerous, unserious "solutions."

Accurate and complete credit reports are the bedrock of this country's robust and competitive consumer credit market. Most, if not all, lenders rely upon credit history data found in credit reports to identify and evaluate potential risks a consumer may pose before entering into a financial relationship with that consumer. That information is critical for lenders to evaluate the applicant's ability to repay and to establish interest rates and other loan terms. A degradation of reporting standards could lead to more borrowers being eligible for a taxpayer-backed mortgage by Fannie Mae and Freddie Mac, or insured by the Federal Housing Administration which may not be able to handle additional credit obligations. Under such a scenario, if more unqualified borrowers default on their mortgages, it could threaten the housing system and lead to another significant bailout of the GSEs.

Instead of putting bureaucrats over consumers, lawmakers should expand the amount of data and other information that would make credit reports more predictable and inclusive. For example, bipartisan legislation, the "Credit Access and Inclusion Act" would encourage the reporting of telecommunications data and rental data to help reduce our country's widespread credit invisible population. Additionally, NTU strongly supports the creation of a pilot program that would report the payment or nonpayment of rent by tenants in public housing, which we believe can move the needle for many underserved communities.

However, the proposals on the committee agenda, if enacted, would have a chilling effect on credit reporting and ultimately harm consumers by restricting access to credit or raising interest rates on loans made to borrowers considered "subprime" or less than high quality.

Protecting Your Credit Score Act

Though well-intentioned, this legislation would cede more power to the unaccountable Consumer Financial Protection Bureau (CFPB), jeopardize consumer information, and potentially weaken lending underwriting standards. Perhaps the most problematic provision of the Protecting Your Credit Score Act is the requirement for the three major consumer credit agencies, which are entirely private businesses, to jointly create an online consumer portal for consumers to access their credit reports and scores, dispute errors, and place or lift security freezes. While a one-stop shop may seem to offer consumer benefits, having one location containing every credit report, personal information, and social security number of every individual could have disastrous consequences in the event of a cyber hack or data breach.

Further, this legislation provides no legal protection to these entities in the event of a large-scale cyber breach, leaving these businesses vulnerable to big class-action lawsuits. This proposal also changes how consumers dispute adverse information found in their credit reports, allowing individuals to flood reporting agencies and lenders with false claims of inaccuracies that must be resolved in a timely manner. Ultimately, this proposal shifts the burden on dispute resolution from the individual onto the credit bureaus.

Additionally, this bill establishes a second, duplicative ombudsman at the CFPB who will have sole control over credit reporting. The ombudsperson would help resolve persistent errors in credit reports that aren't addressed in a timely manner, and make referrals for supervisory or enforcement actions against credit reporting companies. This situation sets up a new opportunity for the CFPB to specifically target certain companies that may become "unsavory" and be subject to political targeting.

NTU also questions the need for such legislation, as the Fair Credit Reporting Act (FCRA) currently provides consumers ample opportunity to dispute inaccurate information on their credit reports. The FCRA already requires these disputes to be resolved in a timely manner and, if the disputed information is incorrect, the information in question is eliminated from a report. In essence, this legislation does not bring any new meaningful benefits to the credit reporting process

The National Credit Reporting Agency Act

This legislation is perhaps the most significant proposal of government overreach into private credit markets ever considered by this committee. While some portray the National Credit Reporting Act as a "public option" for credit reporting, in reality it is a government-run credit bureau that will socialize credit information and access. Under such a scheme, the Consumer Financial Protection Bureau would be charged with maintaining a database with the financial data of every American and determining how creditworthy each person is. In short, the government would be deciding who does, or doesn't, qualify for a mortgage, car loan, or other sources of credit. It takes away the ability of financial institutions to make loans and instead puts it in the hands of bureaucrats.

To be clear: consumers won't benefit from a government-run credit reporting system. Innovation led by private market actors is working well, and delivering the most efficient outcomes for consumers and small businesses alike. If the government moves forward with a competing scheme, it could have a chilling effect on innovation in credit markets. Should the government develop its own reporting platform, it would be expensive, duplicative, inefficient and curtail development of new, more predictive private models.

NTU explored the potential issues of a government-run credit reporting system in October of 2020, which may be of interest to this committee. In that blog post, I argued that there are three primary interests that would limit the success of such a government-run system: cost, functional viability, and usability. As we wrote back then:

NTU identifies three major problems that could arise if Trump's Office of the Comptroller of the Currency (OCC), or a future Biden administration, creates a government utility entrusted with credit reporting and credit scoring.

1. Cost

The federal government currently has no existing infrastructure when it comes to maintaining credit reports and computing a numerical credit score. Given this reality, the government either needs to build their own system or buy one. No matter which avenue, the cost is likely to be expensive. To build a new system will require thousands of employees and untold resources that will take years to complete. By that time private companies will be years ahead with innovative new models that are more predictive than whatever outdated system the government creates. Once complete, the federal government would have to retain a significant workforce to continuously update credit files, settle disputes, and derive the credit score. According to a quick internet search, the three major credit bureaus employ 36,000 people. Taxpayers may be forgiven for worrying that a government entity would have a much bigger payroll to accomplish what the private sector can do now.

2. Functional Viability

If the government continues ahead with its plan, the creation and operation of a public reporting agency will be a significant expense that will be paid for by taxpayers. Once up and running, how would pricing work and would it be profitable? If the government decides to not charge a fee, or one that is below market rates, it could impact the viability of private businesses already operating in this space. To this end, if the government runs a yearly loss would it fall on taxpayers to keep an unprofitable system running?

The OCC claims it will help the 28 million Americans that currently do not have a credit score. However, how will the OCC by itself determine who is or isn't scored? Will it go through census data and cross reference it through data from private companies? By that time, the federal government may say it's just easier for everyone to have a national credit score and potentially monitor every portion of an individual's financial life. Be careful, "big brother" might literally judge you for spending too much money at the grocery store or your local coffee shop.

3. Usability

Nearly all lenders already have trusted experience with private sector firms that provide credit scores. Since the overwhelming majority already have some level of credit file, and by extension a credit score, it may not be worth the additional hassle of trying out the government-run score. As newly developed models and products move to market to meet evolving credit scoring challenges, by the time the government creates its own system it could be years behind the industry when it comes to data inclusive models. Plus, if lenders choose not to accept the government-run credit score, consumers who are forced to have this score would not have equal access to credit and would be no better off.

Aside from these aforementioned general concerns, this bill also contains many issues that should concern every consumer or business. For example, there includes a requirement that anyone who furnishes to any CRA must also furnish to the government-run credit bureau; hefty financial penalties for data furnishers who report inaccurate or incomplete information to the government run credit bureau; and an unprecedented amount of power given to the already powerful, unaccountable CFPB.

Comprehensive CREDIT Act

Finally, the Comprehensive CREDIT Act (H.R. 4120) would drastically reduce the accuracy and predictiveness of credit reports and credit scores - thereby putting stress on the foundation of sound lending standards. This will lead to a less stable financial system, undermining safety and soundness of private sector credit reporting that has built up over the last decade. As a result, the Comprehensive CREDIT Act will socialize credit scoring and, therefore, affect credit allocation.

Lawmakers should be cautious in their approach to amending credit reporting laws due to the unforeseen impacts it could have on consumers and government programs. Credit reports are an integral piece for companies to determine a person's individual credit score through consumer credit-scoring models. The use of credit scores is incredibly far-reaching and the credit report information is used to help determine the likelihood that prospective borrowers will repay their loans.

First and foremost, this legislation mandates that credit scores be made available - free of charge - to all consumers. It is wholly un-American to mandate that products produced by private-sector actors be forced to give away their product for free. Moreover, Section 204 would require nationwide CRAs to provide a credit score for free to consumers on request via a government-mandated central website and through companies' individual websites. If certain companies wish to allow consumers to check their credit score for free, that is entirely their choice, but it should not be required by the Congress.

Additionally, H.R. 4120 proposes to hide negative, but accurate, information associated with certain credit obligations. This means credit reports will be incomplete and ultimately less predictive of credit scores. With less accurate consumer reports and scores, creditors will be inevitably forced to reduce the amount of credit extended and/or raise prices to cover for the additional risk. As it relates to medical debt, this legislation simply hides certain obligations and pretends that they don't exist. There are some targeted reforms that could be considered when it comes to the furnishing of medical debt - both paid and unpaid - such as the substitute amendment from Rep. Patrick McHenry (R-NC) that was rejected during the markup of H.R. 2547. Simply passing a law pretending certain debt doesn't exist is an unworkable attempt at trying to solve a real problem many consumers face.

Thank you for considering our viewpoints on these critical issues. Should you be interested in engaging on any of the above proposals or should you have any questions, we are at your disposal.

Sincerely,

Thomas Aiello
Director of Federal Affairs

Written Responses of Chi Chi Wu to Questions for the Record from Representative William Timmons

**Chi Chi Wu Answer to
Rep. William Timmons Question for the Record: June 29, 2021 House Financial Services Full Committee Hybrid Hearing Entitled: A Biased, Broken System: Examining Proposals to Overhaul Credit Reporting to Achieve Equity**

For Ms. Chi Chi Wu:

On your website it states that your Partners Council is charged with ensuring the National Consumer Law Center (NCLC) has the revenue necessary to operate. Every member of that council is a trial lawyer.

***Question**: Can you please tell us who primarily funds the NCLC?*

Answer: For a breakdown of NCLC's primary funding sources, please see our most recently filed IRS Form 990, which is attached. It provides extensive detail on all our sources of revenue in both 2019 and 2018.

EXTENDED TO NOVEMBER 16, 2020

Form **990** (Rev. January 2020) Department of the Treasury Internal Revenue Service

Return of Organization Exempt From Income Tax

Under section 501(c), 527, or 4947(a)(1) of the Internal Revenue Code (except private foundations)

▶ Do not enter social security numbers on this form as it may be made public.

▶ Go to www.irs.gov/Form990 for instructions and the latest information.

OMB No. 1545-0047 **2019** Open to Public Inspection

A For the 2019 calendar year, or tax year beginning and ending

B Check if applicable: ☐ Address change ☐ Name change ☐ Initial return ☐ Final return/terminated ☐ Amended return ☐ Application pending

C Name of organization: NATIONAL CONSUMER LAW CENTER, INC.

Doing business as

Number and street (or P.O. box if mail is not delivered to street address): 7 WINTHROP SQUARE, 4TH FLOOR Room/suite

City or town, state or province, country, and ZIP or foreign postal code: BOSTON, MA 02110-1006

D Employer identification number: 04-2488502

E Telephone number: 617-542-8010

G Gross receipts $ 24,940,391.

F Name and address of principal officer: RICHARD DUBOIS SAME AS C ABOVE

H(a) Is this a group return for subordinates? ☐ Yes ☒ No

H(b) Are all subordinates included? ☐ Yes ☐ No If "No," attach a list. (see instructions)

H(c) Group exemption number ▶

I Tax-exempt status: ☒ 501(c)(3) ☐ 501(c) ( ) ◀ (insert no.) ☐ 4947(a)(1) or ☐ 527

J Website: ▶ WWW.NCLC.ORG

K Form of organization: ☒ Corporation ☐ Trust ☐ Association ☐ Other ▶

L Year of formation: 1971 M State of legal domicile: MA

Part I Summary

Activities & Governance

1 Briefly describe the organization's mission or most significant activities: SINCE 1969, THE NONPROFIT NATIONAL CONSUMER LAW CENTER HAS USED ITS EXPERTISE IN CONSUMER LAW

2 Check this box ▶ ☐ if the organization discontinued its operations or disposed of more than 25% of its net assets.

3	Number of voting members of the governing body (Part VI, line 1a)	3	12
4	Number of independent voting members of the governing body (Part VI, line 1b)	4	12
5	Total number of individuals employed in calendar year 2019 (Part V, line 2a)	5	67
6	Total number of volunteers (estimate if necessary)	6	13
7a	Total unrelated business revenue from Part VIII, column (C), line 12	7a	0.
b	Net unrelated business taxable income from Form 990-T, line 39	7b	0.

			Prior Year	Current Year
Revenue	8	Contributions and grants (Part VIII, line 1h)	3,237,235.	3,147,226.
	9	Program service revenue (Part VIII, line 2g)	8,550,241.	6,529,320.
	10	Investment income (Part VIII, column (A), lines 3, 4, and 7d)	1,549,835.	1,342,615.
	11	Other revenue (Part VIII, column (A), lines 5, 6d, 8c, 9c, 10c, and 11e)	241,432.	173,221.
	12	Total revenue - add lines 8 through 11 (must equal Part VIII, column (A), line 12)	13,578,743.	11,192,382.
Expenses	13	Grants and similar amounts paid (Part IX, column (A), lines 1-3)	0.	0.
	14	Benefits paid to or for members (Part IX, column (A), line 4)	0.	0.
	15	Salaries, other compensation, employee benefits (Part IX, column (A), lines 5-10)	6,053,485.	6,596,419.
	16a	Professional fundraising fees (Part IX, column (A), line 11e)	0.	0.
	b	Total fundraising expenses (Part IX, column (D), line 25) ▶ 674,156.		
	17	Other expenses (Part IX, column (A), lines 11a-11d, 11f-24e)	2,994,577.	3,293,282.
	18	Total expenses. Add lines 13-17 (must equal Part IX, column (A), line 25)	9,048,062.	9,889,701.
	19	Revenue less expenses. Subtract line 18 from line 12	4,530,681.	1,302,681.
Net Assets or Fund Balances			Beginning of Current Year	End of Year
	20	Total assets (Part X, line 16)	30,855,082.	34,989,182.
	21	Total liabilities (Part X, line 26)	1,672,630.	2,275,656.
	22	Net assets or fund balances. Subtract line 21 from line 20	29,182,452.	32,713,526.

Part II Signature Block

Under penalties of perjury, I declare that I have examined this return, including accompanying schedules and statements, and to the best of my knowledge and belief, it is true, correct, and complete. Declaration of preparer (other than officer) is based on all information of which preparer has any knowledge.

Sign Here ▶ [signature] Signature of officer — Date 11/2/2020

▶ RICHARD DUBOIS, EXECUTIVE DIRECTOR — Type or print name and title

Paid Preparer Use Only

Print/Type preparer's name	Preparer's signature	Date	Check ☐ if self-employed	PTIN
JOHN BUCKLEY, CPA	JOHN BUCKLEY, CPA	10/27/20		P00830631

Firm's name ▶ AAFCPAS, INC. — Firm's EIN ▶ 04-2571788

Firm's address ▶ 50 WASHINGTON STREET WESTBOROUGH, MA 01581 — Phone no. 508-366-9100

May the IRS discuss this return with the preparer shown above? (see instructions) ☒ Yes ☐ No

932001 01-20-20 LHA **For Paperwork Reduction Act Notice, see the separate instructions.** Form **990** (2019)

SEE SCHEDULE O FOR ORGANIZATION MISSION STATEMENT CONTINUATION

Form 990 (2019) NATIONAL CONSUMER LAW CENTER, INC. 04-2488502 Page 2

Part III | Statement of Program Service Accomplishments

Check if Schedule O contains a response or note to any line in this Part III [X]

1 Briefly describe the organization's mission:
SINCE 1969, THE NONPROFIT NATIONAL CONSUMER LAW CENTER HAS USED ITS EXPERTISE IN CONSUMER LAW AND ENERGY POLICY TO WORK FOR CONSUMER JUSTICE AND ECONOMIC SECURITY FOR LOW-INCOME AND OTHER DISADVANTAGED PEOPLE. NCLC'S EXPERTISE INCLUDES POLICY ANALYSIS AND ADVOCACY;

2 Did the organization undertake any significant program services during the year which were not listed on the prior Form 990 or 990-EZ? [ ] Yes [X] No
If "Yes," describe these new services on Schedule O.

3 Did the organization cease conducting, or make significant changes in how it conducts, any program services? [ ] Yes [X] No
If "Yes," describe these changes on Schedule O.

4 Describe the organization's program service accomplishments for each of its three largest program services, as measured by expenses. Section 501(c)(3) and 501(c)(4) organizations are required to report the amount of grants and allocations to others, the total expenses, and revenue, if any, for each program service reported.

4a (Code:) (Expenses $ 6,044,713. including grants of $) (Revenue $ 5,153,398.)
BUILDING FAMILY AND INDIVIDUAL ECONOMIC SECURITY

LOW-INCOME FAMILIES HAVE LITTLE OR NO SAVINGS TO PROVIDE A SAFETY NET, LIVING WEEK TO WEEK AND MONTH TO MONTH TO MEET BASIC EXPENSES. THIS POPULATION IS DISPROPORTIONATELY TARGETED FOR OVERPRICED FINANCIAL SERVICES, SUCH AS EXCESSIVE BANK FEES, HIGH-COST LOANS, AND PREDATORY HOME MORTGAGES. LAX REGULATION HAS LEFT MANY FAMILIES VULNERABLE TO WEALTH-STRIPPING PRACTICES AND DEEPLY IN DEBT, REDUCING OPPORTUNITIES FOR HIGHER EDUCATION, JOB TRAINING AND HOMEOWNERSHIP. TO COUNTER THESE TRENDS AND HELP LOW-INCOME PEOPLE BUILD ASSETS AND ECONOMIC SECURITY, NCLC PROMOTES THE ADOPTION AND ENFORCEMENT OF STRONG CONSUMER PROTECTIONS IN THE FINANCIAL SERVICES MARKETPLACE.

4b (Code:) (Expenses $ 943,100. including grants of $) (Revenue $ 750,503.)
IMPROVING ACCESS TO ENERGY, UTILITIES, & TELECOMMUNICATIONS SERVICES

ACCESS TO AFFORDABLE AND EFFICIENT ELECTRICITY, HEATING FUEL, WATER, AND TELECOMMUNICATIONS SERVICES IS ESSENTIAL FOR ALL AMERICANS. UNFORTUNATELY, MILLIONS OF STRUGGLING FAMILIES CANNOT PAY FOR BASIC UTILITIES, PUTTING THEIR HEALTH, SAFETY, AND WELL-BEING AT RISK. IN ADDITION, LOW-INCOME HOUSEHOLDS TEND TO LIVE IN LESS ENERGY EFFICIENT HOMES AND USE LESS EFFICIENT APPLIANCES, BOTH OF WHICH LEAD TO HIGHER OVERALL ENERGY COSTS. NCLC PROMOTES THE ADOPTION AND ENFORCEMENT OF PUBLIC POLICIES THAT DELIVER AFFORDABLE AND EFFICIENT UTILITY SERVICES FOR LOW-INCOME HOUSEHOLDS.

4c (Code:) (Expenses $ 807,904. including grants of $) (Revenue $ 625,419.)
WORKING WITH DISTINCT POPULATIONS

NCLC SEEKS TO FORM PARTNERSHIPS WITH GRASSROOTS ORGANIZATIONS, HUMAN SERVICE PROVIDERS, COUNSELING GROUPS, AND OTHERS INTERESTED IN PROTECTING CONSUMER RIGHTS. WE PROVIDE SPECIAL PUBLICATIONS THAT ARE TAILORED TO ATTORNEYS AND HUMAN SERVICE PROVIDERS; CONDUCT HANDS-ON, PRACTICAL TRAINING WORKSHOPS; AND OFFER CASE CONSULTING EXPERTISE ON DIFFICULT CLIENT MATTERS. NCLC HAS ESTABLISHED STRONG RELATIONSHIPS WITH ORGANIZATIONS NATIONWIDE SERVING A BROAD RANGE OF DISTINCT POPULATIONS.

4d Other program services (Describe on Schedule O.)
(Expenses $ including grants of $) (Revenue $)

4e Total program service expenses ▶ 7,795,717.

Form **990** (2019)

932002 01-20-20

SEE SCHEDULE O FOR CONTINUATION(S)

Form 990 (2019) NATIONAL CONSUMER LAW CENTER, INC. 04-2488502 Page 3

Part IV Checklist of Required Schedules

			Yes	No
1	Is the organization described in section 501(c)(3) or 4947(a)(1) (other than a private foundation)? *If "Yes," complete Schedule A*	1	X	
2	Is the organization required to complete *Schedule B, Schedule of Contributors*?	2	X	
3	Did the organization engage in direct or indirect political campaign activities on behalf of or in opposition to candidates for public office? *If "Yes," complete Schedule C, Part I*	3		X
4	**Section 501(c)(3) organizations.** Did the organization engage in lobbying activities, or have a section 501(h) election in effect during the tax year? *If "Yes," complete Schedule C, Part II*	4	X	
5	Is the organization a section 501(c)(4), 501(c)(5), or 501(c)(6) organization that receives membership dues, assessments, or similar amounts as defined in Revenue Procedure 98-19? *If "Yes," complete Schedule C, Part III*	5		X
6	Did the organization maintain any donor advised funds or any similar funds or accounts for which donors have the right to provide advice on the distribution or investment of amounts in such funds or accounts? *If "Yes," complete Schedule D, Part I*	6		X
7	Did the organization receive or hold a conservation easement, including easements to preserve open space, the environment, historic land areas, or historic structures? *If "Yes," complete Schedule D, Part II*	7		X
8	Did the organization maintain collections of works of art, historical treasures, or other similar assets? *If "Yes," complete Schedule D, Part III*	8		X
9	Did the organization report an amount in Part X, line 21, for escrow or custodial account liability, serve as a custodian for amounts not listed in Part X; or provide credit counseling, debt management, credit repair, or debt negotiation services? *If "Yes," complete Schedule D, Part IV*	9		X
10	Did the organization, directly or through a related organization, hold assets in donor-restricted endowments or in quasi endowments? *If "Yes," complete Schedule D, Part V*	10	X	
11	If the organization's answer to any of the following questions is "Yes," then complete Schedule D, Parts VI, VII, VIII, IX, or X as applicable.			
a	Did the organization report an amount for land, buildings, and equipment in Part X, line 10? *If "Yes," complete Schedule D, Part VI*	11a	X	
b	Did the organization report an amount for investments - other securities in Part X, line 12, that is 5% or more of its total assets reported in Part X, line 16? *If "Yes," complete Schedule D, Part VII*	11b		X
c	Did the organization report an amount for investments - program related in Part X, line 13, that is 5% or more of its total assets reported in Part X, line 16? *If "Yes," complete Schedule D, Part VIII*	11c		X
d	Did the organization report an amount for other assets in Part X, line 15, that is 5% or more of its total assets reported in Part X, line 16? *If "Yes," complete Schedule D, Part IX*	11d		X
e	Did the organization report an amount for other liabilities in Part X, line 25? *If "Yes," complete Schedule D, Part X*	11e		X
f	Did the organization's separate or consolidated financial statements for the tax year include a footnote that addresses the organization's liability for uncertain tax positions under FIN 48 (ASC 740)? *If "Yes," complete Schedule D, Part X*	11f	X	
12a	Did the organization obtain separate, independent audited financial statements for the tax year? *If "Yes," complete Schedule D, Parts XI and XII*	12a		X
b	Was the organization included in consolidated, independent audited financial statements for the tax year? *If "Yes," and if the organization answered "No" to line 12a, then completing Schedule D, Parts XI and XII is optional*	12b	X	
13	Is the organization a school described in section 170(b)(1)(A)(ii)? *If "Yes," complete Schedule E*	13		X
14a	Did the organization maintain an office, employees, or agents outside of the United States?	14a		X
b	Did the organization have aggregate revenues or expenses of more than $10,000 from grantmaking, fundraising, business, investment, and program service activities outside the United States, or aggregate foreign investments valued at $100,000 or more? *If "Yes," complete Schedule F, Parts I and IV*	14b		X
15	Did the organization report on Part IX, column (A), line 3, more than $5,000 of grants or other assistance to or for any foreign organization? *If "Yes," complete Schedule F, Parts II and IV*	15		X
16	Did the organization report on Part IX, column (A), line 3, more than $5,000 of aggregate grants or other assistance to or for foreign individuals? *If "Yes," complete Schedule F, Parts III and IV*	16		X
17	Did the organization report a total of more than $15,000 of expenses for professional fundraising services on Part IX, column (A), lines 6 and 11e? *If "Yes," complete Schedule G, Part I*	17		X
18	Did the organization report more than $15,000 total of fundraising event gross income and contributions on Part VIII, lines 1c and 8a? *If "Yes," complete Schedule G, Part II*	18	X	
19	Did the organization report more than $15,000 of gross income from gaming activities on Part VIII, line 9a? *If "Yes," complete Schedule G, Part III*	19		X
20a	Did the organization operate one or more hospital facilities? *If "Yes," complete Schedule H*	20a		X
b	If "Yes" to line 20a, did the organization attach a copy of its audited financial statements to this return?	20b		
21	Did the organization report more than $5,000 of grants or other assistance to any domestic organization or domestic government on Part IX, column (A), line 1? *If "Yes," complete Schedule I, Parts I and II*	21		X

932003 01-20-20 Form **990** (2019)

Form 990 (2019) NATIONAL CONSUMER LAW CENTER, INC. 04-2488502 Page 4

Part IV Checklist of Required Schedules *(continued)*

			Yes	No
22	Did the organization report more than $5,000 of grants or other assistance to or for domestic individuals on Part IX, column (A), line 2? *If "Yes," complete Schedule I, Parts I and III*	22		X
23	Did the organization answer "Yes" to Part VII, Section A, line 3, 4, or 5 about compensation of the organization's current and former officers, directors, trustees, key employees, and highest compensated employees? *If "Yes," complete Schedule J*	23	X	
24a	Did the organization have a tax-exempt bond issue with an outstanding principal amount of more than $100,000 as of the last day of the year, that was issued after December 31, 2002? *If "Yes," answer lines 24b through 24d and complete Schedule K. If "No," go to line 25a*	24a		X
b	Did the organization invest any proceeds of tax-exempt bonds beyond a temporary period exception?	24b		
c	Did the organization maintain an escrow account other than a refunding escrow at any time during the year to defease any tax-exempt bonds?	24c		
d	Did the organization act as an "on behalf of" issuer for bonds outstanding at any time during the year?	24d		
25a	**Section 501(c)(3), 501(c)(4), and 501(c)(29) organizations.** Did the organization engage in an excess benefit transaction with a disqualified person during the year? *If "Yes," complete Schedule L, Part I*	25a		X
b	Is the organization aware that it engaged in an excess benefit transaction with a disqualified person in a prior year, and that the transaction has not been reported on any of the organization's prior Forms 990 or 990-EZ? *If "Yes," complete Schedule L, Part I*	25b		X
26	Did the organization report any amount on Part X, line 5 or 22, for receivables from or payables to any current or former officer, director, trustee, key employee, creator or founder, substantial contributor, or 35% controlled entity or family member of any of these persons? *If "Yes," complete Schedule L, Part II*	26		X
27	Did the organization provide a grant or other assistance to any current or former officer, director, trustee, key employee, creator or founder, substantial contributor or employee thereof, a grant selection committee member, or to a 35% controlled entity (including an employee thereof) or family member of any of these persons? *If "Yes," complete Schedule L, Part III*	27		X
28	Was the organization a party to a business transaction with one of the following parties (see Schedule L, Part IV instructions, for applicable filing thresholds, conditions, and exceptions):			
a	A current or former officer, director, trustee, key employee, creator or founder, or substantial contributor? *If "Yes," complete Schedule L, Part IV*	28a		X
b	A family member of any individual described in line 28a? *If "Yes," complete Schedule L, Part IV*	28b		X
c	A 35% controlled entity of one or more individuals and/or organizations described in lines 28a or 28b? *If "Yes," complete Schedule L, Part IV*	28c		X
29	Did the organization receive more than $25,000 in non-cash contributions? *If "Yes," complete Schedule M*	29		X
30	Did the organization receive contributions of art, historical treasures, or other similar assets, or qualified conservation contributions? *If "Yes," complete Schedule M*	30		X
31	Did the organization liquidate, terminate, or dissolve and cease operations? *If "Yes," complete Schedule N, Part I*	31		X
32	Did the organization sell, exchange, dispose of, or transfer more than 25% of its net assets? *If "Yes," complete Schedule N, Part II*	32		X
33	Did the organization own 100% of an entity disregarded as separate from the organization under Regulations sections 301.7701-2 and 301.7701-3? *If "Yes," complete Schedule R, Part I*	33		X
34	Was the organization related to any tax-exempt or taxable entity? *If "Yes," complete Schedule R, Part II, III, or IV, and Part V, line 1*	34	X	
35a	Did the organization have a controlled entity within the meaning of section 512(b)(13)?	35a		X
b	If "Yes" to line 35a, did the organization receive any payment from or engage in any transaction with a controlled entity within the meaning of section 512(b)(13)? *If "Yes," complete Schedule R, Part V, line 2*	35b		
36	**Section 501(c)(3) organizations.** Did the organization make any transfers to an exempt non-charitable related organization? *If "Yes," complete Schedule R, Part V, line 2*	36		X
37	Did the organization conduct more than 5% of its activities through an entity that is not a related organization and that is treated as a partnership for federal income tax purposes? *If "Yes," complete Schedule R, Part VI*	37		X
38	Did the organization complete Schedule O and provide explanations in Schedule O for Part VI, lines 11b and 19? **Note:** All Form 990 filers are required to complete Schedule O	38	X	

Part V Statements Regarding Other IRS Filings and Tax Compliance

Check if Schedule O contains a response or note to any line in this Part V ☐

					Yes	No
1a	Enter the number reported in Box 3 of Form 1096. Enter -0- if not applicable	1a	21			
b	Enter the number of Forms W-2G included in line 1a. Enter -0- if not applicable	1b	0			
c	Did the organization comply with backup withholding rules for reportable payments to vendors and reportable gaming (gambling) winnings to prize winners?			1c	X	

932004 01-20-20 Form **990** (2019)

Form 990 (2019) NATIONAL CONSUMER LAW CENTER, INC. 04-248 8502 Page 5

Part V Statements Regarding Other IRS Filings and Tax Compliance *(continued)*

				Yes	No
2a	Enter the number of employees reported on Form W-3, Transmittal of Wage and Tax Statements, filed for the calendar year ending with or within the year covered by this return	2a	67		
b	If at least one is reported on line 2a, did the organization file all required federal employment tax returns?		2b	X	
	Note: If the sum of lines 1a and 2a is greater than 250, you may be required to *e-file* (see instructions)				
3a	Did the organization have unrelated business gross income of $1,000 or more during the year?		3a		X
b	If "Yes," has it filed a Form 990-T for this year? *If "No" to line 3b, provide an explanation on Schedule O*		3b		
4a	At any time during the calendar year, did the organization have an interest in, or a signature or other authority over, a financial account in a foreign country (such as a bank account, securities account, or other financial account)?		4a		X
b	If "Yes," enter the name of the foreign country ▶				
	See instructions for filing requirements for FinCEN Form 114, Report of Foreign Bank and Financial Accounts (FBAR).				
5a	Was the organization a party to a prohibited tax shelter transaction at any time during the tax year?		5a		X
b	Did any taxable party notify the organization that it was or is a party to a prohibited tax shelter transaction?		5b		X
c	If "Yes" to line 5a or 5b, did the organization file Form 8886-T?		5c		
6a	Does the organization have annual gross receipts that are normally greater than $100,000, and did the organization solicit any contributions that were not tax deductible as charitable contributions?		6a		X
b	If "Yes," did the organization include with every solicitation an express statement that such contributions or gifts were not tax deductible?		6b		
7	**Organizations that may receive deductible contributions under section 170(c).**				
a	Did the organization receive a payment in excess of $75 made partly as a contribution and partly for goods and services provided to the payor?		7a	X	
b	If "Yes," did the organization notify the donor of the value of the goods or services provided?		7b	X	
c	Did the organization sell, exchange, or otherwise dispose of tangible personal property for which it was required to file Form 8282?		7c		X
d	If "Yes," indicate the number of Forms 8282 filed during the year	7d			
e	Did the organization receive any funds, directly or indirectly, to pay premiums on a personal benefit contract?		7e		X
f	Did the organization, during the year, pay premiums, directly or indirectly, on a personal benefit contract?		7f		X
g	If the organization received a contribution of qualified intellectual property, did the organization file Form 8899 as required?		7g		
h	If the organization received a contribution of cars, boats, airplanes, or other vehicles, did the organization file a Form 1098-C?		7h		
8	**Sponsoring organizations maintaining donor advised funds.** Did a donor advised fund maintained by the sponsoring organization have excess business holdings at any time during the year?		8		
9	**Sponsoring organizations maintaining donor advised funds.**				
a	Did the sponsoring organization make any taxable distributions under section 4966?		9a		
b	Did the sponsoring organization make a distribution to a donor, donor advisor, or related person?		9b		
10	**Section 501(c)(7) organizations.** Enter:				
a	Initiation fees and capital contributions included on Part VIII, line 12	10a			
b	Gross receipts, included on Form 990, Part VIII, line 12, for public use of club facilities	10b			
11	**Section 501(c)(12) organizations.** Enter:				
a	Gross income from members or shareholders	11a			
b	Gross income from other sources (Do not net amounts due or paid to other sources against amounts due or received from them.)	11b			
12a	**Section 4947(a)(1) non-exempt charitable trusts.** Is the organization filing Form 990 in lieu of Form 1041?		12a		
b	If "Yes," enter the amount of tax-exempt interest received or accrued during the year	12b			
13	**Section 501(c)(29) qualified nonprofit health insurance issuers.**				
a	Is the organization licensed to issue qualified health plans in more than one state?		13a		
	Note: See the instructions for additional information the organization must report on Schedule O.				
b	Enter the amount of reserves the organization is required to maintain by the states in which the organization is licensed to issue qualified health plans	13b			
c	Enter the amount of reserves on hand	13c			
14a	Did the organization receive any payments for indoor tanning services during the tax year?		14a		X
b	If "Yes," has it filed a Form 720 to report these payments? *If "No," provide an explanation on Schedule O*		14b		
15	Is the organization subject to the section 4960 tax on payment(s) of more than $1,000,000 in remuneration or excess parachute payment(s) during the year?		15		X
	If "Yes," see instructions and file Form 4720, Schedule N.				
16	Is the organization an educational institution subject to the section 4968 excise tax on net investment income?		16		X
	If "Yes," complete Form 4720, Schedule O.				

Form **990** (2019)

932005 01-20-20

Form 990 (2019) NATIONAL CONSUMER LAW CENTER, INC. 04-2488502 Page 6

Part VI Governance, Management, and Disclosure *For each "Yes" response to lines 2 through 7b below, and for a "No" response to line 8a, 8b, or 10b below, describe the circumstances, processes, or changes on Schedule O. See instructions.*

Check if Schedule O contains a response or note to any line in this Part VI [X]

Section A. Governing Body and Management

				Yes	No
1a	Enter the number of voting members of the governing body at the end of the tax year	1a 12			
	If there are material differences in voting rights among members of the governing body, or if the governing body delegated broad authority to an executive committee or similar committee, explain on Schedule O.				
b	Enter the number of voting members included on line 1a, above, who are independent	1b 12			
2	Did any officer, director, trustee, or key employee have a family relationship or a business relationship with any other officer, director, trustee, or key employee?		2		X
3	Did the organization delegate control over management duties customarily performed by or under the direct supervision of officers, directors, trustees, or key employees to a management company or other person?		3		X
4	Did the organization make any significant changes to its governing documents since the prior Form 990 was filed?		4		X
5	Did the organization become aware during the year of a significant diversion of the organization's assets?		5		X
6	Did the organization have members or stockholders?		6		X
7a	Did the organization have members, stockholders, or other persons who had the power to elect or appoint one or more members of the governing body?		7a		X
b	Are any governance decisions of the organization reserved to (or subject to approval by) members, stockholders, or persons other than the governing body?		7b		X
8	Did the organization contemporaneously document the meetings held or written actions undertaken during the year by the following:				
a	The governing body?		8a	X	
b	Each committee with authority to act on behalf of the governing body?		8b	X	
9	Is there any officer, director, trustee, or key employee listed in Part VII, Section A, who cannot be reached at the organization's mailing address? *If "Yes," provide the names and addresses on Schedule O*		9		X

Section B. Policies *(This Section B requests information about policies not required by the Internal Revenue Code.)*

			Yes	No
10a	Did the organization have local chapters, branches, or affiliates?	10a		X
b	If "Yes," did the organization have written policies and procedures governing the activities of such chapters, affiliates, and branches to ensure their operations are consistent with the organization's exempt purposes?	10b		
11a	Has the organization provided a complete copy of this Form 990 to all members of its governing body before filing the form?	11a	X	
b	Describe in Schedule O the process, if any, used by the organization to review this Form 990.			
12a	Did the organization have a written conflict of interest policy? *If "No," go to line 13*	12a	X	
b	Were officers, directors, or trustees, and key employees required to disclose annually interests that could give rise to conflicts?	12b	X	
c	Did the organization regularly and consistently monitor and enforce compliance with the policy? *If "Yes," describe in Schedule O how this was done*	12c	X	
13	Did the organization have a written whistleblower policy?	13	X	
14	Did the organization have a written document retention and destruction policy?	14	X	
15	Did the process for determining compensation of the following persons include a review and approval by independent persons, comparability data, and contemporaneous substantiation of the deliberation and decision?			
a	The organization's CEO, Executive Director, or top management official	15a	X	
b	Other officers or key employees of the organization	15b	X	
	If "Yes" to line 15a or 15b, describe the process in Schedule O (see instructions).			
16a	Did the organization invest in, contribute assets to, or participate in a joint venture or similar arrangement with a taxable entity during the year?	16a		X
b	If "Yes," did the organization follow a written policy or procedure requiring the organization to evaluate its participation in joint venture arrangements under applicable federal tax law, and take steps to safeguard the organization's exempt status with respect to such arrangements?	16b		

Section C. Disclosure

17 List the states with which a copy of this Form 990 is required to be filed ▶MA,AK,CA,FL,MD,MI,MS,NY,OR,PA,WI,WA

18 Section 6104 requires an organization to make its Forms 1023 (1024 or 1024-A, if applicable), 990, and 990-T (Section 501(c)(3)s only) available for public inspection. Indicate how you made these available. Check all that apply.
[ ] Own website [ ] Another's website [X] Upon request [ ] Other *(explain on Schedule O)*

19 Describe on Schedule O whether (and if so, how) the organization made its governing documents, conflict of interest policy, and financial statements available to the public during the tax year.

20 State the name, address, and telephone number of the person who possesses the organization's books and records ▶
MARGARET KOHLER - 617-542-8010
7 WINTHROP SQUARE, 4TH FLOOR, BOSTON, MA 02110-1006

932006 01-20-20 SEE SCHEDULE O FOR FULL LIST OF STATES Form **990** (2019)

Form 990 (2019) NATIONAL CONSUMER LAW CENTER, INC. 04-2488502 Page 7

Part VII Compensation of Officers, Directors, Trustees, Key Employees, Highest Compensated Employees, and Independent Contractors

Check if Schedule O contains a response or note to any line in this Part VII ☐

Section A. Officers, Directors, Trustees, Key Employees, and Highest Compensated Employees

1a Complete this table for all persons required to be listed. Report compensation for the calendar year ending with or within the organization's tax year.

- List all of the organization's **current** officers, directors, trustees (whether individuals or organizations), regardless of amount of compensation. Enter -0- in columns (D), (E), and (F) if no compensation was paid.
- List all of the organization's **current** key employees, if any. See instructions for definition of "key employee."
- List the organization's five **current** highest compensated employees (other than an officer, director, trustee, or key employee) who received reportable compensation (Box 5 of Form W-2 and/or Box 7 of Form 1099-MISC) of more than $100,000 from the organization and any related organizations.
- List all of the organization's **former** officers, key employees, and highest compensated employees who received more than $100,000 of reportable compensation from the organization and any related organizations.
- List all of the organization's **former directors or trustees** that received, in the capacity as a former director or trustee of the organization, more than $10,000 of reportable compensation from the organization and any related organizations.

See instructions for the order in which to list the persons above.

☐ Check this box if neither the organization nor any related organization compensated any current officer, director, or trustee.

(A) Name and title	(B) Average hours per week (list any hours for related organizations below line)	(C) Position (do not check more than one box, unless person is both an officer and a director/trustee): Individual trustee or director	Institutional trustee	Officer	Key employee	Highest compensated employee	Former	(D) Reportable compensation from the organization (W-2/1099-MISC)	(E) Reportable compensation from related organizations (W-2/1099-MISC)	(F) Estimated amount of other compensation from the organization and related organizations
(1) RICHARD DUBOIS EXECUTIVE DIRECTOR	40.00			X				177,482.	0.	33,377.
(2) MARGOT SAUNDERS STAFF ATTORNEY	40.00					X		145,090.	0.	31,724.
(3) GEOFFRY WALSH STAFF ATTORNEY	40.00					X		144,636.	0.	31,405.
(4) STUART ROSSMAN DIRECTOR OF LITIGATION	40.00					X		149,073.	0.	25,827.
(5) CHARLES DELBAUM STAFF ATTORNEY	40.00					X		146,748.	0.	24,609.
(6) CAROLYN CARTER DEPUTY DIRECTOR	40.00			X				149,665.	0.	17,555.
(7) MARGARET KOHLER CHIEF FINANCIAL OFFICER	40.00			X				127,475.	0.	32,705.
(8) JOHN HOWAT STAFF ATTORNEY	40.00					X		143,492.	0.	15,908.
(9) STEPHEN HURLEY CHIEF DEVELOPMENT OFFICER	40.00			X				129,147.	0.	30,051.
(10) MICHAEL FERRY PRESIDENT	1.00	X		X				0.	0.	0.
(11) DONNA DALEY VICE PRESIDENT	1.00	X		X				0.	0.	0.
(12) BEVERLY COURTNEY DIRECTOR	1.00	X						0.	0.	0.
(13) DAVID VLADECK DIRECTOR	1.00	X						0.	0.	0.
(14) DOLORES S. SMITH DIRECTOR	1.00	X						0.	0.	0.
(15) JONATHAN L. KRAVETZ DIRECTOR	1.00	X						0.	0.	0.
(16) LATRYNA CARLTON DIRECTOR	1.00	X						0.	0.	0.
(17) MARK E. BUDNITZ DIRECTOR	1.00	X						0.	0.	0.

932007 01-20-20 Form **990** (2019)

Form 990 (2019) NATIONAL CONSUMER LAW CENTER, INC. 04-2488502 Page 8

Part VII Section A. Officers, Directors, Trustees, Key Employees, and Highest Compensated Employees *(continued)*

(A) Name and title	(B) Average hours per week (list any hours for related organizations below line)	(C) Position (do not check more than one box, unless person is both an officer and a director/trustee): Individual trustee or director	Institutional trustee	Officer	Key employee	Highest compensated employee	Former	(D) Reportable compensation from the organization (W-2/1099-MISC)	(E) Reportable compensation from related organizations (W-2/1099-MISC)	(F) Estimated amount of other compensation from the organization and related organizations
(18) NANCY BARRON DIRECTOR	1.00	X						0.	0.	0.
(19) DANCY MCKINNEY-PARKER DIRECTOR	1.00	X						0.	0.	0.
(20) DEEPAK GUPTA DIRECTOR	1.00	X						0.	0.	0.
(21) MARTHA TAMAYO DIRECTOR	1.00	X						0.	0.	0.

	(D)	(E)	(F)
1b Subtotal ▶	1,312,808.	0.	243,161.
c Total from continuation sheets to Part VII, Section A ▶	0.	0.	0.
d Total (add lines 1b and 1c) ▶	1,312,808.	0.	243,161.

2 Total number of individuals (including but not limited to those listed above) who received more than $100,000 of reportable compensation from the organization ▶ 20

		Yes	No
3 Did the organization list any **former** officer, director, trustee, key employee, or highest compensated employee on line 1a? *If "Yes," complete Schedule J for such individual*	3		X
4 For any individual listed on line 1a, is the sum of reportable compensation and other compensation from the organization and related organizations greater than $150,000? *If "Yes," complete Schedule J for such individual*	4	X	
5 Did any person listed on line 1a receive or accrue compensation from any unrelated organization or individual for services rendered to the organization? *If "Yes," complete Schedule J for such person*	5		X

Section B. Independent Contractors

1 Complete this table for your five highest compensated independent contractors that received more than $100,000 of compensation from the organization. Report compensation for the calendar year ending with or within the organization's tax year.

(A) Name and business address NONE	(B) Description of services	(C) Compensation

2 Total number of independent contractors (including but not limited to those listed above) who received more than $100,000 of compensation from the organization ▶ 0

Form **990** (2019)

932008 01-20-20

Form 990 (2019) NATIONAL CONSUMER LAW CENTER, INC. 04-2488502 Page 9

Part VIII Statement of Revenue

Check if Schedule O contains a response or note to any line in this Part VIII ☐

				(A) Total revenue	(B) Related or exempt function revenue	(C) Unrelated business revenue	(D) Revenue excluded from tax under sections 512 - 514
Contributions, Gifts, Grants and Other Similar Amounts	1 a Federated campaigns	1a					
	b Membership dues	1b					
	c Fundraising events	1c	114,201.				
	d Related organizations	1d					
	e Government grants (contributions)	1e	95,906.				
	f All other contributions, gifts, grants, and similar amounts not included above	1f	2,937,119.				
	g Noncash contributions included in lines 1a-1f	1g	$				
	h **Total.** Add lines 1a-1f ▶			3,147,226.			
Program Service Revenue			Business Code				
	2 a ATTORNEY FEE AWARDS		541100	3,287,839.	3,287,839.		
	b PUBLICATIONS		511120	2,272,410.	2,272,410.		
	c CONFERENCES		900099	918,589.	918,589.		
	d ADVICE AND ASSISTANCE		541100	44,878.	44,878.		
	e MISCELLANEOUS		900099	5,604.	5,604.		
	f All other program service revenue						
	g **Total.** Add lines 2a-2f ▶			6,529,320.			
Other Revenue	3 Investment income (including dividends, interest, and other similar amounts) ▶			1,369,131.			1,369,131.
	4 Income from investment of tax-exempt bond proceeds ▶						
	5 Royalties ▶						
			(i) Real / (ii) Personal				
	6 a Gross rents	6a	192,900. /				
	b Less: rental expenses	6b	0. /				
	c Rental income or (loss)	6c	192,900. /				
	d Net rental income or (loss) ▶			192,900.			192,900.
			(i) Securities / (ii) Other				
	7 a Gross amount from sales of assets other than inventory	7a	13,598,376. /				
	b Less: cost or other basis and sales expenses	7b	13,624,892. /				
	c Gain or (loss)	7c	-26,516. /				
	d Net gain or (loss) ▶			-26,516.			-26,516.
	8 a Gross income from fundraising events (not including $ 114,201. of contributions reported on line 1c). See Part IV, line 18	8a	103,438.				
	b Less: direct expenses	8b	123,117.				
	c Net income or (loss) from fundraising events ▶			-19,679.			-19,679.
	9 a Gross income from gaming activities. See Part IV, line 19	9a					
	b Less: direct expenses	9b					
	c Net income or (loss) from gaming activities ▶						
	10 a Gross sales of inventory, less returns and allowances	10a					
	b Less: cost of goods sold	10b					
	c Net income or (loss) from sales of inventory ▶						
Miscellaneous Revenue			Business Code				
	11 a						
	b						
	c						
	d All other revenue						
	e **Total.** Add lines 11a-11d ▶						
	12 **Total revenue.** See instructions ▶			11,192,382.	6,529,320.	0.	1,515,836.

932009 01-20-20 Form **990** (2019)

Form 990 (2019) NATIONAL CONSUMER LAW CENTER, INC. 04-2488502 Page **10**

Part IX Statement of Functional Expenses

Section 501(c)(3) and 501(c)(4) organizations must complete all columns. All other organizations must complete column (A).

Check if Schedule O contains a response or note to any line in this Part IX ☐

Do not include amounts reported on lines 6b, 7b, 8b, 9b, and 10b of Part VIII.	(A) Total expenses	(B) Program service expenses	(C) Management and general expenses	(D) Fundraising expenses
1 Grants and other assistance to domestic organizations and domestic governments. See Part IV, line 21				
2 Grants and other assistance to domestic individuals. See Part IV, line 22				
3 Grants and other assistance to foreign organizations, foreign governments, and foreign individuals. See Part IV, lines 15 and 16				
4 Benefits paid to or for members				
5 Compensation of current officers, directors, trustees, and key employees	697,456.	120,398.	385,868.	191,190.
6 Compensation not included above to disqualified persons (as defined under section 4958(f)(1)) and persons described in section 4958(c)(3)(B)				
7 Other salaries and wages	4,533,172.	3,926,336.	283,368.	323,468.
8 Pension plan accruals and contributions (include section 401(k) and 403(b) employer contributions)	169,512.	146,882.	8,808.	13,822.
9 Other employee benefits	826,735.	717,772.	53,181.	55,782.
10 Payroll taxes	369,544.	292,088.	42,709.	34,747.
11 Fees for services (nonemployees):				
a Management				
b Legal				
c Accounting	44,405.		44,405.	
d Lobbying				
e Professional fundraising services. See Part IV, line 17				
f Investment management fees	96,432.		96,432.	
g Other. (If line 11g amount exceeds 10% of line 25, column (A) amount, list line 11g expenses on Sch O.)	581,504.	390,924.	161,420.	29,160.
12 Advertising and promotion				
13 Office expenses	242,089.	87,052.	155,037.	
14 Information technology				
15 Royalties				
16 Occupancy	949,097.	870,130.	52,980.	25,987.
17 Travel	140,139.	87,176.	52,963.	
18 Payments of travel or entertainment expenses for any federal, state, or local public officials				
19 Conferences, conventions, and meetings	555,863.	544,093.	11,770.	
20 Interest				
21 Payments to affiliates				
22 Depreciation, depletion, and amortization	103,752.	83,453.	20,299.	
23 Insurance	23,669.	20,590.	3,079.	
24 Other expenses. Itemize expenses not covered above (List miscellaneous expenses on line 24e. If line 24e amount exceeds 10% of line 25, column (A) amount, list line 24e expenses on Schedule O.)				
a PUBLICATIONS	321,689.	321,689.		
b MISCELLANEOUS	112,510.	104,778.	7,732.	
c EQUIPMENT	109,632.	82,356.	27,276.	
d PERIODICALS	12,501.		12,501.	
e All other expenses				
25 **Total functional expenses.** Add lines 1 through 24e	9,889,701.	7,795,717.	1,419,828.	674,156.
26 **Joint costs.** Complete this line only if the organization reported in column (B) joint costs from a combined educational campaign and fundraising solicitation. Check here ▶ ☐ if following SOP 98-2 (ASC 958-720)				

932010 01-20-20 Form **990** (2019)

Form 990 (2019) NATIONAL CONSUMER LAW CENTER, INC. 04-2488502 Page 11

Part X Balance Sheet

Check if Schedule O contains a response or note to any line in this Part X ☐

Section	Line	Description		(A) Beginning of year	Line	(B) End of year
Assets	1	Cash - non-interest-bearing		752,006.	1	2,070,921.
	2	Savings and temporary cash investments		1,207,297.	2	1,651,455.
	3	Pledges and grants receivable, net		2,166,150.	3	1,606,878.
	4	Accounts receivable, net		236,924.	4	318,076.
	5	Loans and other receivables from any current or former officer, director, trustee, key employee, creator or founder, substantial contributor, or 35% controlled entity or family member of any of these persons			5	
	6	Loans and other receivables from other disqualified persons (as defined under section 4958(f)(1)), and persons described in section 4958(c)(3)(B)			6	
	7	Notes and loans receivable, net			7	
	8	Inventories for sale or use			8	
	9	Prepaid expenses and deferred charges		109,277.	9	85,380.
	10a	Land, buildings, and equipment: cost or other basis. Complete Part VI of Schedule D	10a 961,557.			
	b	Less: accumulated depreciation	10b 759,365.	290,762.	10c	202,192.
	11	Investments - publicly traded securities		25,757,859.	11	28,713,899.
	12	Investments - other securities. See Part IV, line 11			12	
	13	Investments - program-related. See Part IV, line 11			13	
	14	Intangible assets			14	
	15	Other assets. See Part IV, line 11		334,807.	15	340,381.
	16	**Total assets.** Add lines 1 through 15 (must equal line 33)		30,855,082.	16	34,989,182.
Liabilities	17	Accounts payable and accrued expenses		874,705.	17	1,368,597.
	18	Grants payable			18	
	19	Deferred revenue		797,925.	19	907,059.
	20	Tax-exempt bond liabilities			20	
	21	Escrow or custodial account liability. Complete Part IV of Schedule D			21	
	22	Loans and other payables to any current or former officer, director, trustee, key employee, creator or founder, substantial contributor, or 35% controlled entity or family member of any of these persons			22	
	23	Secured mortgages and notes payable to unrelated third parties			23	
	24	Unsecured notes and loans payable to unrelated third parties			24	
	25	Other liabilities (including federal income tax, payables to related third parties, and other liabilities not included on lines 17-24). Complete Part X of Schedule D			25	
	26	**Total liabilities.** Add lines 17 through 25		1,672,630.	26	2,275,656.
Net Assets or Fund Balances		**Organizations that follow FASB ASC 958, check here ▶ [X] and complete lines 27, 28, 32, and 33.**				
	27	Net assets without donor restrictions		25,196,367.	27	28,489,490.
	28	Net assets with donor restrictions		3,986,085.	28	4,224,036.
		Organizations that do not follow FASB ASC 958, check here ▶ ☐ and complete lines 29 through 33.				
	29	Capital stock or trust principal, or current funds			29	
	30	Paid-in or capital surplus, or land, building, or equipment fund			30	
	31	Retained earnings, endowment, accumulated income, or other funds			31	
	32	Total net assets or fund balances		29,182,452.	32	32,713,526.
	33	Total liabilities and net assets/fund balances		30,855,082.	33	34,989,182.

Form **990** (2019)

932011 01-20-20

Form 990 (2019) NATIONAL CONSUMER LAW CENTER, INC. 04-2488502 Page **12**

Part XI Reconciliation of Net Assets

Check if Schedule O contains a response or note to any line in this Part XI ☐

1	Total revenue (must equal Part VIII, column (A), line 12)	1	11,192,382.
2	Total expenses (must equal Part IX, column (A), line 25)	2	9,889,701.
3	Revenue less expenses. Subtract line 2 from line 1	3	1,302,681.
4	Net assets or fund balances at beginning of year (must equal Part X, line 32, column (A))	4	29,182,452.
5	Net unrealized gains (losses) on investments	5	2,228,393.
6	Donated services and use of facilities	6	
7	Investment expenses	7	
8	Prior period adjustments	8	
9	Other changes in net assets or fund balances (explain on Schedule O)	9	0.
10	Net assets or fund balances at end of year. Combine lines 3 through 9 (must equal Part X, line 32, column (B))	10	32,713,526.

Part XII Financial Statements and Reporting

Check if Schedule O contains a response or note to any line in this Part XII ☒

			Yes	No
1	Accounting method used to prepare the Form 990: ☐ Cash ☒ Accrual ☐ Other ______ If the organization changed its method of accounting from a prior year or checked "Other," explain in Schedule O.			
2a	Were the organization's financial statements compiled or reviewed by an independent accountant?	2a		X
	If "Yes," check a box below to indicate whether the financial statements for the year were compiled or reviewed on a separate basis, consolidated basis, or both: ☐ Separate basis ☐ Consolidated basis ☐ Both consolidated and separate basis			
b	Were the organization's financial statements audited by an independent accountant?	2b	X	
	If "Yes," check a box below to indicate whether the financial statements for the year were audited on a separate basis, consolidated basis, or both: ☐ Separate basis ☒ Consolidated basis ☐ Both consolidated and separate basis			
c	If "Yes" to line 2a or 2b, does the organization have a committee that assumes responsibility for oversight of the audit, review, or compilation of its financial statements and selection of an independent accountant?	2c	X	
	If the organization changed either its oversight process or selection process during the tax year, explain on Schedule O.			
3a	As a result of a federal award, was the organization required to undergo an audit or audits as set forth in the Single Audit Act and OMB Circular A-133?	3a		X
b	If "Yes," did the organization undergo the required audit or audits? If the organization did not undergo the required audit or audits, explain why on Schedule O and describe any steps taken to undergo such audits	3b		

Form **990** (2019)

932012 01-20-20

SCHEDULE A
(Form 990 or 990-EZ)

Department of the Treasury
Internal Revenue Service

Public Charity Status and Public Support

Complete if the organization is a section 501(c)(3) organization or a section 4947(a)(1) nonexempt charitable trust.
▶ Attach to Form 990 or Form 990-EZ.
▶ Go to www.irs.gov/Form990 for instructions and the latest information.

OMB No. 1545-0047
2019
Open to Public Inspection

Name of the organization: NATIONAL CONSUMER LAW CENTER, INC.
Employer identification number: 04-2488502

Part I Reason for Public Charity Status (All organizations must complete this part.) See instructions.

The organization is not a private foundation because it is: (For lines 1 through 12, check only one box.)

1 ☐ A church, convention of churches, or association of churches described in **section 170(b)(1)(A)(i).**
2 ☐ A school described in **section 170(b)(1)(A)(ii).** (Attach Schedule E (Form 990 or 990-EZ).)
3 ☐ A hospital or a cooperative hospital service organization described in **section 170(b)(1)(A)(iii).**
4 ☐ A medical research organization operated in conjunction with a hospital described in **section 170(b)(1)(A)(iii).** Enter the hospital's name, city, and state: ____
5 ☐ An organization operated for the benefit of a college or university owned or operated by a governmental unit described in **section 170(b)(1)(A)(iv).** (Complete Part II.)
6 ☐ A federal, state, or local government or governmental unit described in **section 170(b)(1)(A)(v).**
7 ☒ An organization that normally receives a substantial part of its support from a governmental unit or from the general public described in **section 170(b)(1)(A)(vi).** (Complete Part II.)
8 ☐ A community trust described in **section 170(b)(1)(A)(vi).** (Complete Part II.)
9 ☐ An agricultural research organization described in **section 170(b)(1)(A)(ix)** operated in conjunction with a land-grant college or university or a non-land-grant college of agriculture (see instructions). Enter the name, city, and state of the college or university: ____
10 ☐ An organization that normally receives: (1) more than 33 1/3% of its support from contributions, membership fees, and gross receipts from activities related to its exempt functions - subject to certain exceptions, and (2) no more than 33 1/3% of its support from gross investment income and unrelated business taxable income (less section 511 tax) from businesses acquired by the organization after June 30, 1975. See **section 509(a)(2).** (Complete Part III.)
11 ☐ An organization organized and operated exclusively to test for public safety. See **section 509(a)(4).**
12 ☐ An organization organized and operated exclusively for the benefit of, to perform the functions of, or to carry out the purposes of one or more publicly supported organizations described in **section 509(a)(1)** or **section 509(a)(2).** See **section 509(a)(3).** Check the box in lines 12a through 12d that describes the type of supporting organization and complete lines 12e, 12f, and 12g.

a ☐ **Type I.** A supporting organization operated, supervised, or controlled by its supported organization(s), typically by giving the supported organization(s) the power to regularly appoint or elect a majority of the directors or trustees of the supporting organization. **You must complete Part IV, Sections A and B.**
b ☐ **Type II.** A supporting organization supervised or controlled in connection with its supported organization(s), by having control or management of the supporting organization vested in the same persons that control or manage the supported organization(s). **You must complete Part IV, Sections A and C.**
c ☐ **Type III functionally integrated.** A supporting organization operated in connection with, and functionally integrated with, its supported organization(s) (see instructions). **You must complete Part IV, Sections A, D, and E.**
d ☐ **Type III non-functionally integrated.** A supporting organization operated in connection with its supported organization(s) that is not functionally integrated. The organization generally must satisfy a distribution requirement and an attentiveness requirement (see instructions). **You must complete Part IV, Sections A and D, and Part V.**
e ☐ Check this box if the organization received a written determination from the IRS that it is a Type I, Type II, Type III functionally integrated, or Type III non-functionally integrated supporting organization.
f Enter the number of supported organizations ☐
g Provide the following information about the supported organization(s).

(i) Name of supported organization	(ii) EIN	(iii) Type of organization (described on lines 1-10 above (see instructions))	(iv) Is the organization listed in your governing document? Yes	No	(v) Amount of monetary support (see instructions)	(vi) Amount of other support (see instructions)
Total						

Schedule A (Form 990 or 990-EZ) 2019 NATIONAL CONSUMER LAW CENTER, INC. 04-2488502 Page 2

Part II **Support Schedule for Organizations Described in Sections 170(b)(1)(A)(iv) and 170(b)(1)(A)(vi)**

(Complete only if you checked the box on line 5, 7, or 8 of Part I or if the organization failed to qualify under Part III. If the organization fails to qualify under the tests listed below, please complete Part III.)

Section A. Public Support

Calendar year (or fiscal year beginning in) ▶	(a) 2015	(b) 2016	(c) 2017	(d) 2018	(e) 2019	(f) Total
1 Gifts, grants, contributions, and membership fees received. (Do not include any "unusual grants.")	2,404,461.	3,240,839.	3,869,842.	3,237,235.	3,147,226.	15,899,603.
2 Tax revenues levied for the organization's benefit and either paid to or expended on its behalf						
3 The value of services or facilities furnished by a governmental unit to the organization without charge						
4 **Total.** Add lines 1 through 3	2,404,461.	3,240,839.	3,869,842.	3,237,235.	3,147,226.	15,899,603.
5 The portion of total contributions by each person (other than a governmental unit or publicly supported organization) included on line 1 that exceeds 2% of the amount shown on line 11, column (f)						3,747,753.
6 **Public support.** Subtract line 5 from line 4.						12,151,850.

Section B. Total Support

Calendar year (or fiscal year beginning in) ▶	(a) 2015	(b) 2016	(c) 2017	(d) 2018	(e) 2019	(f) Total
7 Amounts from line 4	2,404,461.	3,240,839.	3,869,842.	3,237,235.	3,147,226.	15,899,603.
8 Gross income from interest, dividends, payments received on securities loans, rents, royalties, and income from similar sources	994,840.	922,899.	1,135,859.	1,481,020.	1,562,031.	6,096,649.
9 Net income from unrelated business activities, whether or not the business is regularly carried on						
10 Other income. Do not include gain or loss from the sale of capital assets (Explain in Part VI.)						
11 **Total support.** Add lines 7 through 10						21,996,252.

12 Gross receipts from related activities, etc. (see instructions) | 12 | 36,640,072.

13 **First five years.** If the Form 990 is for the organization's first, second, third, fourth, or fifth tax year as a section 501(c)(3) organization, check this box and **stop here** ▶ ☐

Section C. Computation of Public Support Percentage

14 Public support percentage for 2019 (line 6, column (f) divided by line 11, column (f)) | 14 | 55.25 %

15 Public support percentage from 2018 Schedule A, Part II, line 14 | 15 | 65.99 %

16a **33 1/3% support test - 2019.** If the organization did not check the box on line 13, and line 14 is 33 1/3% or more, check this box and **stop here.** The organization qualifies as a publicly supported organization ▶ ☒

b **33 1/3% support test - 2018.** If the organization did not check a box on line 13 or 16a, and line 15 is 33 1/3% or more, check this box and **stop here.** The organization qualifies as a publicly supported organization ▶ ☐

17a **10% -facts-and-circumstances test - 2019.** If the organization did not check a box on line 13, 16a, or 16b, and line 14 is 10% or more, and if the organization meets the "facts-and-circumstances" test, check this box and **stop here.** Explain in Part VI how the organization meets the "facts-and-circumstances" test. The organization qualifies as a publicly supported organization ▶ ☐

b **10% -facts-and-circumstances test - 2018.** If the organization did not check a box on line 13, 16a, 16b, or 17a, and line 15 is 10% or more, and if the organization meets the "facts-and-circumstances" test, check this box and **stop here.** Explain in Part VI how the organization meets the "facts-and-circumstances" test. The organization qualifies as a publicly supported organization ▶ ☐

18 **Private foundation.** If the organization did not check a box on line 13, 16a, 16b, 17a, or 17b, check this box and see instructions ▶ ☐

Schedule A (Form 990 or 990-EZ) 2019

932022 09-25-19

Schedule A (Form 990 or 990-EZ) 2019 NATIONAL CONSUMER LAW CENTER, INC. 04-2488502 Page 3

Part III Support Schedule for Organizations Described in Section 509(a)(2)

(Complete only if you checked the box on line 10 of Part I or if the organization failed to qualify under Part II. If the organization fails to qualify under the tests listed below, please complete Part II.)

Section A. Public Support

Calendar year (or fiscal year beginning in) ▶	(a) 2015	(b) 2016	(c) 2017	(d) 2018	(e) 2019	(f) Total
1 Gifts, grants, contributions, and membership fees received. (Do not include any "unusual grants.")						
2 Gross receipts from admissions, merchandise sold or services performed, or facilities furnished in any activity that is related to the organization's tax-exempt purpose						
3 Gross receipts from activities that are not an unrelated trade or business under section 513						
4 Tax revenues levied for the organization's benefit and either paid to or expended on its behalf						
5 The value of services or facilities furnished by a governmental unit to the organization without charge						
6 **Total.** Add lines 1 through 5						
7a Amounts included on lines 1, 2, and 3 received from disqualified persons						
b Amounts included on lines 2 and 3 received from other than disqualified persons that exceed the greater of $5,000 or 1% of the amount on line 13 for the year						
c Add lines 7a and 7b						
8 **Public support.** (Subtract line 7c from line 6.)						

Section B. Total Support

Calendar year (or fiscal year beginning in) ▶	(a) 2015	(b) 2016	(c) 2017	(d) 2018	(e) 2019	(f) Total
9 Amounts from line 6						
10a Gross income from interest, dividends, payments received on securities loans, rents, royalties, and income from similar sources						
b Unrelated business taxable income (less section 511 taxes) from businesses acquired after June 30, 1975						
c Add lines 10a and 10b						
11 Net income from unrelated business activities not included in line 10b, whether or not the business is regularly carried on						
12 Other income. Do not include gain or loss from the sale of capital assets (Explain in Part VI.)						
13 **Total support.** (Add lines 9, 10c, 11, and 12.)						

14 **First five years.** If the Form 990 is for the organization's first, second, third, fourth, or fifth tax year as a section 501(c)(3) organization, check this box and **stop here** ▶ ☐

Section C. Computation of Public Support Percentage

15 Public support percentage for 2019 (line 8, column (f), divided by line 13, column (f))	15	%
16 Public support percentage from 2018 Schedule A, Part III, line 15	16	%

Section D. Computation of Investment Income Percentage

17 Investment income percentage for **2019** (line 10c, column (f), divided by line 13, column (f))	17	%
18 Investment income percentage from **2018** Schedule A, Part III, line 17	18	%

19a **33 1/3% support tests - 2019.** If the organization did not check the box on line 14, and line 15 is more than 33 1/3%, and line 17 is not more than 33 1/3%, check this box and **stop here.** The organization qualifies as a publicly supported organization ▶ ☐

b **33 1/3% support tests - 2018.** If the organization did not check a box on line 14 or line 19a, and line 16 is more than 33 1/3%, and line 18 is not more than 33 1/3%, check this box and **stop here.** The organization qualifies as a publicly supported organization ▶ ☐

20 **Private foundation.** If the organization did not check a box on line 14, 19a, or 19b, check this box and see instructions ▶ ☐

932023 09-25-19 **Schedule A (Form 990 or 990-EZ) 2019**

Schedule A (Form 990 or 990-EZ) 2019 NATIONAL CONSUMER LAW CENTER, INC. 04-2488502 Page 4

Part IV Supporting Organizations

(Complete only if you checked a box in line 12 on Part I. If you checked 12a of Part I, complete Sections A and B. If you checked 12b of Part I, complete Sections A and C. If you checked 12c of Part I, complete Sections A, D, and E. If you checked 12d of Part I, complete Sections A and D, and complete Part V.)

Section A. All Supporting Organizations

			Yes	No
1	Are all of the organization's supported organizations listed by name in the organization's governing documents? *If "No," describe in* **Part VI** *how the supported organizations are designated. If designated by class or purpose, describe the designation. If historic and continuing relationship, explain.*	1		
2	Did the organization have any supported organization that does not have an IRS determination of status under section 509(a)(1) or (2)? *If "Yes," explain in* **Part VI** *how the organization determined that the supported organization was described in section 509(a)(1) or (2).*	2		
3a	Did the organization have a supported organization described in section 501(c)(4), (5), or (6)? *If "Yes," answer (b) and (c) below.*	3a		
b	Did the organization confirm that each supported organization qualified under section 501(c)(4), (5), or (6) and satisfied the public support tests under section 509(a)(2)? *If "Yes," describe in* **Part VI** *when and how the organization made the determination.*	3b		
c	Did the organization ensure that all support to such organizations was used exclusively for section 170(c)(2)(B) purposes? *If "Yes," explain in* **Part VI** *what controls the organization put in place to ensure such use.*	3c		
4a	Was any supported organization not organized in the United States ("foreign supported organization")? *If "Yes," and if you checked 12a or 12b in Part I, answer (b) and (c) below.*	4a		
b	Did the organization have ultimate control and discretion in deciding whether to make grants to the foreign supported organization? *If "Yes," describe in* **Part VI** *how the organization had such control and discretion despite being controlled or supervised by or in connection with its supported organizations.*	4b		
c	Did the organization support any foreign supported organization that does not have an IRS determination under sections 501(c)(3) and 509(a)(1) or (2)? *If "Yes," explain in* **Part VI** *what controls the organization used to ensure that all support to the foreign supported organization was used exclusively for section 170(c)(2)(B) purposes.*	4c		
5a	Did the organization add, substitute, or remove any supported organizations during the tax year? *If "Yes," answer (b) and (c) below (if applicable). Also, provide detail in* **Part VI,** *including (i) the names and EIN numbers of the supported organizations added, substituted, or removed; (ii) the reasons for each such action; (iii) the authority under the organization's organizing document authorizing such action; and (iv) how the action was accomplished (such as by amendment to the organizing document).*	5a		
b	**Type I or Type II only.** Was any added or substituted supported organization part of a class already designated in the organization's organizing document?	5b		
c	**Substitutions only.** Was the substitution the result of an event beyond the organization's control?	5c		
6	Did the organization provide support (whether in the form of grants or the provision of services or facilities) to anyone other than (i) its supported organizations, (ii) individuals that are part of the charitable class benefited by one or more of its supported organizations, or (iii) other supporting organizations that also support or benefit one or more of the filing organization's supported organizations? *If "Yes," provide detail in* **Part VI.**	6		
7	Did the organization provide a grant, loan, compensation, or other similar payment to a substantial contributor (as defined in section 4958(c)(3)(C)), a family member of a substantial contributor, or a 35% controlled entity with regard to a substantial contributor? *If "Yes," complete Part I of Schedule L (Form 990 or 990-EZ).*	7		
8	Did the organization make a loan to a disqualified person (as defined in section 4958) not described in line 7? *If "Yes," complete Part I of Schedule L (Form 990 or 990-EZ).*	8		
9a	Was the organization controlled directly or indirectly at any time during the tax year by one or more disqualified persons as defined in section 4946 (other than foundation managers and organizations described in section 509(a)(1) or (2))? *If "Yes," provide detail in* **Part VI.**	9a		
b	Did one or more disqualified persons (as defined in line 9a) hold a controlling interest in any entity in which the supporting organization had an interest? *If "Yes," provide detail in* **Part VI.**	9b		
c	Did a disqualified person (as defined in line 9a) have an ownership interest in, or derive any personal benefit from, assets in which the supporting organization also had an interest? *If "Yes," provide detail in* **Part VI.**	9c		
10a	Was the organization subject to the excess business holdings rules of section 4943 because of section 4943(f) (regarding certain Type II supporting organizations, and all Type III non-functionally integrated supporting organizations)? *If "Yes," answer 10b below.*	10a		
b	Did the organization have any excess business holdings in the tax year? *(Use Schedule C, Form 4720, to determine whether the organization had excess business holdings.)*	10b		

932024 09-25-19 **Schedule A (Form 990 or 990-EZ) 2019**

Schedule A (Form 990 or 990-EZ) 2019 NATIONAL CONSUMER LAW CENTER, INC. 04-2488502 Page 5

Part IV Supporting Organizations *(continued)*

		Yes	No
11 Has the organization accepted a gift or contribution from any of the following persons?			
a A person who directly or indirectly controls, either alone or together with persons described in (b) and (c) below, the governing body of a supported organization?	11a		
b A family member of a person described in (a) above?	11b		
c A 35% controlled entity of a person described in (a) or (b) above? *If "Yes" to a, b, or c, provide detail in* **Part VI.**	11c		

Section B. Type I Supporting Organizations

		Yes	No
1 Did the directors, trustees, or membership of one or more supported organizations have the power to regularly appoint or elect at least a majority of the organization's directors or trustees at all times during the tax year? *If "No," describe in* **Part VI** *how the supported organization(s) effectively operated, supervised, or controlled the organization's activities. If the organization had more than one supported organization, describe how the powers to appoint and/or remove directors or trustees were allocated among the supported organizations and what conditions or restrictions, if any, applied to such powers during the tax year.*	1		
2 Did the organization operate for the benefit of any supported organization other than the supported organization(s) that operated, supervised, or controlled the supporting organization? *If "Yes," explain in* **Part VI** *how providing such benefit carried out the purposes of the supported organization(s) that operated, supervised, or controlled the supporting organization.*	2		

Section C. Type II Supporting Organizations

		Yes	No
1 Were a majority of the organization's directors or trustees during the tax year also a majority of the directors or trustees of each of the organization's supported organization(s)? *If "No," describe in* **Part VI** *how control or management of the supporting organization was vested in the same persons that controlled or managed the supported organization(s).*	1		

Section D. All Type III Supporting Organizations

		Yes	No
1 Did the organization provide to each of its supported organizations, by the last day of the fifth month of the organization's tax year, (i) a written notice describing the type and amount of support provided during the prior tax year, (ii) a copy of the Form 990 that was most recently filed as of the date of notification, and (iii) copies of the organization's governing documents in effect on the date of notification, to the extent not previously provided?	1		
2 Were any of the organization's officers, directors, or trustees either (i) appointed or elected by the supported organization(s) or (ii) serving on the governing body of a supported organization? *If "No," explain in* **Part VI** *how the organization maintained a close and continuous working relationship with the supported organization(s).*	2		
3 By reason of the relationship described in (2), did the organization's supported organizations have a significant voice in the organization's investment policies and in directing the use of the organization's income or assets at all times during the tax year? *If "Yes," describe in* **Part VI** *the role the organization's supported organizations played in this regard.*	3		

Section E. Type III Functionally Integrated Supporting Organizations

1 *Check the box next to the method that the organization used to satisfy the Integral Part Test during the year* **(see instructions).**

a ☐ The organization satisfied the Activities Test. *Complete* **line 2** *below.*

b ☐ The organization is the parent of each of its supported organizations. *Complete* **line 3** *below.*

c ☐ The organization supported a governmental entity. *Describe in* **Part VI** *how you supported a government entity (see instructions).*

		Yes	No
2 Activities Test. **Answer (a) and (b) below.**			
a Did substantially all of the organization's activities during the tax year directly further the exempt purposes of the supported organization(s) to which the organization was responsive? *If "Yes," then in* **Part VI identify those supported organizations and explain** *how these activities directly furthered their exempt purposes, how the organization was responsive to those supported organizations, and how the organization determined that these activities constituted substantially all of its activities.*	2a		
b Did the activities described in (a) constitute activities that, but for the organization's involvement, one or more of the organization's supported organization(s) would have been engaged in? *If "Yes," explain in* **Part VI** *the reasons for the organization's position that its supported organization(s) would have engaged in these activities but for the organization's involvement.*	2b		
3 Parent of Supported Organizations. **Answer (a) and (b) below.**			
a Did the organization have the power to regularly appoint or elect a majority of the officers, directors, or trustees of each of the supported organizations? *Provide details in* **Part VI.**	3a		
b Did the organization exercise a substantial degree of direction over the policies, programs, and activities of each of its supported organizations? *If "Yes," describe in* **Part VI** *the role played by the organization in this regard.*	3b		

932025 09-25-19 **Schedule A (Form 990 or 990-EZ) 2019**

Schedule A (Form 990 or 990-EZ) 2019 NATIONAL CONSUMER LAW CENTER, INC. 04-2488502 Page 6

Part V Type III Non-Functionally Integrated 509(a)(3) Supporting Organizations

1 ☐ Check here if the organization satisfied the Integral Part Test as a qualifying trust on Nov. 20, 1970 (explain in Part VI). **See instructions.** All other Type III non-functionally integrated supporting organizations must complete Sections A through E.

Section A - Adjusted Net Income		(A) Prior Year	(B) Current Year (optional)
1 Net short-term capital gain	1		
2 Recoveries of prior-year distributions	2		
3 Other gross income (see instructions)	3		
4 Add lines 1 through 3.	4		
5 Depreciation and depletion	5		
6 Portion of operating expenses paid or incurred for production or collection of gross income or for management, conservation, or maintenance of property held for production of income (see instructions)	6		
7 Other expenses (see instructions)	7		
8 **Adjusted Net Income** (subtract lines 5, 6, and 7 from line 4)	8		

Section B - Minimum Asset Amount		(A) Prior Year	(B) Current Year (optional)
1 Aggregate fair market value of all non-exempt-use assets (see instructions for short tax year or assets held for part of year):			
a Average monthly value of securities	1a		
b Average monthly cash balances	1b		
c Fair market value of other non-exempt-use assets	1c		
d **Total** (add lines 1a, 1b, and 1c)	1d		
e **Discount** claimed for blockage or other factors (explain in detail in **Part VI**):			
2 Acquisition indebtedness applicable to non-exempt-use assets	2		
3 Subtract line 2 from line 1d.	3		
4 Cash deemed held for exempt use. Enter 1-1/2% of line 3 (for greater amount, see instructions).	4		
5 Net value of non-exempt-use assets (subtract line 4 from line 3)	5		
6 Multiply line 5 by .035.	6		
7 Recoveries of prior-year distributions	7		
8 **Minimum Asset Amount** (add line 7 to line 6)	8		

Section C - Distributable Amount			Current Year
1 Adjusted net income for prior year (from Section A, line 8, Column A)	1		
2 Enter 85% of line 1.	2		
3 Minimum asset amount for prior year (from Section B, line 8, Column A)	3		
4 Enter greater of line 2 or line 3.	4		
5 Income tax imposed in prior year	5		
6 **Distributable Amount.** Subtract line 5 from line 4, unless subject to emergency temporary reduction (see instructions).	6		

7 ☐ Check here if the current year is the organization's first as a non-functionally integrated Type III supporting organization (see instructions).

Schedule A (Form 990 or 990-EZ) 2019

932026 09-25-19

Schedule A (Form 990 or 990-EZ) 2019 NATIONAL CONSUMER LAW CENTER, INC. 04-2488502 Page 7

Part V | Type III Non-Functionally Integrated 509(a)(3) Supporting Organizations *(continued)*

Section D - Distributions	Current Year
1 Amounts paid to supported organizations to accomplish exempt purposes	
2 Amounts paid to perform activity that directly furthers exempt purposes of supported organizations, in excess of income from activity	
3 Administrative expenses paid to accomplish exempt purposes of supported organizations	
4 Amounts paid to acquire exempt-use assets	
5 Qualified set-aside amounts (prior IRS approval required)	
6 Other distributions (describe in **Part VI**). See instructions.	
7 **Total annual distributions.** Add lines 1 through 6.	
8 Distributions to attentive supported organizations to which the organization is responsive (provide details in **Part VI**). See instructions.	
9 Distributable amount for 2019 from Section C, line 6	
10 Line 8 amount divided by line 9 amount	

Section E - Distribution Allocations (see instructions)	(i) **Excess Distributions**	(ii) **Underdistributions Pre-2019**	(iii) **Distributable Amount for 2019**
1 Distributable amount for 2019 from Section C, line 6			
2 Underdistributions, if any, for years prior to 2019 (reasonable cause required- explain in **Part VI**). See instructions.			
3 Excess distributions carryover, if any, to 2019			
a From 2014			
b From 2015			
c From 2016			
d From 2017			
e From 2018			
f **Total** of lines 3a through e			
g Applied to underdistributions of prior years			
h Applied to 2019 distributable amount			
i Carryover from 2014 not applied (see instructions)			
j Remainder. Subtract lines 3g, 3h, and 3i from 3f.			
4 Distributions for 2019 from Section D, line 7: $			
a Applied to underdistributions of prior years			
b Applied to 2019 distributable amount			
c Remainder. Subtract lines 4a and 4b from 4.			
5 Remaining underdistributions for years prior to 2019, if any. Subtract lines 3g and 4a from line 2. For result greater than zero, explain in **Part VI**. See instructions.			
6 Remaining underdistributions for 2019. Subtract lines 3h and 4b from line 1. For result greater than zero, explain in **Part VI**. See instructions.			
7 **Excess distributions carryover to 2020.** Add lines 3j and 4c.			
8 Breakdown of line 7:			
a Excess from 2015			
b Excess from 2016			
c Excess from 2017			
d Excess from 2018			
e Excess from 2019			

Schedule A (Form 990 or 990-EZ) 2019

932027 09-25-19

Schedule A (Form 990 or 990-EZ) 2019 NATIONAL CONSUMER LAW CENTER, INC. 04-2488502 Page 8

Part VI **Supplemental Information.** Provide the explanations required by Part II, line 10; Part II, line 17a or 17b; Part III, line 12; Part IV, Section A, lines 1, 2, 3b, 3c, 4b, 4c, 5a, 6, 9a, 9b, 9c, 11a, 11b, and 11c; Part IV, Section B, lines 1 and 2; Part IV, Section C, line 1; Part IV, Section D, lines 2 and 3; Part IV, Section E, lines 1c, 2a, 2b, 3a, and 3b; Part V, line 1; Part V, Section B, line 1e; Part V, Section D, lines 5, 6, and 8; and Part V, Section E, lines 2, 5, and 6. Also complete this part for any additional information. (See instructions.)

SCHEDULE C
(Form 990 or 990-EZ)

Department of the Treasury
Internal Revenue Service

Political Campaign and Lobbying Activities

For Organizations Exempt From Income Tax Under section 501(c) and section 527

▶ Complete if the organization is described below. ▶ Attach to Form 990 or Form 990-EZ.

▶ Go to www.irs.gov/Form990 for instructions and the latest information.

OMB No. 1545-0047

2019

Open to Public Inspection

If the organization answered "Yes," on Form 990, Part IV, line 3, or Form 990-EZ, Part V, line 46 (Political Campaign Activities), then
- Section 501(c)(3) organizations: Complete Parts I-A and B. Do not complete Part I-C.
- Section 501(c) (other than section 501(c)(3)) organizations: Complete Parts I-A and C below. Do not complete Part I-B.
- Section 527 organizations: Complete Part I-A only.

If the organization answered "Yes," on Form 990, Part IV, line 4, or Form 990-EZ, Part VI, line 47 (Lobbying Activities), then
- Section 501(c)(3) organizations that have filed Form 5768 (election under section 501(h)): Complete Part II-A. Do not complete Part II-B.
- Section 501(c)(3) organizations that have NOT filed Form 5768 (election under section 501(h)): Complete Part II-B. Do not complete Part II-A.

If the organization answered "Yes," on Form 990, Part IV, line 5 (Proxy Tax) (see separate instructions) or Form 990-EZ, Part V, line 35c (Proxy Tax) (see separate instructions), then
- Section 501(c)(4), (5), or (6) organizations: Complete Part III.

Name of organization	Employer identification number
NATIONAL CONSUMER LAW CENTER, INC.	04-2488502

Part I-A Complete if the organization is exempt under section 501(c) or is a section 527 organization.

1 Provide a description of the organization's direct and indirect political campaign activities in Part IV.
2 Political campaign activity expenditures ▶ $ ______
3 Volunteer hours for political campaign activities ______

Part I-B Complete if the organization is exempt under section 501(c)(3).

1 Enter the amount of any excise tax incurred by the organization under section 4955 ▶ $ ______
2 Enter the amount of any excise tax incurred by organization managers under section 4955 ▶ $ ______
3 If the organization incurred a section 4955 tax, did it file Form 4720 for this year? ☐ Yes ☐ No
4a Was a correction made? ☐ Yes ☐ No
b If "Yes," describe in Part IV.

Part I-C Complete if the organization is exempt under section 501(c), except section 501(c)(3).

1 Enter the amount directly expended by the filing organization for section 527 exempt function activities ▶ $ ______
2 Enter the amount of the filing organization's funds contributed to other organizations for section 527 exempt function activities ▶ $ ______
3 Total exempt function expenditures. Add lines 1 and 2. Enter here and on Form 1120-POL, line 17b ▶ $ ______
4 Did the filing organization file **Form 1120-POL** for this year? ☐ Yes ☐ No
5 Enter the names, addresses and employer identification number (EIN) of all section 527 political organizations to which the filing organization made payments. For each organization listed, enter the amount paid from the filing organization's funds. Also enter the amount of political contributions received that were promptly and directly delivered to a separate political organization, such as a separate segregated fund or a political action committee (PAC). If additional space is needed, provide information in Part IV.

(a) Name	(b) Address	(c) EIN	(d) Amount paid from filing organization's funds. If none, enter -0-.	(e) Amount of political contributions received and promptly and directly delivered to a separate political organization. If none, enter -0-.

For Paperwork Reduction Act Notice, see the Instructions for Form 990 or 990-EZ. **Schedule C (Form 990 or 990-EZ) 2019**

LHA

932041 11-26-19

Schedule C (Form 990 or 990-EZ) 2019 NATIONAL CONSUMER LAW CENTER, INC. 04-2488502 Page 2

Part II-A Complete if the organization is exempt under section 501(c)(3) and filed Form 5768 (election under section 501(h)).

A Check ▶ ☐ if the filing organization belongs to an affiliated group (and list in Part IV each affiliated group member's name, address, EIN, expenses, and share of excess lobbying expenditures).

B Check ▶ ☐ if the filing organization checked box A and "limited control" provisions apply.

Limits on Lobbying Expenditures (The term "expenditures" means amounts paid or incurred.)	(a) Filing organization's totals	(b) Affiliated group totals
1a Total lobbying expenditures to influence public opinion (grassroots lobbying)	1,640.	
b Total lobbying expenditures to influence a legislative body (direct lobbying)	95,683.	
c Total lobbying expenditures (add lines 1a and 1b)	97,323.	
d Other exempt purpose expenditures	9,792,378.	
e Total exempt purpose expenditures (add lines 1c and 1d)	9,889,701.	
f Lobbying nontaxable amount. Enter the amount from the following table in both columns.	644,485.	

If the amount on line 1e, column (a) or (b) is:	The lobbying nontaxable amount is:
Not over $500,000	20% of the amount on line 1e.
Over $500,000 but not over $1,000,000	$100,000 plus 15% of the excess over $500,000.
Over $1,000,000 but not over $1,500,000	$175,000 plus 10% of the excess over $1,000,000.
Over $1,500,000 but not over $17,000,000	$225,000 plus 5% of the excess over $1,500,000.
Over $17,000,000	$1,000,000.

	(a)	(b)
g Grassroots nontaxable amount (enter 25% of line 1f)	161,121.	
h Subtract line 1g from line 1a. If zero or less, enter -0-	0.	
i Subtract line 1f from line 1c. If zero or less, enter -0-	0.	
j If there is an amount other than zero on either line 1h or line 1i, did the organization file Form 4720 reporting section 4911 tax for this year?	☐ Yes	☐ No

4-Year Averaging Period Under Section 501(h)

(Some organizations that made a section 501(h) election do not have to complete all of the five columns below. See the separate instructions for lines 2a through 2f.)

Lobbying Expenditures During 4-Year Averaging Period

Calendar year (or fiscal year beginning in)	(a) 2016	(b) 2017	(c) 2018	(d) 2019	(e) Total
2a Lobbying nontaxable amount	554,718.	568,256.	602,403.	644,485.	2,369,862.
b Lobbying ceiling amount (150% of line 2a, column(e))					3,554,793.
c Total lobbying expenditures	10,624.	118,576.	85,380.	97,323.	311,903.
d Grassroots nontaxable amount	138,680.	142,064.	150,601.	161,121.	592,466.
e Grassroots ceiling amount (150% of line 2d, column (e))					888,699.
f Grassroots lobbying expenditures	823.	42,890.	4,925.	1,640.	50,278.

Schedule C (Form 990 or 990-EZ) 2019

932042 11-26-19

Schedule C (Form 990 or 990-EZ) 2019 NATIONAL CONSUMER LAW CENTER, INC. 04-2488502 Page 3

Part II-B **Complete if the organization is exempt under section 501(c)(3) and has NOT filed Form 5768 (election under section 501(h)).**

For each "Yes" response on lines 1a through 1i below, provide in Part IV a detailed description of the lobbying activity.	(a) Yes	(a) No	(b) Amount
1 During the year, did the filing organization attempt to influence foreign, national, state, or local legislation, including any attempt to influence public opinion on a legislative matter or referendum, through the use of:			
a Volunteers?			
b Paid staff or management (include compensation in expenses reported on lines 1c through 1i)?			
c Media advertisements?			
d Mailings to members, legislators, or the public?			
e Publications, or published or broadcast statements?			
f Grants to other organizations for lobbying purposes?			
g Direct contact with legislators, their staffs, government officials, or a legislative body?			
h Rallies, demonstrations, seminars, conventions, speeches, lectures, or any similar means?			
i Other activities?			
j Total. Add lines 1c through 1i			
2a Did the activities in line 1 cause the organization to be not described in section 501(c)(3)?			
b If "Yes," enter the amount of any tax incurred under section 4912			
c If "Yes," enter the amount of any tax incurred by organization managers under section 4912			
d If the filing organization incurred a section 4912 tax, did it file Form 4720 for this year?			

Part III-A **Complete if the organization is exempt under section 501(c)(4), section 501(c)(5), or section 501(c)(6).**

		Yes	No
1 Were substantially all (90% or more) dues received nondeductible by members?	1		
2 Did the organization make only in-house lobbying expenditures of $2,000 or less?	2		
3 Did the organization agree to carry over lobbying and political campaign activity expenditures from the prior year?	3		

Part III-B **Complete if the organization is exempt under section 501(c)(4), section 501(c)(5), or section 501(c)(6) and if either (a) BOTH Part III-A, lines 1 and 2, are answered "No" OR (b) Part III-A, line 3, is answered "Yes."**

1 Dues, assessments and similar amounts from members	1	
2 Section 162(e) nondeductible lobbying and political expenditures (**do not include amounts of political expenses for which the section 527(f) tax was paid).**		
a Current year	2a	
b Carryover from last year	2b	
c Total	2c	
3 Aggregate amount reported in section 6033(e)(1)(A) notices of nondeductible section 162(e) dues	3	
4 If notices were sent and the amount on line 2c exceeds the amount on line 3, what portion of the excess does the organization agree to carryover to the reasonable estimate of nondeductible lobbying and political expenditure next year?	4	
5 Taxable amount of lobbying and political expenditures (see instructions)	5	

Part IV **Supplemental Information**

Provide the descriptions required for Part I-A, line 1; Part I-B, line 4; Part I-C, line 5; Part II-A (affiliated group list); Part II-A, lines 1 and 2 (see instructions); and Part II-B, line 1. Also, complete this part for any additional information.

Schedule C (Form 990 or 990-EZ) 2019

932043 11-26-19

SCHEDULE D (Form 990)

Department of the Treasury
Internal Revenue Service

Supplemental Financial Statements

▶ Complete if the organization answered "Yes" on Form 990, Part IV, line 6, 7, 8, 9, 10, 11a, 11b, 11c, 11d, 11e, 11f, 12a, or 12b.
▶ Attach to Form 990.
▶Go to www.irs.gov/Form990 for instructions and the latest information.

OMB No. 1545-0047
2019
Open to Public Inspection

Name of the organization: NATIONAL CONSUMER LAW CENTER, INC.

Employer identification number: 04-2488502

Part I **Organizations Maintaining Donor Advised Funds or Other Similar Funds or Accounts.** Complete if the organization answered "Yes" on Form 990, Part IV, line 6.

		(a) Donor advised funds	(b) Funds and other accounts
1	Total number at end of year		
2	Aggregate value of contributions to (during year)		
3	Aggregate value of grants from (during year)		
4	Aggregate value at end of year		

5 Did the organization inform all donors and donor advisors in writing that the assets held in donor advised funds are the organization's property, subject to the organization's exclusive legal control? ☐ Yes ☐ No

6 Did the organization inform all grantees, donors, and donor advisors in writing that grant funds can be used only for charitable purposes and not for the benefit of the donor or donor advisor, or for any other purpose conferring impermissible private benefit? ☐ Yes ☐ No

Part II **Conservation Easements.** Complete if the organization answered "Yes" on Form 990, Part IV, line 7.

1 Purpose(s) of conservation easements held by the organization (check all that apply).
- ☐ Preservation of land for public use (for example, recreation or education)
- ☐ Protection of natural habitat
- ☐ Preservation of open space
- ☐ Preservation of a historically important land area
- ☐ Preservation of a certified historic structure

2 Complete lines 2a through 2d if the organization held a qualified conservation contribution in the form of a conservation easement on the last day of the tax year.

			Held at the End of the Tax Year
a	Total number of conservation easements	2a	
b	Total acreage restricted by conservation easements	2b	
c	Number of conservation easements on a certified historic structure included in (a)	2c	
d	Number of conservation easements included in (c) acquired after 7/25/06, and not on a historic structure listed in the National Register	2d	

3 Number of conservation easements modified, transferred, released, extinguished, or terminated by the organization during the tax year ▶ ______

4 Number of states where property subject to conservation easement is located ▶ ______

5 Does the organization have a written policy regarding the periodic monitoring, inspection, handling of violations, and enforcement of the conservation easements it holds? ☐ Yes ☐ No

6 Staff and volunteer hours devoted to monitoring, inspecting, handling of violations, and enforcing conservation easements during the year ▶ ______

7 Amount of expenses incurred in monitoring, inspecting, handling of violations, and enforcing conservation easements during the year ▶ $ ______

8 Does each conservation easement reported on line 2(d) above satisfy the requirements of section 170(h)(4)(B)(i) and section 170(h)(4)(B)(ii)? ☐ Yes ☐ No

9 In Part XIII, describe how the organization reports conservation easements in its revenue and expense statement and balance sheet, and include, if applicable, the text of the footnote to the organization's financial statements that describes the organization's accounting for conservation easements.

Part III **Organizations Maintaining Collections of Art, Historical Treasures, or Other Similar Assets.** Complete if the organization answered "Yes" on Form 990, Part IV, line 8.

1a If the organization elected, as permitted under FASB ASC 958, not to report in its revenue statement and balance sheet works of art, historical treasures, or other similar assets held for public exhibition, education, or research in furtherance of public service, provide in Part XIII the text of the footnote to its financial statements that describes these items.

b If the organization elected, as permitted under FASB ASC 958, to report in its revenue statement and balance sheet works of art, historical treasures, or other similar assets held for public exhibition, education, or research in furtherance of public service, provide the following amounts relating to these items:

(i) Revenue included on Form 990, Part VIII, line 1 ▶ $ ______

(ii) Assets included in Form 990, Part X ▶ $ ______

2 If the organization received or held works of art, historical treasures, or other similar assets for financial gain, provide the following amounts required to be reported under FASB ASC 958 relating to these items:

a Revenue included on Form 990, Part VIII, line 1 ▶ $ ______

b Assets included in Form 990, Part X ▶ $ ______

LHA **For Paperwork Reduction Act Notice, see the Instructions for Form 990.** **Schedule D (Form 990) 2019**

932051 10-02-19

Schedule D (Form 990) 2019 NATIONAL CONSUMER LAW CENTER, INC. 04-2488502 Page 2

Part III Organizations Maintaining Collections of Art, Historical Treasures, or Other Similar Assets *(continued)*

3 Using the organization's acquisition, accession, and other records, check any of the following that make significant use of its collection items (check all that apply):

- a ☐ Public exhibition
- b ☐ Scholarly research
- c ☐ Preservation for future generations
- d ☐ Loan or exchange program
- e ☐ Other

4 Provide a description of the organization's collections and explain how they further the organization's exempt purpose in Part XIII.

5 During the year, did the organization solicit or receive donations of art, historical treasures, or other similar assets to be sold to raise funds rather than to be maintained as part of the organization's collection? ☐ Yes ☐ No

Part IV Escrow and Custodial Arrangements. Complete if the organization answered "Yes" on Form 990, Part IV, line 9, or reported an amount on Form 990, Part X, line 21.

1a Is the organization an agent, trustee, custodian or other intermediary for contributions or other assets not included on Form 990, Part X? ☐ Yes ☐ No

b If "Yes," explain the arrangement in Part XIII and complete the following table:

		Amount
c Beginning balance	1c	
d Additions during the year	1d	
e Distributions during the year	1e	
f Ending balance	1f	

2a Did the organization include an amount on Form 990, Part X, line 21, for escrow or custodial account liability? ☐ Yes ☐ No

b If "Yes," explain the arrangement in Part XIII. Check here if the explanation has been provided on Part XIII ☐

Part V Endowment Funds. Complete if the organization answered "Yes" on Form 990, Part IV, line 10.

	(a) Current year	(b) Prior year	(c) Two years back	(d) Three years back	(e) Four years back
1a Beginning of year balance	8,672,626.	8,792,488.	5,765,455.	5,088,931.	5,075,000.
b Contributions	146,938.	8,332.	2,582,446.	500,000.	251,000.
c Net investment earnings, gains, and losses	1,096,206.	-128,194.	444,587.	176,524.	-237,069.
d Grants or scholarships					
e Other expenditures for facilities and programs					
f Administrative expenses					
g End of year balance	9,915,770.	8,672,626.	8,792,488.	5,765,455.	5,088,931.

2 Provide the estimated percentage of the current year end balance (line 1g, column (a)) held as:

a Board designated or quasi-endowment ▶ 89.60 %

b Permanent endowment ▶ %

c Term endowment ▶ 10.40 %

The percentages on lines 2a, 2b, and 2c should equal 100%.

3a Are there endowment funds not in the possession of the organization that are held and administered for the organization by:

		Yes	No
(i) Unrelated organizations	3a(i)		X
(ii) Related organizations	3a(ii)		X
b If "Yes" on line 3a(ii), are the related organizations listed as required on Schedule R?	3b		

4 Describe in Part XIII the intended uses of the organization's endowment funds.

Part VI Land, Buildings, and Equipment.

Complete if the organization answered "Yes" on Form 990, Part IV, line 11a. See Form 990, Part X, line 10.

Description of property	(a) Cost or other basis (investment)	(b) Cost or other basis (other)	(c) Accumulated depreciation	(d) Book value
1a Land				
b Buildings				
c Leasehold improvements		220,765.	101,360.	119,405.
d Equipment		740,792.	658,005.	82,787.
e Other				

Total. Add lines 1a through 1e. *(Column (d) must equal Form 990, Part X, column (B), line 10c.)* ▶ 202,192.

Schedule D (Form 990) 2019

932052 10-02-19

Schedule D (Form 990) 2019 NATIONAL CONSUMER LAW CENTER, INC. 04-2488502 Page 3

Part VII Investments - Other Securities.

Complete if the organization answered "Yes" on Form 990, Part IV, line 11b. See Form 990, Part X, line 12.

(a) Description of security or category (including name of security)	(b) Book value	(c) Method of valuation: Cost or end-of-year market value
(1) Financial derivatives		
(2) Closely held equity interests		
(3) Other		
(A)		
(B)		
(C)		
(D)		
(E)		
(F)		
(G)		
(H)		
Total. (Col. (b) must equal Form 990, Part X, col. (B) line 12.) ▶		

Part VIII Investments - Program Related.

Complete if the organization answered "Yes" on Form 990, Part IV, line 11c. See Form 990, Part X, line 13.

(a) Description of investment	(b) Book value	(c) Method of valuation: Cost or end-of-year market value
(1)		
(2)		
(3)		
(4)		
(5)		
(6)		
(7)		
(8)		
(9)		
Total. (Col. (b) must equal Form 990, Part X, col. (B) line 13.) ▶		

Part IX Other Assets.

Complete if the organization answered "Yes" on Form 990, Part IV, line 11d. See Form 990, Part X, line 15.

(a) Description	(b) Book value
(1)	
(2)	
(3)	
(4)	
(5)	
(6)	
(7)	
(8)	
(9)	
Total. *(Column (b) must equal Form 990, Part X, col. (B) line 15.)* ▶	

Part X Other Liabilities.

Complete if the organization answered "Yes" on Form 990, Part IV, line 11e or 11f. See Form 990, Part X, line 25.

1. (a) Description of liability	(b) Book value
(1) Federal income taxes	
(2)	
(3)	
(4)	
(5)	
(6)	
(7)	
(8)	
(9)	
Total. *(Column (b) must equal Form 990, Part X, col. (B) line 25.)* ▶	

2. Liability for uncertain tax positions. In Part XIII, provide the text of the footnote to the organization's financial statements that reports the organization's liability for uncertain tax positions under FASB ASC 740. Check here if the text of the footnote has been provided in Part XIII [X]

Schedule D (Form 990) 2019

932053 10-02-19

Schedule D (Form 990) 2019 NATIONAL CONSUMER LAW CENTER, INC. 04-2488502 Page 4

Part XI Reconciliation of Revenue per Audited Financial Statements With Revenue per Return.

Complete if the organization answered "Yes" on Form 990, Part IV, line 12a.

1	Total revenue, gains, and other support per audited financial statements			1	
2	Amounts included on line 1 but not on Form 990, Part VIII, line 12:				
a	Net unrealized gains (losses) on investments	2a			
b	Donated services and use of facilities	2b			
c	Recoveries of prior year grants	2c			
d	Other (Describe in Part XIII.)	2d			
e	Add lines **2a** through **2d**			2e	
3	Subtract line **2e** from line **1**			3	
4	Amounts included on Form 990, Part VIII, line 12, but not on line 1:				
a	Investment expenses not included on Form 990, Part VIII, line 7b	4a			
b	Other (Describe in Part XIII.)	4b			
c	Add lines **4a** and **4b**			4c	
5	Total revenue. Add lines **3** and **4c.** *(This must equal Form 990, Part I, line 12.)*			5	

Part XII Reconciliation of Expenses per Audited Financial Statements With Expenses per Return.

Complete if the organization answered "Yes" on Form 990, Part IV, line 12a.

1	Total expenses and losses per audited financial statements			1	
2	Amounts included on line 1 but not on Form 990, Part IX, line 25:				
a	Donated services and use of facilities	2a			
b	Prior year adjustments	2b			
c	Other losses	2c			
d	Other (Describe in Part XIII.)	2d			
e	Add lines **2a** through **2d**			2e	
3	Subtract line **2e** from line **1**			3	
4	Amounts included on Form 990, Part IX, line 25, but not on line 1:				
a	Investment expenses not included on Form 990, Part VIII, line 7b	4a			
b	Other (Describe in Part XIII.)	4b			
c	Add lines **4a** and **4b**			4c	
5	Total expenses. Add lines **3** and **4c.** *(This must equal Form 990, Part I, line 18.)*			5	

Part XIII Supplemental Information.

Provide the descriptions required for Part II, lines 3, 5, and 9; Part III, lines 1a and 4; Part IV, lines 1b and 2b; Part V, line 4; Part X, line 2; Part XI, lines 2d and 4b; and Part XII, lines 2d and 4b. Also complete this part to provide any additional information.

PART X, LINE 2:

THE AGENCY ACCOUNTS FOR UNCERTAINTY IN INCOME TAXES IN ACCORDANCE WITH ASC TOPIC, INCOME TAXES. THIS STANDARD CLARIFIES THE ACCOUNTING FOR UNCERTAINTY IN TAX POSITIONS AND PRESCRIBES A RECOGNITION THRESHOLD AND MEASUREMENT ATTRIBUTE FOR THE CONSOLIDATED FINANCIAL STATEMENTS REGARDING A TAX POSITION TAKEN OR EXPECTED TO BE TAKEN IN A TAX RETURN. THE AGENCY HAS DETERMINED THAT THERE ARE NO UNCERTAIN TAX POSITIONS WHICH QUALIFY FOR EITHER RECOGNITION OR DISCLOSURE IN THE CONSOLIDATED FINANCIAL STATEMENTS AT DECEMBER 31, 2019.

932054 10-02-19 Schedule D (Form 990) 2019

Schedule D (Form 990) 2019 NATIONAL CONSUMER LAW CENTER, INC. 04-2488502 Page 5

Part XIII Supplemental Information *(continued)*

SCHEDULE G (Form 990 or 990-EZ)

Department of the Treasury
Internal Revenue Service

Supplemental Information Regarding Fundraising or Gaming Activities

Complete if the organization answered "Yes" on Form 990, Part IV, line 17, 18, or 19, or if the organization entered more than $15,000 on Form 990-EZ, line 6a.

▶ Attach to Form 990 or Form 990-EZ.

▶ Go to **www.irs.gov/Form990 for instructions and the latest information.**

OMB No. 1545-0047

2019

Open to Public Inspection

Name of the organization: NATIONAL CONSUMER LAW CENTER, INC.

Employer identification number: 04-2488502

Part I **Fundraising Activities.** Complete if the organization answered "Yes" on Form 990, Part IV, line 17. Form 990-EZ filers are not required to complete this part.

1 Indicate whether the organization raised funds through any of the following activities. Check all that apply.

a ☐ Mail solicitations
b ☐ Internet and email solicitations
c ☐ Phone solicitations
d ☐ In-person solicitations
e ☐ Solicitation of non-government grants
f ☐ Solicitation of government grants
g ☐ Special fundraising events

2 a Did the organization have a written or oral agreement with any individual (including officers, directors, trustees, or key employees listed in Form 990, Part VII) or entity in connection with professional fundraising services? ☐ **Yes** ☐ **No**

b If "Yes," list the 10 highest paid individuals or entities (fundraisers) pursuant to agreements under which the fundraiser is to be compensated at least $5,000 by the organization.

(i) Name and address of individual or entity (fundraiser)	(ii) Activity	(iii) Did fundraiser have custody or control of contributions? Yes	No	(iv) Gross receipts from activity	(v) Amount paid to (or retained by) fundraiser listed in col. (i)	(vi) Amount paid to (or retained by) organization
Total ▶						

3 List all states in which the organization is registered or licensed to solicit contributions or has been notified it is exempt from registration or licensing.

LHA **For Paperwork Reduction Act Notice, see the Instructions for Form 990 or 990-EZ.** **Schedule G (Form 990 or 990-EZ) 2019**

932081 09-11-19

Schedule G (Form 990 or 990-EZ) 2019 NATIONAL CONSUMER LAW CENTER, INC. 04-2488502 Page 2

Part II **Fundraising Events.** Complete if the organization answered "Yes" on Form 990, Part IV, line 18, or reported more than $15,000 of fundraising event contributions and gross income on Form 990-EZ, lines 1 and 6b. List events with gross receipts greater than $5,000.

		(a) Event #1 50TH ANNIVERSARY GALA (event type)	(b) Event #2 (event type)	(c) Other events NONE (total number)	(d) Total events (add col. (a) through col. (c))
Revenue	1 Gross receipts	217,639.			217,639.
	2 Less: Contributions	114,201.			114,201.
	3 Gross income (line 1 minus line 2)	103,438.			103,438.
Direct Expenses	4 Cash prizes				
	5 Noncash prizes				
	6 Rent/facility costs				
	7 Food and beverages	112,456.			112,456.
	8 Entertainment	4,000.			4,000.
	9 Other direct expenses	6,661.			6,661.
	10 Direct expense summary. Add lines 4 through 9 in column (d) ▶				123,117.
	11 Net income summary. Subtract line 10 from line 3, column (d) ▶				-19,679.

Part III **Gaming.** Complete if the organization answered "Yes" on Form 990, Part IV, line 19, or reported more than $15,000 on Form 990-EZ, line 6a.

		(a) Bingo	(b) Pull tabs/instant bingo/progressive bingo	(c) Other gaming	(d) Total gaming (add col. (a) through col. (c))
Revenue	1 Gross revenue				
Direct Expenses	2 Cash prizes				
	3 Noncash prizes				
	4 Rent/facility costs				
	5 Other direct expenses				
	6 Volunteer labor	☐ Yes ____ % ☐ No	☐ Yes ____ % ☐ No	☐ Yes ____ % ☐ No	
	7 Direct expense summary. Add lines 2 through 5 in column (d) ▶				
	8 Net gaming income summary. Subtract line 7 from line 1, column (d) ▶				

9 Enter the state(s) in which the organization conducts gaming activities: ____

a Is the organization licensed to conduct gaming activities in each of these states? ☐ Yes ☐ No

b If "No," explain: ____

10a Were any of the organization's gaming licenses revoked, suspended, or terminated during the tax year? ☐ Yes ☐ No

b If "Yes," explain: ____

932082 09-11-19 Schedule G (Form 990 or 990-EZ) 2019

Schedule G (Form 990 or 990-EZ) 2019 NATIONAL CONSUMER LAW CENTER, INC. 04-2488502 Page 3

11 Does the organization conduct gaming activities with nonmembers? ☐ Yes ☐ No

12 Is the organization a grantor, beneficiary or trustee of a trust, or a member of a partnership or other entity formed to administer charitable gaming? ☐ Yes ☐ No

13 Indicate the percentage of gaming activity conducted in:

a The organization's facility 13a %

b An outside facility 13b %

14 Enter the name and address of the person who prepares the organization's gaming/special events books and records:

Name ▶

Address ▶

15a Does the organization have a contract with a third party from whom the organization receives gaming revenue? ☐ Yes ☐ No

b If "Yes," enter the amount of gaming revenue received by the organization ▶ $ ______ and the amount of gaming revenue retained by the third party ▶ $ ______

c If "Yes," enter name and address of the third party:

Name ▶

Address ▶

16 Gaming manager information:

Name ▶

Gaming manager compensation ▶ $ ______

Description of services provided ▶

☐ Director/officer ☐ Employee ☐ Independent contractor

17 Mandatory distributions:

a Is the organization required under state law to make charitable distributions from the gaming proceeds to retain the state gaming license? ☐ Yes ☐ No

b Enter the amount of distributions required under state law to be distributed to other exempt organizations or spent in the organization's own exempt activities during the tax year ▶ $

Part IV Supplemental Information. Provide the explanations required by Part I, line 2b, columns (iii) and (v); and Part III, lines 9, 9b, 10b, 15b, 15c, 16, and 17b, as applicable. Also provide any additional information. See instructions.

932083 09-11-19 Schedule G (Form 990 or 990-EZ) 2019

Schedule G (Form 990 or 990-EZ) NATIONAL CONSUMER LAW CENTER, INC. 04-2488502 Page 4

Part IV Supplemental Information *(continued)*

SCHEDULE J (Form 990)

Department of the Treasury
Internal Revenue Service

Compensation Information

For certain Officers, Directors, Trustees, Key Employees, and Highest Compensated Employees
▶ Complete if the organization answered "Yes" on Form 990, Part IV, line 23.
▶ Attach to Form 990.
▶ Go to www.irs.gov/Form990 for instructions and the latest information.

OMB No. 1545-0047
2019
Open to Public Inspection

Name of the organization: NATIONAL CONSUMER LAW CENTER, INC.
Employer identification number: 04-2488502

Part I Questions Regarding Compensation

			Yes	No
1a	Check the appropriate box(es) if the organization provided any of the following to or for a person listed on Form 990, Part VII, Section A, line 1a. Complete Part III to provide any relevant information regarding these items. ☐ First-class or charter travel ☐ Housing allowance or residence for personal use ☐ Travel for companions ☐ Payments for business use of personal residence ☐ Tax indemnification and gross-up payments ☐ Health or social club dues or initiation fees ☐ Discretionary spending account ☐ Personal services (such as maid, chauffeur, chef)			
b	If any of the boxes on line 1a are checked, did the organization follow a written policy regarding payment or reimbursement or provision of all of the expenses described above? If "No," complete Part III to explain	1b		
2	Did the organization require substantiation prior to reimbursing or allowing expenses incurred by all directors, trustees, and officers, including the CEO/Executive Director, regarding the items checked on line 1a?	2		
3	Indicate which, if any, of the following the organization used to establish the compensation of the organization's CEO/Executive Director. Check all that apply. Do not check any boxes for methods used by a related organization to establish compensation of the CEO/Executive Director, but explain in Part III. ☐ Compensation committee ☐ Written employment contract ☒ Independent compensation consultant ☒ Compensation survey or study ☐ Form 990 of other organizations ☒ Approval by the board or compensation committee			
4	During the year, did any person listed on Form 990, Part VII, Section A, line 1a, with respect to the filing organization or a related organization:			
a	Receive a severance payment or change-of-control payment?	4a		X
b	Participate in, or receive payment from, a supplemental nonqualified retirement plan?	4b		X
c	Participate in, or receive payment from, an equity-based compensation arrangement?	4c		X
	If "Yes" to any of lines 4a-c, list the persons and provide the applicable amounts for each item in Part III.			
	Only section 501(c)(3), 501(c)(4), and 501(c)(29) organizations must complete lines 5-9.			
5	For persons listed on Form 990, Part VII, Section A, line 1a, did the organization pay or accrue any compensation contingent on the revenues of:			
a	The organization?	5a		X
b	Any related organization?	5b		X
	If "Yes" on line 5a or 5b, describe in Part III.			
6	For persons listed on Form 990, Part VII, Section A, line 1a, did the organization pay or accrue any compensation contingent on the net earnings of:			
a	The organization?	6a		X
b	Any related organization?	6b		X
	If "Yes" on line 6a or 6b, describe in Part III.			
7	For persons listed on Form 990, Part VII, Section A, line 1a, did the organization provide any nonfixed payments not described on lines 5 and 6? If "Yes," describe in Part III	7		X
8	Were any amounts reported on Form 990, Part VII, paid or accrued pursuant to a contract that was subject to the initial contract exception described in Regulations section 53.4958-4(a)(3)? If "Yes," describe in Part III	8		X
9	If "Yes" on line 8, did the organization also follow the rebuttable presumption procedure described in Regulations section 53.4958-6(c)?	9		

LHA **For Paperwork Reduction Act Notice, see the Instructions for Form 990.** **Schedule J (Form 990) 2019**

932111 10-21-19

Schedule J (Form 990) 2019 NATIONAL CONSUMER LAW CENTER, INC. 04-2488502 Page 2

Part II Officers, Directors, Trustees, Key Employees, and Highest Compensated Employees. Use duplicate copies if additional space is needed.

For each individual whose compensation must be reported on Schedule J, report compensation from the organization on row (i) and from related organizations, described in the instructions, on row (ii). Do not list any individuals that aren't listed on Form 990, Part VII.

Note: The sum of columns (B)(i)-(iii) for each listed individual must equal the total amount of Form 990, Part VII, Section A, line 1a, applicable column (D) and (E) amounts for that individual.

(A) Name and Title		(B) Breakdown of W-2 and/or 1099-MISC compensation (i) Base compensation	(ii) Bonus & incentive compensation	(iii) Other reportable compensation	(C) Retirement and other deferred compensation	(D) Nontaxable benefits	(E) Total of columns (B)(i)-(D)	(F) Compensation in column (B) reported as deferred on prior Form 990
(1) RICHARD DUBOIS	(i)	177,482.	0.	0.	6,765.	26,612.	210,859.	0.
EXECUTIVE DIRECTOR	(ii)	0.	0.	0.	0.	0.	0.	0.
(2) MARGOT SAUNDERS	(i)	145,090.	0.	0.	5,290.	26,434.	176,814.	0.
STAFF ATTORNEY	(ii)	0.	0.	0.	0.	0.	0.	0.
(3) GEOFFRY WALSH	(i)	144,636.	0.	0.	4,529.	26,876.	176,041.	0.
STAFF ATTORNEY	(ii)	0.	0.	0.	0.	0.	0.	0.
(4) STUART ROSSMAN	(i)	149,073.	0.	0.	6,107.	19,720.	174,900.	0.
DIRECTOR OF LITIGATION	(ii)	0.	0.	0.	0.	0.	0.	0.
(5) CHARLES DELBAUM	(i)	146,748.	0.	0.	4,886.	19,723.	171,357.	0.
STAFF ATTORNEY	(ii)	0.	0.	0.	0.	0.	0.	0.
(6) CAROLYN CARTER	(i)	149,665.	0.	0.	4,372.	13,183.	167,220.	0.
DEPUTY DIRECTOR	(ii)	0.	0.	0.	0.	0.	0.	0.
(7) MARGARET KOHLER	(i)	127,475.	0.	0.	6,059.	26,646.	160,180.	0.
CHIEF FINANCIAL OFFICER	(ii)	0.	0.	0.	0.	0.	0.	0.
(8) JOHN DONAT	(i)	143,492.	0.	0.	6,087.	9,841.	159,480.	0.
STAFF ATTORNEY	(ii)	0.	0.	0.	0.	0.	0.	0.
(9) STEPHEN HURLEY	(i)	129,147.	0.	0.	3,061.	26,990.	159,198.	0.
CHIEF DEVELOPMENT OFFICER	(ii)	0.	0.	0.	0.	0.	0.	0.
	(i)							
	(ii)							
	(i)							
	(ii)							
	(i)							
	(ii)							
	(i)							
	(ii)							
	(i)							
	(ii)							
	(i)							
	(ii)							
	(i)							
	(ii)							

Schedule J (Form 990) 2019

932112 10-21-19

Schedule J (Form 990) 2019 NATIONAL CONSUMER LAW CENTER, INC. 04-2488502 Page 3

Part III Supplemental Information

Provide the information, explanation, or descriptions required for Part I, lines 1a, 1b, 3, 4a, 4b, 4c, 5a, 5b, 6a, 6b, 7, and 8, and for Part II. Also complete this part for any additional information.

Schedule J (Form 990) 2019

932112 10-21-19

SCHEDULE O (Form 990 or 990-EZ)
Department of the Treasury Internal Revenue Service

Supplemental Information to Form 990 or 990-EZ

Complete to provide information for responses to specific questions on Form 990 or 990-EZ or to provide any additional information.
▶ Attach to Form 990 or 990-EZ.
▶ Go to www.irs.gov/Form990 for the latest information.

OMB No. 1545-0047
2019
Open to Public Inspection

Name of the organization	Employer identification number
NATIONAL CONSUMER LAW CENTER, INC.	04-2488502

FORM 990, PART I, LINE 1, DESCRIPTION OF ORGANIZATION MISSION:
AND ENERGY POLICY TO WORK FOR CONSUMER JUSTICE AND ECONOMIC SECURITY FOR LOW-INCOME AND OTHER DISADVANTAGED PEOPLE. NCLC'S EXPERTISE INCLUDES POLICY ANALYSIS AND ADVOCACY; CONSUMER LAW AND ENERGY PUBLICATIONS; LITIGATION; EXPERT WITNESS SERVICES, AND TRAINING AND ADVICE FOR ADVOCATES. NCLC WORKS WITH NONPROFIT AND LEGAL SERVICES ORGANIZATIONS, PRIVATE ATTORNEYS, POLICYMAKERS, AND FEDERAL AND STATE GOVERNMENT AND COURTS ACROSS THE NATION TO STOP EXPLOITIVE PRACTICES, HELP FINANCIALLY STRESSED FAMILIES BUILD AND RETAIN WEALTH, AND ADVANCE ECONOMIC FAIRNESS.

FORM 990, PART III, LINE 1, DESCRIPTION OF ORGANIZATION MISSION:
CONSUMER LAW AND ENERGY PUBLICATIONS; LITIGATION; EXPERT WITNESS SERVICES, AND TRAINING AND ADVICE FOR ADVOCATES. NCLC WORKS WITH NONPROFIT AND LEGAL SERVICES ORGANIZATIONS, PRIVATE ATTORNEYS, POLICYMAKERS, AND FEDERAL AND STATE GOVERNMENT AND COURTS ACROSS THE NATION TO STOP EXPLOITIVE PRACTICES, HELP FINANCIALLY STRESSED FAMILIES BUILD AND RETAIN WEALTH, AND ADVANCE ECONOMIC FAIRNESS.

SPECIFIC ACHIEVEMENTS IN 2019:

NCLC MARKED ITS 50TH YEAR OF ADVOCACY DURING ITS LARGEST-EVER CONSUMER RIGHTS LITIGATION CONFERENCE (CRLC) NOVEMBER 14-17, 2019 IN BOSTON. THIS ANNUAL EVENT INCLUDED OVER 800 ATTORNEYS AND ADVOCATES WHO GATHERED TO LEARN ABOUT THE LATEST DEVELOPMENTS IN CONSUMER LITIGATION AND INDUSTRY TRENDS.

Schedule O (Form 990 or 990-EZ) (2019) Page 2

Name of the organization NATIONAL CONSUMER LAW CENTER, INC.

Employer identification number 04-2488502

FORM 990, PART III, LINE 4A, PROGRAM SERVICE ACCOMPLISHMENTS:

SPECIFIC ACHIEVEMENTS INCLUDE:

NCLC FOCUSED ON STATE AUTHORITY TO PROTECT DEBTORS BY COORDINATING ADVOCACY AT THE STATE LEVEL AND PROVIDING TECHNICAL EXPERTISE TO STATE ADVOCATES. ASTRONOMIC GROWTH OF THE DEBT BUYER AND COLLECTION INDUSTRIES MAKES LOW INCOME FAMILIES INCREASINGLY VULNERABLE TO SEIZURE OF ESSENTIAL WAGES AND PROPERTY TO PAY THEIR OLDEST DEBTS. IN 2019, ADVOCATES IN CALIFORNIA, COLORADO, AND WASHINGTON SUCCEEDED IN WINNING STRONGER PROTECTIONS FOR DEBTORS' WAGES AND ASSETS WHEN THEY ARE SUED BY DEBT COLLECTORS. WE ALSO ISSUED A SIGNIFICANT ISSUE BRIEF ON THE POTENTIAL BENEFITS AND DANGERS OF ON-LINE SYSTEMS FOR RESOLVING CONSUMER DEBT CLAIMS, A RAPIDLY GROWING AREA. NCLC ALSO PUBLISHED THE REPORT NO FRESH START IN 2019: HOW STATES STILL LET DEBT COLLECTORS PUSH FAMILIES INTO POVERTY -- NO FRESH START, SURVEYING THE EXEMPTION LAWS OF THE 50 STATES, THE DISTRICT OF COLUMBIA, PUERTO RICO, AND THE VIRGIN ISLANDS.

IMPROVED CREDIT REPORTING STANDARDS TO ADDRESS INACCURACIES AND IMPROVE THE FLAWED DISPUTE PROCESS, WERE ESTABLISHED WITH THE PASSAGE OF THE COMPREHENSIVE CREDIT ACT. NCLC HAS LONG ADVOCATED FOR MAJOR REFORMS TO THE CREDIT REPORTING INDUSTRY AND THE RECENT PASSAGE OF THE COMPREHENSIVE CREDIT (CREDIT REPORTING ENHANCEMENT, DISCLOSURE, INNOVATION, AND TRANSPARENCY) ACT OF 2020 (H.R. 3621) BY THE U.S. HOUSE OF REPRESENTATIVES IS AN IMPORTANT STEP TOWARD THESE REFORMS. THE BILL WOULD REDUCE THE PUNITIVE IMPACT OF NEGATIVE INFORMATION BY REDUCING

Schedule O (Form 990 or 990-EZ) (2019) Page 2

Name of the organization NATIONAL CONSUMER LAW CENTER, INC.

Employer identification number 04-2488502

THE TIME PERIOD IT CAN STAY ON A CONSUMER'S CREDIT - A RECOMMENDATION THAT NCLC MADE.

OVERDRAFT FEES WILL EFFECTIVELY BE REMOVED FROM PAYROLL CARDS AND PREPAID CARDS. NCLC PRODUCED NUMEROUS MATERIALS EXPLAINING IMPORTANT NEW PROTECTIONS FOR PREPAID CARDS THAT WE WORKED HARD TO ACHIEVE AND THAT WENT INTO EFFECT APRIL 1, 2019. WE WORKED TO HIGHLIGHT CERTAIN PREPAID CARDS THAT ARE EVADING THE RULES LIMITING OVERDRAFT FEES, BY SPEAKING TO REPORTERS AND HIGHLIGHTING THAT THOSE CARDS ARE MISSING FROM THE NEW PREPAID CARDS DATABASE. NCLC FILED COMMENTS WITH THE CFPB URGING IT NOT TO WEAKEN ITS EXISTING RULES REQUIRING CONSUMER OPT-IN FOR OVERDRAFT FEES AND TO STRENGTHEN THE OVERDRAFT FEE RULES.

REVERSE MORTGAGES: FOLLOWING A MAJOR POLICY SHIFT BY HUD (AND ADVOCATED BY NCLC) AIMED AT HELPING WIDOWS AND WIDOWERS REMAIN IN THEIR HOMES AFTER THE DEATH OF A SPOUSE WHO HAD TAKEN OUT A REVERSE MORTGAGE ON THE HOME, NCLC ATTORNEY SARAH BOLLING MANCINI TESTIFIED BEFORE THE U.S. HOUSE FINANCIAL SERVICES COMMITTEE HOUSING, COMMUNITY DEVELOPMENT, AND INSURANCE SUBCOMMITTEE AT A HEARING ENTITLED "PROTECTING SENIORS: A REVIEW OF THE FHA'S HOME EQUITY CONVERSION MORTGAGE (HECM) PROGRAM." PRIOR TO THE POLICY SHIFT THESE SO-CALLED NON-BORROWING SPOUSES HAD BEEN BLOCKED FROM A FORECLOSURE DEFERRAL PROGRAM BY UNWORKABLE DEADLINES. MANCINI TESTIFIED ABOUT THE IMPORTANCE OF THIS POLICY SHIFT, WHICH WILL BENEFIT MANY VULNERABLE SURVIVING SPOUSES, AND HIGHLIGHTED THE CHALLENGES THAT REMAIN.

DISCRIMINATION IN AUTO SALES AND FINANCING: IN MAY 2019 NCLC ATTORNEY JOHN VAN ALST TESTIFIED BEFORE THE U.S. HOUSE SUBCOMMITTEE ON OVERSIGHT

Schedule O (Form 990 or 990-EZ) (2019) Page 2

Name of the organization NATIONAL CONSUMER LAW CENTER, INC. | Employer identification number 04-2488502

AND INVESTIGATIONS REGARDING DISCRIMINATION ON THE BASIS OF RACE AND NATIONAL ORIGIN IN THE SALE AND FINANCING OF CARS. AND IN APRIL 2019, TIMED TO COINCIDE WITH THIS TESTIMONY, NCLC PUBLISHED AN ISSUE BRIEF DETAILING THE RESEARCH DOCUMENTING DISCRIMINATORY PRACTICES IN AUTO SALES.

FORM 990, PART III, LINE 4B, PROGRAM SERVICE ACCOMPLISHMENTS:

SPECIFIC ACHIEVEMENTS INCLUDE:

PROMOTING ACCESS TO ESSENTIAL UTILITY SERVICES: NCLC WORKED WITH FEDERAL AND STATE POLICYMAKERS, UTILITY COMPANIES, AND ADVOCATES ON POLICIES AND PROGRAMS TO MAINTAIN FAIR AND AFFORDABLE UTILITY SERVICES FOR LOW-INCOME FAMILIES AND WORKED TO ADDRESS SYSTEMATIC PROBLEMS THOSE HOUSEHOLDS (OR THE AGENCIES THAT HELP THEM) ENCOUNTER.

FUEL ASSISTANCE FOR MASSACHUSETTS RESIDENTS: NCLC ASSISTED THE MASSACHUSETTS COMMUNITY ACTION PROGRAM DIRECTORS ASSOCIATION IN THEIR ADVOCACY EFFORTS TO MAKE APPROVAL OF A $30 MILLION INCREASE IN FUEL ASSISTANCE A REALITY FOR LOW INCOME HOUSEHOLDS AFTER THE MASSACHUSETTS LEGISLATURE SENT TO THE GOVERNOR'S DESK A SUPPLEMENTAL BUDGET THAT INCLUDED $30 MILLION FOR FUEL ASSISTANCE ON MARCH 29TH, 2019. ALSO, IN RESPONSE TO NCLC'S REQUEST, BOTH NATIONAL GRID AND EVERSOURCE UTILITIES SENT LETTERS TO THE GOVERNOR URGING HIM TO APPROVE THE $30 MILLION, AND TO ENSURE THAT ALL INCOME-ELIGIBLE HOUSEHOLDS -- WHETHER THEY HEAT WITH OIL, PROPANE, ELECTRICITY OR GAS - WOULD RECEIVE AN INCREASE IN THEIR MAXIMUM BENEFIT LEVELS.

FORM 990, PART III, LINE 4C, PROGRAM SERVICE ACCOMPLISHMENTS:

Schedule O (Form 990 or 990-EZ) (2019) Page 2

Name of the organization: NATIONAL CONSUMER LAW CENTER, INC.

Employer identification number 04-2488502

SPECIFIC ACHIEVEMENTS INCLUDE:

- TO CONTINUE TO ELEVATE THE INTERESTS OF LOW-INCOME STUDENT LOAN BORROWERS AND THEIR FAMILIES, NCLC PROVIDED EXPERTISE TO CONGRESSIONAL STAFF AND POLICYMAKERS, CULMINATING IN FOUR APPEARANCES BEFORE CONGRESSIONAL SUBCOMMITTEES IN 2019. NCLC HAS LONG ADVOCATED FOR AN END TO THE SEIZURE OF THE EARNED INCOME TAX CREDIT (EITC) TO REPAY STUDENT LOANS AS THE (EITC) PROVIDES SUBSTANTIAL SUPPORT TO LOW- AND MODERATE-INCOME WORKING PARENTS AND THEIR FAMILIES. THE STOP EITC AND CHILD TAX CREDIT (CTC) SEIZURES ACT, INTRODUCED IN NOVEMBER 2019, WOULD PROTECT STUDENT LOAN BORROWERS FROM HAVING THEIR EITCS AND CTCS SEIZED TO REPAY THEIR DEFAULTED FEDERAL LOANS. NCLC ORGANIZED A COALITION OF 29 NATIONAL, STATE AND LOCAL CIVIL LEGAL AID, CIVIL RIGHTS, CONSUMER, LABOR, RELIGIOUS, VETERAN, AND PUBLIC INTEREST ORGANIZATIONS TO RAISE AWARENESS ON THIS ISSUE AND EDUCATE POLICYMAKERS AND THE PUBLIC ON THE IMPACT OF THE PROBLEM AND NEED FOR A SOLUTION.

- LIMITS WILL BE PLACED ON THE HARMFUL COLLECTION PRACTICES ASSOCIATED WITH CRIMINAL JUSTICE DEBT, AND PROGRESS MADE IN PROTECTING INDIVIDUALS AND PROVIDING OPPORTUNITIES FOR FRESH STARTS. NCLC'S CONFRONTING CRIMINAL JUSTICE DEBT PROJECT EXPANDED IN 2019 IN ITS CONSULTING, SUPPORT AND COALITION WORK PROVIDING CONSUMER PROTECTION EXPERTISE TO THE COALITION OF ORGANIZATIONS WORKING ON CRIMINAL JUSTICE DEBT ISSUES. NCLC ALSO PUBLISHED TWO REPORTS RELATED TO CRIMINAL JUSTICE DEBT: COMMERCIALIZED (IN)JUSTICE: THE GROWING PROBLEM OF CONSUMER ABUSES PERPETUATED BY COMPANIES PROFITING FROM MASS INCARCERATION AND THE RENT-TO-OWN RACKET: USING CRIMINAL COURTS TO COERCE PAYMENTS FROM VULNERABLE FAMILIES, DETAILING THAT THE DISTRICT OF COLUMBIA AND 47

STATES HAVE LAWS THAT CAN BE USED TO CRIMINALIZE THE FAILURE TO RETURN RENTAL PROPERTY AT THE END OF AN RTO LEASE TERM. NCLC ALSO PUBLISHED A FACT SHEET FOR STATES: WHAT STATES CAN DO: CRIMINAL JUSTICE DEBT AND PRESENTED THE WEBINAR DRIVING WITH DEBT: WHAT ATTORNEYS AND ORGANIZERS CAN DO TO ADDRESS THE PROBLEM OF DRIVER'S LICENSE SUSPENSIONS FOR COURT DEBT.

- PROGRESS WAS MADE IN PROVIDING ACCESS TO CREDIT REPORTS FOR U.S. SERVICE MEMBERS WHEN THE FTC ADOPTED NCLC'S RECOMMENDATION TO REQUIRE THAT SERVICE MEMBERS HAVE ACCESS TO FREE ONLINE CREDIT REPORTS WHEN A SERVICE MEMBER GETS AN ALERT. NCLC CONTINUED ITS ADVOCACY HIGHLIGHTING ONGOING PROBLEMS WITH ERRORS IN BACKGROUND CHECK AND CREDIT REPORTS, ISSUING THE REPORT BROKEN RECORDS REDUX ON DECEMBER 19, 2019 AND ALSO APPEARING, THE SAME DAY, AS PANELISTS (NCLC ATTORNEYS ARIEL NELSON AND CHI CHI WU) AT A JOINT FTC/CFPB WORKSHOP ON ACCURACY IN CONSUMER REPORTING DISCUSSING THE CONSEQUENCES OF ERRORS IN BACKGROUND CHECK AND CREDIT REPORTS FOR CONSUMERS.

- NCLC ALSO RELEASED THE REPORTS: TIME TO STOP RACING CARS: THE ROLE OF RACE AND ETHNICITY IN BUYING AND USING A CAR; AND DON'T ADD INSULT TO INJURY: MEDICAL DEBT & CREDIT REPORTS.

FORM 990, PART VI, SECTION B, LINE 11B:

THE 990 IS SENT BY THE PREPARER VIA EMAIL AND IS REVIEWED AND REVISED BY THE FINANCE COMMITTEE BEFORE IT IS FILED. THE FULL BOARD OF DIRECTORS ALSO RECEIVES A COPY.

FORM 990, PART VI, SECTION B, LINE 12C:

Schedule O (Form 990 or 990-EZ) (2019) Page 2

Name of the organization NATIONAL CONSUMER LAW CENTER, INC.

Employer identification number 04-2488502

EVERY YEAR, BOARD MEMBERS ARE CALLED UPON TO MAKE FULL CONFLICT OF INTEREST DISCLOSURES AT THE BOARD'S ANNUAL MEETING. THE EXECUTIVE DIRECTOR IS RESPONSIBLE FOR PUTTING THIS ITEM ON THE MEETING AGENDA AND THE BOARD SECRETARY RECORDS THE RESULTS IN THE MINUTES.

FORM 990, PART VI, SECTION B, LINE 15:

EVERY 3 YEARS, NCLC CONTRACTS WITH AN OUTSIDE PROFESSIONAL SALARY CONSULTANT FIRM TO DO A SALARY COMPARABILITY STUDY. THE BOARD APPROVES THE RESULTS OF THE STUDY AND SALARIES FOR ALL STAFF (INCLUDING THE EXECUTIVE DIRECTOR AND OTHER KEY EMPLOYEES) ARE SET ACCORDINGLY.

FORM 990, PART VI, LINE 17, LIST OF STATES RECEIVING COPY OF FORM 990:

MA,AK,CA,FL,MD,MI,MS,NY,OR,PA,WI,WA,AR,IL,MN,NJ,OH,UT,VA,CT,DC

FORM 990, PART VI, SECTION C, LINE 19:

THE 990 AND AUDITED FINANCIAL STATEMENTS ARE AVAILABLE TO THE PUBLIC UPON REQUEST.

FORM 990, PART XII, LINE 2C

THIS PROCESS HAS NOT CHANGED FROM THE PRIOR YEAR.

932212 09-06-19 Schedule O (Form 990 or 990-EZ) (2019)

SCHEDULE R (Form 990)

Department of the Treasury Internal Revenue Service

Related Organizations and Unrelated Partnerships

▶ Complete if the organization answered "Yes" on Form 990, Part IV, line 33, 34, 35b, 36, or 37.

▶ Attach to Form 990.

▶ Go to www.irs.gov/Form990 for instructions and the latest information.

OMB No. 1545-0047

2019

Open to Public Inspection

Name of the organization: NATIONAL CONSUMER LAW CENTER, INC.

Employer identification number: 04-2488502

Part I Identification of Disregarded Entities. Complete if the organization answered "Yes" on Form 990, Part IV, line 33.

(a) Name, address, and EIN (if applicable) of disregarded entity	(b) Primary activity	(c) Legal domicile (state or foreign country)	(d) Total income	(e) End-of-year assets	(f) Direct controlling entity

Part II Identification of Related Tax-Exempt Organizations. Complete if the organization answered "Yes" on Form 990, Part IV, line 34, because it had one or more related tax-exempt organizations during the tax year.

(a) Name, address, and EIN of related organization	(b) Primary activity	(c) Legal domicile (state or foreign country)	(d) Exempt Code section	(e) Public charity status (if section 501(c)(3))	(f) Direct controlling entity	(g) Section 512(b)(13) controlled entity? Yes	(g) No
CONSUMER LAW BUILDING CORPORATION - 26-1991555, 7 WINTHROP SQUARE, 4TH FLOOR, BOSTON, MA 02110	TO OWN AND DEVELOP 7 WINTHROP SQUARE	MASSACHUSETTS	501(C)(3)	509(A)(3)	NATIONAL CONSUMER LAW CENTER		X

For Paperwork Reduction Act Notice, see the Instructions for Form 990. Schedule R (Form 990) 2019

932161 09-10-19 LHA

Schedule R (Form 990) 2019 NATIONAL CONSUMER LAW CENTER, INC. 04-2488502 Page 2

Part III Identification of Related Organizations Taxable as a Partnership. Complete if the organization answered "Yes" on Form 990, Part IV, line 34, because it had one or more related organizations treated as a partnership during the tax year.

(a) Name, address, and EIN of related organization	(b) Primary activity	(c) Legal domicile (state or foreign country)	(d) Direct controlling entity	(e) Predominant income (related, unrelated, excluded from tax under sections 512-514)	(f) Share of total income	(g) Share of end-of-year assets	(h) Disproportionate allocations? Yes	(h) No	(i) Code V-UBI amount in box 20 of Schedule K-1 (Form 1065)	(j) General or managing partner? Yes	(j) No	(k) Percentage ownership

Part IV Identification of Related Organizations Taxable as a Corporation or Trust. Complete if the organization answered "Yes" on Form 990, Part IV, line 34, because it had one or more related organizations treated as a corporation or trust during the tax year.

(a) Name, address, and EIN of related organization	(b) Primary activity	(c) Legal domicile (state or foreign country)	(d) Direct controlling entity	(e) Type of entity (C corp, S corp, or trust)	(f) Share of total income	(g) Share of end-of-year assets	(h) Percentage ownership	(i) Section 512(b)(13) controlled entity? Yes	(i) No

932162 09-10-19 Schedule R (Form 990) 2019

Schedule R (Form 990) 2019 NATIONAL CONSUMER LAW CENTER, INC. 04-2488502 Page 3

Part V Transactions With Related Organizations. Complete if the organization answered "Yes" on Form 990, Part IV, line 34, 35b, or 36.

Note: Complete line 1 if any entity is listed in Parts II, III, or IV of this schedule.		Yes	No
1 During the tax year, did the organization engage in any of the following transactions with one or more related organizations listed in Parts II-IV?			
a Receipt of (i) interest, (ii) annuities, (iii) royalties, or (iv) rent from a controlled entity	1a		X
b Gift, grant, or capital contribution to related organization(s)	1b		X
c Gift, grant, or capital contribution from related organization(s)	1c		X
d Loans or loan guarantees to or for related organization(s)	1d	X	
e Loans or loan guarantees by related organization(s)	1e		X
f Dividends from related organization(s)	1f		X
g Sale of assets to related organization(s)	1g		X
h Purchase of assets from related organization(s)	1h		X
i Exchange of assets with related organization(s)	1i		X
j Lease of facilities, equipment, or other assets to related organization(s)	1j		X
k Lease of facilities, equipment, or other assets from related organization(s)	1k	X	
l Performance of services or membership or fundraising solicitations for related organization(s)	1l		X
m Performance of services or membership or fundraising solicitations by related organization(s)	1m		X
n Sharing of facilities, equipment, mailing lists, or other assets with related organization(s)	1n		X
o Sharing of paid employees with related organization(s)	1o		X
p Reimbursement paid to related organization(s) for expenses	1p	X	
q Reimbursement paid by related organization(s) for expenses	1q	X	
r Other transfer of cash or property to related organization(s)	1r		X
s Other transfer of cash or property from related organization(s)	1s		X

2 If the answer to any of the above is "Yes," see the instructions for information on who must complete this line, including covered relationships and transaction thresholds.

(a) Name of related organization	(b) Transaction type (a-s)	(c) Amount involved	(d) Method of determining amount involved
(1) CONSUMER LAW BUILDING CORPORATION	D	4,385,336.	FAIR MARKET VALUE
(2) CONSUMER LAW BUILDING CORPORATION	K	780,000.	FAIR MARKET VALUE
(3)			
(4)			
(5)			
(6)			

932163 09-10-19 Schedule R (Form 990) 2019

Schedule R (Form 990) 2019 NATIONAL CONSUMER LAW CENTER, INC. 04-2488502 Page 4

Part VI Unrelated Organizations Taxable as a Partnership. Complete if the organization answered "Yes" on Form 990, Part IV, line 37.

Provide the following information for each entity taxed as a partnership through which the organization conducted more than five percent of its activities (measured by total assets or gross revenue) that was not a related organization. See instructions regarding exclusion for certain investment partnerships.

(a) Name, address, and EIN of entity	(b) Primary activity	(c) Legal domicile (state or foreign country)	(d) Predominant income (related, unrelated, excluded from tax under sections 512-514)	(e) Are all partners sec. 501(c)(3) orgs.? Yes	(e) No	(f) Share of total income	(g) Share of end-of-year assets	(h) Disproportionate allocations? Yes	(h) No	(i) Code V-UBI amount in box 20 of Schedule K-1 (Form 1065)	(j) General or managing partner? Yes	(j) No	(k) Percentage ownership

Schedule R (Form 990) 2019

932164 09-10-19

Schedule R (Form 990) 2019 NATIONAL CONSUMER LAW CENTER, INC. 04-2488502 Page 5

Part VII Supplemental Information

Provide additional information for responses to questions on Schedule R. See instructions.

Written Responses of Chi Chi Wu to Questions for the Record from Representative Nikema Williams

Chi Chi Wu Answers to

Rep. Williams (GA) Questions for the

Record Financial Services Committee

Full Committee Hearing: "A Biased, Broken System: Examining Proposals to Overhaul Credit Reporting to Achieve Equity"

June 29, 2021

Question: *Credit scoring shapes so much for an individual, from their ability to get a credit card to their likelihood of buying a decent home. That's why it's so important to ensure credit scores are determined fairly. How we account for things like racial equity in credit scoring will determine whether people will get ahead or fall behind as we come out of this pandemic.*

1. *Ms. Wu, in your testimony, you mentioned that an equitable credit scoring model would need to take past and present racial discrimination into account. As credit scoring models develop or change, what are the most important principles they must incorporate to intentionally minimize racial disparities?*

Answer: As discussed in my written testimony, traditional credit scores reflect significant racial disparities, with numerous studies finding that Black and Latinx communities have lower credit scores as a group than whites. These lower scores are the result of both historical and present-day discrimination, which have resulted in multiple dimensions of economic inequality for these communities. Most particularly, decades of economic exclusion have resulted in a vast racial wealth gap that makes it much harder for Black and Latinx consumers to weather financial downturns such as the COVID-19 pandemic's economic fallout.

Credit scores are often touted as objective and their developers state that they do not consider race. But supposedly objective measures are not free from the legacy and impacts of racism; indeed, what they are reflecting is those very impacts. We have seen numerous examples of purportedly objective algorithms producing biased results, from healthcare to criminal justice to employment. Using tools that embed racial disparities to make critical decisions results in reinforcing those same disparities, and is one of the key elements of systemic racism.

We must shift from a framework of equality to one of equity. Treating people equally when the playing field is not level, and never has been, is a formula for perpetuating inequality.

In order to minimize racial disparities and make scoring equitable, scoring models need to be refined and improved with *intentionality*, the very concept raised in your question. Intentionality is key - the income disparities and wealth gaps reflected by credit scores were the product of centuries of intentional discrimination – they cannot and will not be reduced or resolved without the same level of intentionality.

Thus, credit scoring models must be actively developed to reduce the impact of race. An example of this sort of effort could be the process known as adversarial debiasing or adversarial learning, which uses two "adversarial" models to maximize the ability of the first model to predict a desired factor (e.g., probability of defaulting on a loan) while the second model that predicts the sensitive attribute (e.g., protected class) is used to minimize disparities in the first model.

Thus, in order to minimize the impact of race, scoring models must be refined by taking race into consideration in their development. Model developers might be concerned that such development techniques could run afoul of the Equal Credit Opportunity Act (ECOA) or Fair Housing Act (FHA). Indeed, many of the civil rights laws written in the 1960s and 1970s were drafted using an equality framework. That was certainly a huge and necessary step forward from the intentional discrimination prior to that time but not entirely sufficient to remedy the generations of economic disinheritance from that discrimination.

However, Congress did include a provision incorporating the concept of equity in the ECOA, by allowing lenders to offer "special purpose credit programs," where consideration of race is acceptable. And of course, Congress could take other actions to promote equity in credit scoring. For example, a public credit registry should have as part of its mission the development of credit scoring models that "maximize predictiveness and minimize racial disparities," which the discussion draft of the National Credit Reporting Agency Act does include.

Question: *Ms. Wu, you also mentioned that there's a big difference between scoring those who have faced hardship through no fault of their own and those who are actually irresponsible borrowers. We have to give those impacted by the pandemic the chance to get ahead even if they've fallen on hard times.*

Congress took a great step in this direction, providing that missed payments during the pandemic on a federal student loan would not adversely impact a borrower's credit standing. But we have to be sure this protection is truly there for all the people

2. *How common is it for missed payments on federal student loans to be reported as adverse information despite the letter of the law, and what steps need to be taken to ensure everyone has the protection that Congress intended?*

Answer: Unfortunately, failure by student loan servicers to comply with the credit reporting protections of the CARES Act has been well-documented. In April 2021, the Student Borrower Protection Center documented numerous instances in which servicers improperly reported adverse student loan information despite these credit reporting protections. The most notorious example occurred in May 2020, when Great Lakes Educational Loan Services reported inaccurate information to the credit bureaus for nearly 5 million borrowers. Great Lakes incorrectly indicated that these borrowers paused payment on their loans (an arrangement known as a "deferment"), rather than that they were "current" on the loans as the CARES Act required. Other examples include:

- Correspondence between the Department of Education and the servicer ECSI revealed that "ECSI reported ~43K borrowers in 'mand[atory] admin[istrative] forbearance' as 'deferred.'" This is the same error as the one that Great Lakes committed.
- In over 5,290 instances, servicers reported borrowers as being in default when that status may not have been appropriate.

See Student Borrower Protection Center, *Adding Insult to Injury: New Evidence of How the Department of Education and the Student Loan Industry Failed Borrowers during COVID—and Why the Biden Administration Must Act, April 2021*, https://protectborrowers.org/wp-content/uploads/2021/04/SBPC_Adding-Insult-to-Injury.pdf

To ensure that everyone has the protection that Congress intended, the Department must not only devote much more of its own resources and attention to supervising the servicers and ensuring their compliance, it must also coordinate with and support investigation and enforcement actions by the CFPB and states. The Department must also make sure borrowers whose repayment status was misreported receive full remedies for the harm.

Question*: Ms. Wu, you also mentioned that we need to do more to give relief for adverse credit events that happened during the pandemic. One of my priorities is making sure private student loan borrowers get the same relief that federal student loan borrowers got. My colleague, Congresswoman Alma Adams, and I passed an amendment that would do just that.*

3. *What would this relief mean for borrowers who are looking to build a better life for themselves and their families in the wake of the pandemic?*

Answer: Private student loan borrowers who miss payments because they are economically struggling due to the COVID-19 pandemic should not be saddled with negative credit reporting information for the next seven years. A private student loan borrower who had to miss payments because they lost their job or got sick from COVID-19 should not be penalized by impaired credit, which will also hinder them from being able to recover financially. In addition to denying them affordable credit, a bad credit report can result in being denied a new job, an apartment, and insurance.

Allowing private student loan borrowers who miss payments during the pandemic to suffer lasting credit damage is particularly concerning because of the racial and gender disparities in the impact of the pandemic. It will exacerbate and extend the financial harm women of color experienced as a result of the pandemic.

Chapter 2

Consumer Credit Reporting, Credit Bureaus, Credit Scoring, and Related Policy Issues*

Cheryl R. Cooper and Darryl E. Getter

Summary

The consumer data industry—generally referred to as credit reporting agencies or credit bureaus—collects and subsequently provides information to firms about the behavior of consumers when they participate in various financial transactions. Firms use consumer information to screen for consumer risks. For example, lenders rely upon credit reports and scores to determine the likelihood that prospective borrowers will repay their loans. Insured depository institutions (i.e., banks and credit unions) rely on consumer data service providers to determine whether to make available checking accounts or loans to individuals. Some insurance companies use consumer data to determine what insuranceproducts to make available and to set policy premiums. Some payday lenders use data regarding the management of checking accounts and payment of telecommunications and utility bills to determinethe likelihood of failure to repay small-dollar cash advances. Merchants rely on the consumer data industry to determine whether to approve payment by check or electronic payment card. Employers may use consumer data information to screen prospective employees to determine the likelihood of fraudulent behavior. In short, numerous firms rely upon consumer data to identify and evaluate potential risks a consumer may pose before entering into a financial relationship with that consumer.

* This is an edited, reformatted and augmented version of the Congressional Research Service Publication No. R44125, dated October 15, 2020.

In: Credit Reporting
Editor: Anthony J. Haley
ISBN: 979-8-88697-414-0

Greater reliance by firms on consumer data significantly affects—and potentially limits—consumer access to financial products or opportunities. Specifically, negative or derogatory information, such as late payments, loan defaults, and multiple overdrafts, may stay on consumer reports for several years and lead firms to deny a consumer access to credit, a financial product, or a job opportunity. Having a nonexistent, insufficient, or stale credit history may also prevent credit access.

Accordingly, various policy issues have been raised about the consumer data industry, including the following:

- How to address inaccurate or disputed consumer data provided in consumer data reports;
- How long negative or derogatory information should remain in consumer data reports;
- How to address differences in billing and collection practices that can adversely affect consumer data reports, an issue of particular concern with medical billing practices;
- How to ensure that consumers are aware of their rights and how to exercise them in the event of aconsumer data dispute;
- Whether uses of consumer data reports outside of the financial services, such as for employment decisions, adversely affect consumers and should be limited;
- Whether the use of *alternative* consumer data or newer versions of credit scores may increaseaccuracy and credit access; and
- How to address data protection and security issues in consumer data reporting.

Congress has shown continuing interest in these and other policy questions surrounding the consumer data industry. In the 116th Congress, the House passed H.R. 3621, the Comprehensive Credit Reporting Enhancement, Disclosure, Innovation, and Transparency Act of 2020 (Comprehensive CREDIT Act). This bill includes legislation from other bills marked up by the House Financial Services Committee: H.R. 3614, H.R. 3618, H.R. 3622, H.R. 3629, H.R. 3642. In the 116th Congress, the House Financial Services Committee marked up two otherbills: H.R. 5332 and H.R. 5330. On March 27, in response to the coronavirus (COVID-19) pandemic, the President signed the CARES Act (P.L. 116-136). Section 4021 of the CARES Act addresses credit reporting during the pandemic. The House also passed two versions of Heroes Act (H.R. 6800 and H.R. 925). Both bills would create a moratorium on furnishing adverse information to credit bureaus during the COVID-19 pandemic period, as well as for other future major natural disasters.

Introduction

The consumer data industry collects and subsequently provides information to firms about behavior when consumers conduct various financial transactions. Firms use this data to determine whether consumers have engaged in behaviors that could be costly or beneficial to the firms. For example, lenders rely upon credit reports and scoring systems to determine the likelihood that prospective borrowers will repay their loans. The data may also be used to predict consumer behaviors that would financially benefit firms.

Although the general public is likely to be more familiar with the use of credit reporting and scoring to qualify for mortgage and other consumer loans, the scope of consumer data use is much broader. Insured depository institutions (i.e., banks and credit unions) rely on consumer data service providers to determine whether to make checking accounts or loans available to individuals. Insurance companies use consumer data to determine what insurance products to make available and to set policy premiums.[1] Some payday lenders use data regarding the management of checking accounts and payment of telecommunications bills to determine the likelihood that a consumer will fail to repay small-dollar cash advances. Merchants rely on the consumer data industry to determine whether to approve payment by check or electronic payment card. Employers may use consumer data information to screen prospective employees to determine, for example, the likelihood of fraudulent behavior. In short, numerous firms rely upon consumer data to identify and evaluate the risks associated with entering into financial relationships or transactions with consumers.

Reliance by firms on consumer data significantly affects consumer access to financial products or opportunities. For example, negative or derogatory information, such as multiple overdrafts, involuntary account closures, loan defaults, and fraud incidents, may influence a lender to deny a consumer access to credit. Further, such information may stay on a consumer's reports for several years. The inclusion of negative information may be particularly limiting to consumers under circumstances in which such information is inaccurate or needs to be updated to reflect more current and possibly more favorable financial situations. Furthermore, consumers may find the process of making corrections to consumer data reports to be time-consuming, complex, and perhaps ineffective. The exclusion of more favorable

[1] See CRS Report RS21341, Credit Scores: Credit-Based Insurance Scores, by Baird Webel.

information, such as the timely repayment of noncredit obligations, from standard credit reporting or scoring models may also limit credit access.

This chapter first provides background information on the consumer data industry and various specialty areas. It examines one prominent specialty area—consumer scoring—and describes various factors used to calculate credit scores. Next, the chapter provides a general description of the current regulatory framework of the consumer data industry. Finally, the chapter discusses selected policy issues pertaining to consumer data reports. Specifically, the chapter addresses policy issues concerning (1) inaccurate or disputed consumer data provided in consumer data reports; (2) how long negative or derogatory information should remain in consumer data reports; (3) differences in billing and collection practices that can adversely affect consumer data reports, an issue of particular concern with medical billing practices; (4) consumers' rights; (5) whether uses of credit bureau data outside of the financial services, such as for employment decisions, adversely affect consumers and should be limited; (6) whether the use of alternative consumer data or newer versions of credit scores may increase accuracy and credit access; and (7) how to address data protection and security issues in consumer data reporting. For each policy issue, the chapter addresses corresponding legislative and regulatory developments.

In the 116th Congress, credit reporting and the consumer data industry is a topic of interest.[2] On January 29, 2020, the House passed the Comprehensive Credit Reporting Enhancement, Disclosure, Innovation, and Transparency Act of 2020 (Comprehensive CREDIT Act; H.R. 3621). Originally a narrower bill, H.R. 3621 was amended in committee to include other bills marked up and ordered reported by the House Financial Services Committee: H.R. 3614 (The Restricting Credit Checks for Employment Decisions Act, Title VI of bill); H.R. 3618 (The Free Credit Scores for Consumers Act of 2019, Title II of bill); H.R. 3622 (Restoring Unfairly Impaired Credit and Protection Consumers Act, Title IV of bill); H.R. 3629 (The Clarity in Credit Score Formation Act of 2019, Title V of bill); and H.R. 3642 (The Improving Credit Reporting for

[2] On February 26, 2019, the House Financial Services Committee held a hearing on the consumer data industry; see U.S. Congress, House Committee on Financial Services, "Who's Keeping Score? Holding Credit Bureaus Accountable and Repairing a Broken System," 116th Cong., February 26, 2019. The Senate has also expressed interest in credit reporting and the consumer data industry; see U.S. Congress, Senate Committee on Banking, Housing, and Urban Affairs, "Crapo Outlines Banking Committee Agenda for 116 th Congress," prepared by Chairman Mike Crapo, 116 th Cong., 1st sess., January 29, 2019, at https://www.banking.senate.gov/newsroom/majority/crapo-outlines-agenda-for-116th-congress.

All Consumers Act, Title I and VII of the bill). In addition, in December 2019, the committee marked up and ordered reported two bills, the Protecting Your Credit Score Act of 2019 (H.R. 5332) and the Consumer Protection for Medical Debt Collections Act (H.R. 5330).[3] Where relevant, this chapter discusses the approach these bills would take to address the policy issues examined. When H.R. 3621 is addressed, the references are to the bill as passed by the House. Where H.R. 5330 and H.R. 5332 are addressed, the references are to the bills after committee amendment.

COVID-19 Pandemic and Credit Reporting

On March 27, in response to the Coronavirus Disease 2019 (COVID-19) pandemic, the President signed the Coronavirus Aid, Relief, and Economic Security Act (CARES Act; P.L. 116-136). Section 4021 of the CARES Act addresses credit reporting during the pandemic. It requires furnishers during the COVID-19 pandemic covered period to report to the credit bureaus that consumers are current on their credit obligations if they enter into an agreement to defer, forbear, modify, make partial payments, or get any other assistance on their loan payments from a financial institution and fulfil those requirements, provided they were current before this period.[4]

Although the CARES Act protects the credit histories of consumers with forbearance agreements, some consumers may still experience harm to their credit record because lenders can choose whether to enter into an assistance agreement for many types of consumer loans. On May 15, 2020, the House passed the Heroes Act (H.R. 6800), and on October 1, 2020, the House passed an updated version of the bill (H.R. 925). Division K, Title IV, Section 110401 of H.R. 6800 and Division O, Title IV, Section 401of H.R. 925 would address this potential harm by creating a moratorium on

[3] H.R. 5332 and H.R. 5330 were marked up and ordered to be reported on December 10, 2019; see https://financialservices.house.gov/calendar/eventsingle.aspx?EventID=404859. H.Rept.116-416 to accompany H.R. 5332 was filed on March 12, 2020.

[4] If the consumer was delinquent before the covered period, then the furnisher should maintain the delinquent status unless the consumer brings the account or obligation current. The covered period starts on January 31, 2020, and extends to the later of 120 days after enactment or 120 days after the national emergency declared by the President on March 13, 2020, terminates. For more information, see CFPB, *Statement on Supervisory and Enforcement Practices Regarding the Fair Credit Reporting Act and Regulation V in Light of the CARES Act*, April 1, 2020, at https://files.consumerfinance.gov/f/documents/cfpb_credit-reporting-policy-statement_cares-act_2020-04.pdf.

furnishing adverse information to credit bureaus during the COVID-19 pandemic and for 120 days afterward, as well as for other future major natural disasters. Although these provisions would protect consumers from lower credit scores, the removal of information may also reduce credit scores' predictability in the future, which could harm some consumers in the long term. For more information on credit reporting, the COVID-19 pandemic, and the CARES Act, see the Appendix.

The Consumer Data Industry and Specialty Services

This section provides background information on the consumer data industry, which generally includes credit reporting agencies (CRAs), also referred to as credit bureaus (both terms are used interchangeably in this chapter). This section also provides background on credit scoring, a specialty service the industry provides, including a summary of the key factors known to affect credit scores.

Consumer Reporting Services

According to the Fair Credit Reporting Act (FCRA), which generally regulates the business of credit reporting, CRAs are firms that prepare consumer reports based upon individuals' financial transactions history data.[5] Such data may include historical information about credit repayment, tenant payment, employment, insurance claims, arrests, bankruptcies, and check writing and account management. Consumer files, however, do not contain information on consumer incomeor assets.[6] Consumer reports generally may not include

---

[5] P.L. 91-508. Title VI, §601, 84 Stat. 1128 (1970), codified as amended at 15 U.S.C. §§1681-1681x. For the legal definition, see 12 C.F.R. §1090.104, "Consumer Reporting Market," at http://www.ecfr.gov/cgi-bin/text-idx?SID=c13cb74ad55c0e8d6abf8d2d1b26a2bc&mc=true&node=se12.9.1090_1104&rgn=div8 The Fair Credit Reporting Act, the Fair Debt Collection Practices Act, and the Equal Credit Opportunity Act are all consumer credit protection amendments included in the Consumer Credit Protection Act (P.L. 90-321).

[6] See Bureau of Consumer Financial Protection (CFPB), *Key Dimensions and Processes in the U.S. Credit Reporting System*, December 2012, at http://files.consumerfinance.gov/f/201212_cfpb_credit-reporting-white-paper.pdf.

information on items such as race or ethnicity, religious or political preference, or medical history.[7]

Equifax, Experian, and TransUnion are the three largest nationwide providers of credit reports.[8] Other CRAs provide a variety of specialized consumer reporting services.[9] Some specialty CRAs collect data regarding payment for phone, utilities (e.g., electric, gas, water), and telecommunication (e.g., cable) services.[10] Utility and telecommunication service providers use the reports to verify the identity of customers and determine down payment requirements for new customers. Property management companies and rent payment services may report to CRAs that specialize in collecting rent payment data for tenant and employment screening.[11] Some CRAs specialize in consumer reporting for the underbanked, near prime, and subprime consumer segments, including consumers with minimal recorded data.[12] Some CRAs specialize in debt collection (recovering past due funds) and fraud verification data.[13]

---

[7] See Federal Reserve Board (FRB), "Federal Fair Lending Regulations and Statutes: Equal Credit Opportunity (Regulation B)," *Consumer Compliance Handbook*, at http://www.federalreserve.gov/boarddocs/supmanual/cch/fair_lend_reg_b.pdf ; and Experian, "Basic Questions About Credit Reports and Credit Reporting," *Reports on Credit issue 1*, at https://www.experian.com/assets/consumer-educationcontent/brochures/Reports_Issue_1.pdf

[8] For a list of consumer reporting agencies, see "List of Consumer Reporting Agencies," issued by CFPB, at https://files.consumerfinance.gov/f/documents/cfpb_consumer-reporting-companies-list.pdf.

[9] Some specialty CRAs are subsidiaries of larger CRAs. Examples include the National Consumer Telecom & Utilities Exchange, at http://www.nctue.com/, which is owned by Equifax; and RentBureau, at http://www.experian.com/rentbureau/renter-credit.html, which is owned by Experian.

[10] For example, see National Consumer Telecom & Utilities Exchange, at http://www.nctue.com/.

[11] For example, see Experian RentBureau, at http://www.experian.com/rentbureau/renter-credit.html.

[12] For example, see Clarity Services, Inc., at https://www.clarityservices.com/about/, which focuses on higher-risk borrowers and collects data from financial service providers, such as auto financers, check cashers, prepaid card issuers, peer-to-peer micro lenders, and small dollar credit lenders.

[13] See Consumer Data Industry Association (CDIA), "About CDIA," at https://www.cdiaonline.org/about/index.cfm?unItemNumber=515.

Examples of Specialty CRA Services: Checking Accounts and Check Verification

When an individual applies for a checking account, a depository institution typically pays a fee to purchase a credit report from a specialty CRA. This is a component of the initial fixed costs the depository institution incurs to begin a financial relationship with a new customer. The institution can use the information about a prospective customer to determine whether to offer the consumer a checking account and, if so, what range of product features (e.g., check-writing privileges, overdraft protection) to offer the consumer.

Specifically, depository institutions use credit reports to screen for certain types of borrower risks.[14] Banks must verify the identities of their customers as required by the Bank Secrecy Act.[15] In addition, depository institutions look for any incidents of fraudulent activity associated with a prospective customer.[16] Depository institutions typically reject consumers when they discover problems verifying identity or incidents of fraud. Next, depository institutions look for information about past banking relationships, particularly to see if any financial institutions closed checking or other accounts due to their inability to collect overdraft or insufficient funds fees.[17] Although some institutions may choose to reject applicants if they discover adverse information in their credit reports, many institutions may offer these applicants specialized checking

---

[14] See ChexSystems, "ChexSystems—Credit System for Checking Accounts," Crediful, at https://www.crediful.com/chexsystems/.

[15] P.L. 91-508.

[16] Fraud may include, but is not limited to, identity theft and check kiting. Real Time Identity Check is a specialty CRA used for this purpose; see Access Payment Systems, "Real Time Check Verification," at http://www.accesspaymentsystems.com/real-time-check-verification/. Another specialty CRA used for this purpose is Early Warning, which offers a product known as *Deposit Chek*, at https://www.earlywarning.com/solutions/payment/deposit-chek.html#real-time-deposit-chek-service. In the payment system, fraud occurs when an unauthorized person accesses the value associated with a payment vehicle. See Mark Furletti and Stephen Smith, *The Laws, Regulations, and Industry Practices That Protect Consumers Who Use Electronic Payment Systems: ACH E-Checks & Prepaid Cards*, Federal Reserve Bank of Philadelphia, Payment Cards Center Discussion Paper, DP05 -04, March 2005, at http://www.philadelphiafed.org/consumer-credit-and-payments/payment-cards-center/publications/discussion-papers/2005/ConsumerProtection.pdf.

[17] For ChexSystems, which is owned by parent company Fidelity National Information Services (FNIS), this product is known as QualiFile. See Rebecca Lake, "What Is a Good ChexSystems (Qualifile) Score?" My BankTracker, July 20, 2018, at https://www.mybanktracker.com/checking/faq/good-chexsystems-qualifile-score-276348. For Early Warning, this product is known as *Deposit Chek* at https://www.earlywarning.com/solutions/payment/deposit-chek.html#real-time-deposit-chek-service.

accounts with less overdraft coverage and fewer check-writing privileges. Institutions may also offer these applicants prepaid cards as a substitute for a checking account. The information the institutions obtain from CRAs may also allow them to infer the probability of cross- selling (or arguably preapproving access to) other financial products (e.g., mortgages, credit cards, savings accounts) to new customers.

Some specialty CRAs help facilitate consumer payments by check. For example, if a customer wants to use a check to pay for purchases, a merchant can electronically and quickly request check authorization from a specialty CRA that provides information at the point of sale (at the cash register).[18] The specialty CRA collects payment history and check-writing patterns, and the merchant pays a check authorization fee to obtain an instant recommendation of accept or decline.[19]

Firms that use consumer reports may also report information to CRAs, thus serving as furnishers. A tradeline is an account attached to a particular consumer that is reported to a CRAby a furnisher.[20] A tradeline serves as a record of the transaction (payment) activity associated with the account. Furnishing tradelines is voluntary, and furnishers are not required to submit tradelines to all CRAs. Furnishers also have different business models and policies, resulting in different reporting practices. Some furnishers may report all unpaid customer obligations that were deemed uncollectible and written off their balance sheets; some report when money balances owed surpass minimum threshold levels; some report only the principal balances owed minus the penalties and fees; and others may report all monies owed. Furnishers also have discretion over the types of obligations they wish to report.[21]

---

[18] Certegy, which is owned by parent company FIS (see http://www.fisglobal.com/products-retailpayments), and Telecheck (see http://www.firstdata.com/telecheck/) are specialty CRAs often used to obtain check authorization at the point of sale (i.e., the moment customers pay for their purchases).

[19] The fee paid by the merchant is analogous to the merchant discount fee that merchants pay when accepting credit or debit card payments. See CRS Report R41913, *Regulation of Debit Interchange Fees*, by Darryl E. Getter.

[20] See Experian, "Glossary of Credit Terms," at https://www.experian.com/blogs/ask-experian/credit-education/faqs/glossary/.

[21] A community bank, for example, may choose to report delinquencies on consumer loans rather than on commercial loans given that it may have greater information regarding the cash flow circumstances of its larger commercial borrowers. See Federal Trade Commission (FTC) and FRB, *Report to Congress on the Fair Credit Reporting Act*

Benefits to users of consumer data increase as more individual companies choose to participate as furnishers, but furnishers do incur costs to report data. To become furnishers, firms must be approved and comply with the policies of a CRA, such as fee registration requirements.[22] The transfer of consumer data involves security risks, and many CRAs have adopted standardized reporting formats and requirements approved by the Consumer Data Industry Association (CDIA) for transferring data.[23] Furnishers must be able to comply with industry data transfer requirements or some CRAs are unlikely to accept their data. Compliance may require investing in technology compatible with the computer systems of a CRA. Compliance costs may be more burdensome for smaller firms, causing some to choose not to be furnishers. In addition, entities that elect to become furnishers face legal obligations under the FCRA.[24] The FCRA requires furnishers to report accurate and complete information as well as to investigate consumer disputes. Hence, reporting obligations could possibly, under some circumstances, result in legal costs, which may also influence a firm's decision to become a furnisher.

Business models and policies of CRAs are also different. Different CRAs may collect the same information on the same individuals but adopt different conventions for storing the information. One CRA may report a delinquent debt obligation separately from the penalties and fees whereas another CRA may choose to combine both items into one entry. Consequently, consumer reports obtained from different CRAs on the same consumer are likely to differ due to different policies adopted by furnishers, CRAs, or both.

Credit Scoring Services

A consumer score is a (numeric) metric that can be used to predict a variety of financial behaviors.[25] Consumer credit scores are prepared for lenders to

---

Dispute Process, August 2006, at http://www.federalreserve.gov/boarddocs/rptcongress/fcradispute/fcradispute200608.htm#toc4.

[22] For examples of some furnisher requirements, see Experian, "Reporting to Credit Agencies," at http://www.experian.com/consumer-information/reporting-to-credit-agencies.html.

[23] The approved formats add security (privacy) protections to the data transfer process. See CDIA, "Metro 2 Format for Credit Reporting," at https://www.cdiaonline.org/resources/furnishers-of-data-overview/metro2-information/.

[24] See FTC, "Consumer Reports: What Information Furnishers Need to Know," at https://www.ftc.gov/tips-advice/business-center/guidance/consumer-reports-what-information-furnishers-need-know.

[25] The predictability power of consumer scores, assuming no significant changes in consumer repayment patterns, may last for approximately one year to two years. For examples of

determine, for example, the likelihood of loan default. Other consumer scores can be prepared to predict the likelihood of filing an insurance claim, overdrawing a bank account, failing to pay a utility bill, committing fraud, or a host of other adverse financial behaviors.

Consumer scores are typically computed using the information obtained from one or more consumer reports. Rather than maintaining a repository of credit records, some firms are primarily engaged in the production of consumer scores.[26] Hence, consumer scoring can be considered a specialty service in the consumer data industry. For example, if a user of a consumer report subsequently wants a consumer score, it may be charged an additional fee.

Given the variety of different financial behaviors to predict, there are many consumer scores that can be calculated. Consumer scores for the same individual and behavior calculated by different scoring firms are also likely to differ. Consumer scoring firms may have purchased consumer information from different CRAs, which have their own policies for storing and reporting information. Each scoring firm has its own proprietary statistical model(s), meaning that each firm decides what consumer information should be included and excluded from calculations.

Each firm can choose its own weighting algorithms. For example, included information can be equally weighted, or heavier weights can be placed on more recent information or on information otherwise deemed more pertinent. Sometimes the consumer scoring firm selects the appropriate weighting scheme, and sometimes the requestor of a consumer score may provide instructions to the preparer. Hence, consumers may not see the actual scores used until after the decision making firms release them, particularly in cases when customized scores were requested and used in the decision making process.

---

various types of scores and corresponding estimated months of predictive power, see TransUnion, "Scores Overview," *TransUnion Scores*, at http://www.transunion.com/docs/financialServices/FS_ScoresOverview.pdf.

[26] FICO (see http://www.fico.com/en/) and VantageScore (see http://www.vantagescore.com/) are examples of firms that specialize in the production of credit scores; their primary business is not to compile consumer reports.

Some Factors Frequently Used to Calculate Credit Scores[27]

Lenders, whether for mortgages or other forms of consumer loans (e.g., credit card loans, installment loans, and automobile loans), rely upon credit scores, which are calculated to represent the risk of delinquency or default of consumers seeking credit. To calculate a credit score, credit scoring models generally obtain the following factors from a credit report.

- *Payment history.* A lender is concerned about the borrower paying past credit accounts on time. The payment history includes information related to late or missed payments, how late, amount owed, bankruptcies, foreclosures, lawsuits, and wage garnishments. Negative information on a credit report negatively affects a credit score.
- *Credit utilization.* This factor measures the amount of outstanding debt a consumer has accumulated relative to his or her credit limit. An individual with $3,000 in charges on a credit card with a $5,000 limit would have a credit utilization rate of 60%. A high credit utilization rate negatively affects a credit score.
- *Length of credit history.* The more experience an individual has using credit, the easier it is for a lender to determine how well or poorly additional credit will be managed. Calculating credit scores may be impossible for "invisible" consumers (i.e., consumers with either no credit history or an insufficient credit history).
- *New credit accounts or requests.* There are two types of inquiries. A *soft* inquiry occurs when consumers request to check their credit reports, typically for accuracies or to dispute information, but there is no corresponding request for credit. Users of credit reports do not receive information regarding soft inquiries. A *hard* inquiry occurs when consumers apply for credit, and action is required by users of credit reports, typically to make approval or rejection decisions. Hence, making numerous different credit requests, particularly over a short period of time, generally can negatively affect a score. If a consumer shops for credit, which would be indicated by applying for the same type of credit within a short period of time (e.g., two to six weeks), then that activity would count only as one hard inquiry in most credit

[27] See Fair Isaac, "What's in My FICO Scores: How My FICO Scores Are Calculated," at http://www.myfico.com/crediteducation/whatsinyourscore.aspx; and FRB, "Credit Reports and Credit Score," at https://www.federalreserveconsumerhelp.gov/learnmore/credit-reports-and-scores?sc_lang=en.

scores.[28] Prescreening, which is used frequently in credit card solicitations, does not count as a "firm offer of credit or insurance" and, therefore, does not affect consumer credit scores.[29]

- *Credit mix.* Demonstrating the ability to manage multiple types of credit obligations (i.e., revolving, installment, mortgage credit, and finance company credit) influences a credit score. For example, the ability to maintain a stable debt-to-income ratio, preferably below 28%, despite having a mix of credit types, indicates the ability to manage credit. Having most of one's credit consist of credit from *indirect lenders,* such as department stores and rent-to-own stores, may not be viewed as favorably in some credit scoring models as credit from *direct lenders,* such as banks and credit unions.

Firms that prepare or users that purchase credit scores can decide how much weight to apply to each factor, and they may include additional predictive factors (e.g., information found on the credit application such as income and employment history) in the calculations. The Equal Credit Opportunity Act, however, prohibits characteristics such as race, sex, marital status, national origin, and religion from being used in credit scoring models.[30] Information for consumers on how to improve and maintain a good credit score is available from the Consumer Financial Protection Bureau (see https://www.consumerfinance.gov/consumer-tools/credit-reports-and-scores/).

Existing Consumer Protections and Regulation of Credit Reporting Agencies

This section provides a brief overview of existing consumer protections and regulation related to credit reporting.

[28] CFPB, What effect will shopping for an auto loan have on my credit? Ask CFPB, June 6, 2016, at https://www.consumerfinance.gov/ask-cfpb/what-effect-will-shopping-for-an-auto-loan-have-on-my-credit-en-763/.

[29] See FRB, "Permissible Purposes of Consumer Reports (FRCA, Section 604) and Investigative Consumer Reports (FRCA, Section 606)," Fair Credit Reporting, at http://www.federalreserve.gov/boarddocs/supmanual/cch/200611/fcra.pdf; CFPB, *Key Dimensions and Processes in the U.S. Credit Reporting System* , December 2012, p. 9, at http://files.consumerfinance.gov/f/201212_cfpb_credit-reporting-white-paper.pdf ; and " New Rules for Prescreening," at https://www.bankersonline.com/articles/103643.

[30] P.L. 93-495, Title 5, 88 Stat. 1520; 15 U.S.C. §1691 et seq.

As noted, the Fair Credit Reporting Act (FCRA), enacted in 1970, is the main statute regulating the credit reporting industry. The FCRA requires "that consumer reporting agencies adopt reasonable procedures for meeting the needs of commerce for consumer credit, personnel, insurance, and other information in a manner which is fair and equitable to the consumer, with regard to the confidentiality, accuracy, relevancy, and proper utilization of such information."[31] The FCRA establishes consumers' rights in relation to their credit reports, as well as permissible uses of credit reports. It also imposes certain responsibilities on those who collect, furnish, and use the information contained in consumers' credit reports.[32]

The FCRA includes consumer protection provisions. Under the FCRA, consumers must be told when their information from a CRA has been used after an adverse action (generally a denial of credit) has occurred, and disclosure of that information must be made free of charge.[33] Consumers have a right to one free credit report every year (from each of the three largest nationwide credit reporting providers) even in the absence of an adverse action (e.g., credit denial). Consumers also have the right to dispute inaccurate or incomplete information in their report. After a consumer alerts a CRA of such a discrepancy, the CRA must investigate and correct errors, usually within 30 days. The FCRA also limits the length of time negative information may remain on reports.

Negative collection tradelines typically stay on credit reports for 7 years, even if the consumer pays in full the item in collection; a tradeline associated with a personal bankruptcy stays on a credit report for 10 years.[34]

The Dodd-Frank Wall Street Reform and Consumer Protection Act (Dodd-Frank)[35] established the Bureau of Consumer Financial Protection (CFPB), consolidating many federal consumer financial protection powers from other federal agencies. The CFPB has rulemaking and enforcement authorities over all CRAs for certain consumer protection laws; it has supervisory authority, or the authority to conduct examinations, over the larger CRAs. In July 2012, the CFPB announced that it would supervise CRAs with

---

[31] 15 U.S.C. §1681.

[32] CRS Insight IN10792, The Equifax Data Breach: An Overview and Issues for Congress, by N. Eric Weiss.

[33] See FTC, *A Summary of your Rights Under the Fair Credit Reporting Act*, at https://www.consumer.ftc.gov/articles/pdf-0096-fair-credit-reporting-act.pdf.

[34] CFPB, *How long does negative information remain on my credit report?* Ask CFPB, August 4, 2016, at https://www.consumerfinance.gov/ask-cfpb/how-long-does-negative-information-remain-on-my-credit-report-en-323/.

[35] P.L. 111-203, §1011.

$7 million or more in annual receipts, which included 30 firms representing approximately 94% of the market.[36]

The CFPB conducts examinations of the CRAs, reviewing procedures and operating systems regarding the management of consumer data and enforcing applicable laws. In 2017, the CFPB released a report of its supervisory work in the credit reporting system.[37] The report discusses the CFPB's efforts to work with credit bureaus and financial firms to improve credit reporting in three specific areas: data accuracy, dispute handling and resolution, and furnisher reporting. As the report describes, credit bureaus and financial firms have developed data governance and quality control programs to monitor data accuracy through working with the CFPB. In addition, the CFPB has encouraged credit bureaus to improve their dispute and resolution processes, including making it easier and more informative for consumers.[38]

Recently, Congress has also been interested in improving consumer protections in the credit reporting system, particularly in response to the 2017 Equifax data breach, which exposed personal information of millions of consumers.[39] The 2018 Economic Growth, Regulatory Relief, and Consumer Protection Act (P.L. 115-174) established new consumer protections relating to credit reporting, including the right to a free credit freeze. Credit freezes allow consumers to stop new credit from being opened in their name, to protect themselves from fraud and identity theft.

---

[36] CFPB, "CFPB to Supervise Credit Reporting," July 16, 2012, at http://www.consumerfinance.gov/newsroom/consumer-financial-protection-bureau-to-superivse-credit-reporting/.

[37] CFPB, Supervisory Highlights Consumer Reporting Special Edition, Issue 14, 2017, at https://files.consumerfinance.gov/f/documents/201703_cfpb_Supervisory-Highlights-Consumer-Reporting-Special- Edition.pdf.

[38] The credit bureaus' efforts to make disputes easier and more informative for consumers include (1) online portals to submit disputes and upload attachments of supporting documentation; (2) improvements to their call center scripts and training regarding solicitation of relevant information from consumers with disputes; (3) no longer requiring that consumers obtain or purchase a recent consumer report before investigations; and (4) notice to consumer of dispute results, including investigation results. CFPB, *Supervisory Highlights Consumer Reporting Special Edition*, Issue 14, 2017, pp.9-11, at https://files.consumerfinance.gov/f/documents/201703_cfpb_Supervisory-Highlights-Consumer-Reporting-Special-Edition.pdf.

[39] Equifax, "Equifax Announces Cybersecurity Incident Involving Consumer Information," press release, September 7, 2017, at https://investor.equifax.com/news-and-events/news/2017/09-07-2017-213000628.

Policy Issues

This section examines selected policy issues pertaining to the use of credit reports and scores in consumer lending decisions. For each policy issue, the report highlights recent legislative and regulatory developments and discusses selected legislative proposals from the 116th Congress thatwould address the issue.

Inaccurate or Disputed Information

The accuracy of consumer information in consumer data reports has been an ongoing policy concern. Inaccurate information in a credit report may limit a consumer's access to credit in somecases or increase the costs to the consumer of obtaining credit in others. In 2012, the Federal Trade Commission (FTC) reported that 26% of participants in a survey of credit report accuracy were able to identify at least one potentially material error on at least one of approximately three different credit reports prepared using their consumer information.[40] After the reports were corrected, 13% of participants in the FTC study saw one or more of their credit scores increase. For those who saw an increase, over 40% of their scores rose by more than 20 points, which could increase the likelihood that the consumer would be offered less expensive credit terms.

Credit reporting inaccuracies may occur for various reasons. Consumers may inadvertently provide inaccurate data when applying for financial services. Furnishers may inadvertently input inaccurate information into their databases. Matching information to the proper individual poses challenges, such as in cases when multiple individuals have similar names and spellings. In somecases, the information may be properly matched, but the individual could be a victim of fraud or identity theft.

The predictive power of consumer data, or the ability to accurately predict a consumer's likelihood to default on a loan, would be enhanced to the extent that consumer tradelines are regularly updated with correct and current information. As mentioned in the previous section, theCFPB has recently

---

[40] See FTC, *Report to Congress Under Section 319 of the Fair and Accurate Credit Transactions Act of 2003*, December 2012, at https://www.ftc.gov/sites/default/files/documents/reports/section-319-fair-and-accurate-credit-transactions-act-2003-fifth-interim-federal-trade-commission/130211factareport.pdf.

encouraged credit bureaus and financial firms to improve data accuracy in credit reporting. For example, since 2014, the CFPB has required the largest consumer reporting firms to provide standardized accuracy reports on a regular basis.[41] The accuracy reports must specify the frequency that consumers dispute information, list furnishers and industries with the most disputes, and provide dispute resolution information. According to the CFPB, the top 100 furnishers provide 76% of tradeline information to the largest nationwide CRAs, and the furnishers regularly update the account status of reported tradelines.[42] In addition, the larger CRAs have also made improvements to the communication tool they use to facilitate the dispute resolution process between consumers and furnishers.[43] Further, effective July 1, 2017, the CRAsenhanced public record data standards for the collection and timely updating of civil judgements and tax liens.[44] Public record data must contain minimum identifying information (i.e., name, address, and Social Security number or date of birth) and must be updated at least every 90 days; otherwise, the tax lien and civil judgment information will no longer be reported. According to the CFPB, this led to the removal of most civil judgements and half of all tax liens in credit reports for the nationwide CRAs.[45] The accuracy of credit reports, nonetheless, ultimately depends upon consumers to monitor and dispute any discrepancies.

H.R. 3621 and H.R. 5332 would address some concerns relating to inaccurate or disputed data byestablishing new consumer rights around the

---

[41] See CFPB, "Prepared Remarks of CFPB Director Richard Cordray at the Medical Debt Collection Hearing," December 11, 2014, at http://www.consumerfinance.gov/newsroom/prepared-remarks-of-cfpb-director-richard-cordray-at-the-medical-debt-collection-hearing/. A sample accuracy report may be found at http://files.consumerfinance.gov/f/201412_cfpb_sample-accuracy-report.pdf.

[42] See CFPB, *Key Dimensions and Processes in the U.S. Credit Reporting System*, December 2012, p. 14, at http://files.consumerfinance.gov/f/201212_cfpb_credit-reporting-white-paper.pdf.

[43] The CRAs use a web-based tool, the Online Solution for Complete and Accurate Reporting (e-OSCAR), to investigate credit reporting disputes. e-OSCAR is owned and operated by four companies: Equifax, Experian, Innovis, and TransUnion. See http://www.e-oscar.org/.

[44] See Consumer Data Industry Association, "New Public Record Credit Reporting Standards to Begin July 1, 2017;
Civil Judgments and some Tax Liens to be removed from many credit reports," press release, June 28, 2017, at http://s3.amazonaws.com/rdcms-cdia/files/production/public/PDFs/CDIA.NCAP.July1Changes.6.28.pdf.

[45] Claire Brennecke, Jasper Clarkberg, and Michelle Kambara, *Public Records, Credit Scores, and Credit Performance*, CFPB, Quarterly Consumer Credit Trends, December 2019, p. 2, at https://files.consumerfinance.gov/f/documents/cfpb_quarterly-consumer-credit-trends_public-records-credit-scores-performance_2019-12.pdf.

dispute process. Both bills would guarantee consumers more information about dispute investigations and would grant consumers the right toappeal disputes to credit bureaus, thus formalizing the process.[46] It also would explicitly establishconsumers' right to seek injunctive relief, a legal remedy where a court requires future behavior change (e.g., removing adverse information from a credit record).[47] Moreover, it would provide credit restoration to consumers who are the victims of some predatory activities, such as deceptive lender acts or fraud.[48] H.R. 5332 would require social security number matches before information could be included in a consumer's credit report.[49] It would also create a CFPB credit reporting ombudsperson to help resolve persistent errors.[50]

Length of Time to Retain Negative Information

Policymakers have also considered the appropriate length of time negative information should be allowed to remain on a credit report. Negative information generally refers to delinquencies or defaults, which typically remain on credit reports for seven years. Negative information in a credit report often results in a consumer appearing to pose a greater risk of default or other negative behavior. This may lead a consumer to either pay more for financial services or, in some cases, be denied access to credit entirely. Limiting a consumer's access to certain financial services, such as depository checking accounts or lower cost loans, may disproportionately affect the consumer's cost of engaging in financial transactions. Similarly, the use of consumer data reports by potential employers, discussed below, may limit job opportunities that could arguably help applicants overcome financial challenges and thereby improve their credit histories.[51]

Retaining negative information on credit reports for an extended period of time may pose benefits and detriments. On the one hand, under circumstances in which the underlying information in a consumer data report is inaccurate or out of date, consumers may improperly be considered to pose a greater risk to

[46] Title I of H.R. 3621; H.R. 5332, §4.
[47] H.R. 3621, §110.
[48] Title IV of H.R. 3621.
[49] H.R. 5332, §3.
[50] H.R. 5332, §4.
[51] See Dana Dratch, "States Weigh Limits on Credit Checks for Employment," CreditCards.com, at http://www.creditcards.com/credit-card-news/states-weigh-limits-credit-checks-for-employment-1282.php.

a firm. In that case, the consumer may be offered costlier credit options (or even face denials of credit) that do not accurately reflect the consumer's actual risk of default. In other cases, consumers also may unfairly be considered to pose a greater risk now due to circumstances in the past that they have since overcome. On the other hand, the longer information remains on the credit report arguably allows lenders to see long-term trends that may be helpful for distinguishing between a rare occurrence and a consistent pattern in a consumer's behavior. Shorter or insufficient periods of time in which negative tradelines appear on consumer reports may also compromise the ability to compute reliable scores. If lenders view credit reports and scores as unreliable due to premature removal of negative information, they could increase down payment requirements across the board for all credit applicants or reduce loan amounts. In short, lenders who are uncertain about data reliability might adopt stricter underwriting and lending policies. In addition to restricting credit access generally, this could reduce competition by allowing lenders with an established relationship and more information on a consumer to provide more favorable terms to that consumer than other companies. In addition, the Association of Certified Fraud Examiners (ACFE) found that poor credit can signal criminal activity, and earlier removal of negative information may make it more difficult for an organization to detect fraud, which may be particularly costly for small businesses and nonprofit organizations.[52]

Many preparers and users of credit scores have adopted weighting schemes that place less weight on older information in a consumer data report. Maintaining longer (rather than shorter) durations of negative tradelines on reports allows preparers to make greater use of variable-weighted algorithms to calculate scores, which may be useful when the importance of a weight needs to be modified over time. In addressing this policy issue, H.R. 3621 would shorten the time period that adverse information could remain on a person's credit report by three years (such that it remainson the report for a total of four years), among other things.[53]

---

[52] See Michelle Long, "Internal Controls for Small Businesses to Reduce the Risk of Fraud," Intuit, at http://longforsuccess.com/wp-content/uploads/2010/09/Good-Internal-Controls.pdf; and Association of Certified Fraud Examiners (ACFE), Report to the Nations on Occupational Fraud and Abuse: 2012 Global Fraud Study, Fraud Q&A with James Ratley, President and CEO of the ACFE, at https://www.acfe.com/uploadedFiles/ACFE_Website/Content/rttn/2012-report-to-nations.pdf. Approximately 36% of fraudsters live beyond their means and 27% undergo personal financial difficulties. See *Preventing and Detecting Fraud in Not-For-Profit Organizations*, at https://www.kellerowens.com/wp-content/uploads/2012/07/Fraud-Booklet-2012-Revised-Version.pdf.

[53] H.R. 3621, §401.

Rehabilitation of Education Loans

Borrowers who default on some federal student loan programs (defined as not having made a payment in more than 270 days) have a one-time loan rehabilitation option.[54] A loan rehabilitation (as opposed to a loan consolidation) requires a defaulted borrower to make nine on-time monthly payments during a period of 10 consecutive months.[55] The loan is considered rehabilitated if the borrower satisfies the requirements, and then the loan may be reinstated. In addition, the borrower's credit report is generally updated to show that the loan is no longer in default (or the default record would be eliminated); however, the information pertaining to the late payments that led up to the rehabilitation would still remain for seven years.[56]

By contrast, students who default on private loans are less likely to receive a rehabilitation option.[57] P.L. 115-174, Section 602, allows a borrower a one-time opportunity to remove a reported default on a qualified (private) student loan from a credit report if the borrower satisfies the requirements of loan rehabilitation programs that private lenders may be willing to offer (with the approval of prudential regulators), which is analogous to the procedures followed when federal student loans are in default.[58] However, depositories (i.e., banks and credit unions), which are regulated for safety and soundness, treat their student loans like all other private consumer loans. Private student loans must still satisfy underwriting requirements, typically requiring co-signers who become responsible for the loans if the students are unable to repay. After 120 days

---

54 See CFPB, "What Does It Mean to 'Default' on My Federal Student Loans?" press release, August 4, 2016, at https://www.consumerfinance.gov/ask-cfpb/what-does-it-mean-to-default-on-my-federal-student-loans-en-649/.

55 See CRS Report R40122, *Federal Student Loans Made Under the Federal Family Education Loan Program and the William D. Ford Federal Direct Loan Program: Terms and Conditions for Borrowers*, by David P. Smole.

56 See Experian, "What Is Student Loan Rehabilitation?" February 3, 2020, at https://www.experian.com/blogs/ask-experian/what-is-student-loan-rehabilitation/.

57 CFPB, *Private Student Loans*, Report to the Senate Committee on Banking, Housing, and Urban Affairs, the Senate Committee on Health, Education, Labor, and Pensions, the House of Representatives Committee on Financial Services, and the House of Representatives Committee on Education and the Workforce, August 29, 2012, at http://files.consumerfinance.gov/f/201207_cfpb_Reports_Private-Student-Loans.pdf.

58 P.L. 115-174, §601 prohibits a private student loan lender from accelerating a debt or declaring a default against a student loan borrower upon the bankruptcy or death of a co-signer. Section 601 also releases a co-signer from the debt obligation upon the death of the student.

past due (closed-end), consumer loans held by depositories are treated as uncollectible.[59] The Office of the Comptroller of the Currency also points out: "Banks have some latitude to offer similar federal workout programs to private student loans. Banks, however, should do so while adhering to safety and soundness requirements and following existing banking guidance and GAAP."[60] Apart from safety and soundness requirements, the information pertaining to the late payments that led up to the rehabilitation would likely remain on the students' credit reports for seven years even if the default records were removed. Hence, this information would still be likely to be incorporated in students' credit scores.

H.R. 3621 would require credit bureaus to remove adverse information for private student loan borrowers who have demonstrated a history of repayment, similarly to federal student loans.[61] Private lenders currently have discretion in offering rehabilitation; under H.R. 3621, however, all private student loan borrowers would have the right to obtain loan rehabilitation. This provision would increase the ability of private student loan borrowers to receive rehabilitation. Because this practice would likely increase costs on financial institutions, as discussed above, this provision might reduce the willingness of lenders to originate private student loans.[62]

Inconsistent Billing and Reporting Practices: Medical Tradelines

Another policy issue that often arises in connection with credit reporting is that different holders of consumer debt bill differently and report to the CRAs differently. Inconsistent reporting practices result in variation of the timing with which unpaid debts appear on consumer reports. For example, medical providers may assign unpaid bills to debt collectors or sell outstanding debts to debt buyers. Some medical providers may assign or sell the debt after 60 days, but some may do so after 30 days (by comparison, most bank credit card

[59] After 120-180 days, a depository firm may hire a debt collector, who receives a percentage of the collected amount, or sell the defaulted loan outright to a collection agency. The debt collection process is guided by the Fair Debt Collection Practices Act (P.L. 90-321).

[60] See Office of the Comptroller of the Currency, *Comptroller's Handbook*, Version 1.0, May 2016, p. 34, at https://www.occ.treas.gov/publications/publications-by-type/comptrollers-handbook/student-lending/pub-ch-student-lending.pdf.

[61] Title III of.

[62] For more information, see CRS Report R45339, *Banking: Current Expected Credit Loss (CECL)*, by Raj Gnanarajah.

delinquencies are assigned or soldafter 180 days). Some firms may turn obligations over to collections as a tool to encourage consumers to settle unpaid balances, blurring the distinction between billing and collecting policies.[63] Debt collectors or buyers subsequently furnish negative information to CRAs, causing tradeline accounts to sometimes appear on consumer reports.

The CFPB used a random sample of approximately 5 million consumers as of December 2012 to determine what types of tradeline accounts were reported most frequently and the amounts.[64] The CFPB found that approximately 33% of credit reports surveyed had collection tradelines, and approximately 52% of those collection tradelines were related to medical collections. After medical obligations, the CFPB found that the remaining collection tradelines of significant relevance were associated with unclassified debts (17.3%), cable or cellular bills (8.2%), utilities (7.3%), and retail stores (7.2%). All other categories of collectible tradelines were approximately 2% or less of the survey. For 85% of the respondents, the amounts owed for medical debt were for less than $1,000. In short, more than half of collection tradelines were associated with medicaldebt, and they were for relatively small amounts. Specifically, the median amount owed for the medical collection tradelines was $207, and 75% of all medical collection tradelines were under $490.

One form of consumer debt—medical debt—is most often disputed by consumers and raises specific policy issues related to inconsistent billing and reporting practices. According to the CFPB study, consumers are unlikely to know when and how much various medical services cost in advance, particularly those associated with accidents and emergencies. People often have difficulty understanding co-pays and health insurance deductibles.[65] Consequently, consumers may delay paying medical obligations as they either assume their insurance companies will pay orattempt to figure out why they

---

[63] See CFPB, *Consumer Credit Reports: A Study of Medical and Non-Medical Collections*, December 2014, p. 36, at http://files.consumerfinance.gov/f/201412_cfpb_reports_consumer-credit-medical-and-non-medical-collections.pdf. Other firms may not immediately employ a collections strategy to encourage repayment of obligations for fears of reputational risk.

[64] See CFPB, *Consumer Credit Reports: A Study of Medical and Non-Medical Collections*, December 2014, at http://files.consumerfinance.gov/f/201412_cfpb_reports_consumer-credit-medical-and-non-medical-collections.pdf.

[65] Confusion about costs and co-pays may increase when medical care is administered outside of a consumer's state of residence, given that health insurers and providers determine costs that vary and are influenced by state regulations. See CRS In Focus IF10043, *Introduction to Financial Services: Insurance*, by Baird Webel.

have been billed, which often results in medical debt appearing unpaid on credit reports.

Regulators and industry have taken actions that may reduce medical tradelines and their associated negative effects on consumer credit data. On December 31, 2014, the Internal RevenueService (IRS) announced a final rule requiring the separation of billing and collection policies of nonprofit hospitals.[66] Under the rule, hospitals that have or are pursuing tax-exempt status are required to make reasonable efforts to determine whether their patients are eligible for financial assistance before engaging in "extraordinary collection actions," which may include turning a debt over to a collection agency (thus creating a medical tradeline) or garnishing wages. In short, tax-exempt hospitals must allow patients 120 days from the date of the first billing statement to pay the obligation before initiating collection procedures.[67] The IRS rule only impacts nonprofit hospitals, but, on September 15, 2017, the three major credit reporting agencies—Experian, Equifax, and TransUnion—established a 180-day (6 month) waiting period before posting a medical collection of any type on a consumer credit report.[68] In addition, P.L. 115-174, Section 302, amended the FCRA to provide credit reporting protections for veterans as follows:

- CRAs must exclude certain medical debt incurred by a veteran from his or her credit report if the hospital care or medical services relating to the debt predatesthe credit report by less than one year.
- CRAs must remove from the credit report a veteran's fully paid or settled medical debt previously characterized as delinquent, charged off, or in collection.
- CRAs must establish a dispute process and verification procedures for veterans' medical debt.
- Active duty military personnel receive free credit monitoring.

---

[66] See Department of the Treasury, Internal Revenue Service, *New Requirements for 501(c)(3) Hospitals Under the Affordable Care Act*, at https://www.irs.gov/charities-non-profits/charitable-organizations/requirements-for-501c3-hospitals-under-the-affordable-care-act-section-501r.

[67] See Department of the Treasury, Internal Revenue Service, "Additional Requirements for Charitable Hospitals; Community Health Needs Assessments for Charitable Hospitals; Requirements of a Section 4959 Excise Tax Returnand Time for Filing the Return," 79 *Federal Register* 78954-79016, December 31, 2014.

[68] See Experian, "Medical Debt and Your Credit Score: Here's What You Need to Know," press release, August 8, 2017, at https://www.experian.com/blogs/ask-experian/medical-debt-and-your-credit-score/.

H.R. 3621 and H.R. 5330 would impose restrictions on the appearance of medical collections on consumer credit reports, extending the CRA's 2017 rule to 365 days and excluding all debts related to medically necessary care.[69] H.R. 3621 would also require expedited removal of all fullyrepaid or settled medical debts.[70]

Consumer Rights in the Credit Reporting System

Consumers sometimes find it difficult to advocate for themselves when credit reporting issues arise because they are not aware of their rights and how to exercise them. According to a CFPB report, some consumers are confused about what credit reports and scores are, find it challenging to obtain credit reports and scores, and struggle to understand the contents of their credit reports.[71] The CFPB receives more credit reporting complaints than complaints in any other industry it regulates.[72] Currently, the CFPB provides financial education resources on its website to help educate consumers about their rights regarding consumer reporting. The credit bureaus' websites also provide information about how to dispute inaccurate information, and consumers can contact them by phone or mail.

H.R. 3621 and H.R. 5332 would require that CRAs provide free credit scores in their annual free credit report.[73] H.R. 3621 would allow consumers to be entitled to free credit reports at other times, for example, whenever they apply for a new mortgage, auto loan, or student loan, or if a consumer's identity is stolen. The report and score used to make underwriting decisions in connection with these events would be provided to the consumer. H.R. 3621 would also direct the credit bureaus to give consumers more information on dispute rights, and it would require hard inquiries to be limited for a longer 120-day shopping window for certain consumer credit products[74] (as described in the box "Some Factors Frequently Used to Calculate Credit Scores" above). H.R. 5332 would require an online consumer portal landing

---

[69] H.R. 3621, §403; H.R. 5330, §§2-3.

[70] H.R. 3621, §403.

[71] CFPB, *Consumer Voices on Credit Reports and Scores*, February 2015, https://files.consumerfinance.gov/f/201502_cfpb_report_consumer-voices-on-credit-reports-and-scores.pdf.

[72] CFPB, *Complaint Snapshot: Mortgage*, January 2019, pp. 3-6, at https://files.consumerfinance.gov/f/documents/cfpb_complaint-snapshot-mortage_2019-01_liwsYNV.pdf.

[73] Title II of H.R. 3621; H.R. 5332, §2.

[74] H.R. 3621, §102 and §705.

page for consumers to access their credit report and initiate disputes and credit freezes.[75] It also would allow consumers to opt out of having their credit report sold to third parties.[76]

Appropriate Purposes for Using Credit Bureau Data: Employment Decisions

Policy questions exist regarding the appropriate uses of credit bureau data, particularly for uses outside of extending credit to consumers.[77] For example, credit information can be used for employment decisions. According to the Society for Human Resource Management (a human resources professional society), in 2012, almost half of surveyed organizations in their membership used credit background checks on some of their job applications.[78] Employers report that they use this information to reduce the likelihood of employee theft or embezzlement and to reduce legal liability for negligent hiring.[79] To comply with the FCRA, employers must inform an applicant that his or her credit report is a part of a hiring decision, and acquire the applicant's written permission to obtain the report. If an applicant is denied a job, or if the employer takes another adverse action due to information on a credit report, then the applicant must be given a copy of the report and a summary of their FCRA rights.[80]

Whether the use of credit information in employment decisions unnecessarily harms prospective job applicants is debatable. For some occupations, past financial difficulties may increase the likelihood, for example, that the employee could be bribed or compromised in some way; however, this information may not be essential for success in all occupations. Currently, many states limit employers' use of credit information for

---

[75] H.R. 5332, §2.

[76] H.R. 5332, §2.

[77] Whether credit information should be used in insurance decisions is also a topic of congressional interest, see H.R. 1756.

[78] Society for Human Resource Management (SHRM), *Background Checking—The Use of Credit Background Checks in Hiring Decisions*, SHRM Blog, August 27, 2012, at https://blog.shrm.org/trends/background-checkingthe-use-of-credit-background-checks-in-hiring-decisions.

[79] SHRM, *Background Checking—The Use of Credit Background Checks in Hiring Decisions.*

[80] FTC, *Using Credit Reports: What Employers Need to Know*, October 2016, at https://www.ftc.gov/tips-advice/business-center/guidance/using-consumer-reports-what-employers-need-know.

employment decisions.[81] H.R. 3621 would ban the use of credit information for employment decisions, unless required by law or for anational security investigation.[82]

Consumers with Limited Credit Histories and Use of Alternative Scoring Methods

The CFPB estimates that credit scores cannot be generated for approximately 20% of the U.S. population due to their limited credit histories.[83] The CFPB distinguishes between different types of consumers with limited credit histories.[84] One category of consumers, referred to as credit invisibles, have no credit record at the three largest credit bureaus and, thus, do not exist for the purposes of credit reporting. According to the CFPB, this group represents 11.0% of the U.S. adult population, or 26 million consumers. Another category of consumers do exist (have a credit record), but they still cannot be scored or are considered nonscorable. Nonscorable consumers either have insufficient (short) histories or outdated (stale) histories. The insufficient and stale unscored groups, each containing more than 9 million individuals, collectively represent 8.3% of the U.S. adult population, or approximately 19 million consumers according to the CFPB. Younger adults may be part of the credit invisible or nonscorable population because they lack a sufficient credit history. As consumers get older, however, the problem of being credit invisible or belonging to the insufficient part of the nonscorable group typically declines, but may begin to reoccur after the age of 60. Older adults, who may have considerably reduced their credit usage, perhaps as they prepare to enter retirement years, may encounter the problem of having stale credit records.[85] Because credit scoring models vary by firms, consumers that cannot

---

[81] Rosemarie Lally, *Using Workers' Credit Information Increasingly Prohibited*, Society for Human Resource Management, July 28, 2015, at https://www.shrm.org/resourcesandtools/legal-and-compliance/state-and-local-updates/pages/states-credit-history.aspx.

[82] Title VI of H.R. 3621.

[83] For more information on credit access policy issues, see CRS Report R45979, *Financial Inclusion and Credit Access Policy Issues*, by Cheryl R. Cooper.

[84] See Kenneth P. Brevoort, Philipp Grimm, and Michelle Kambara, *Data Point: Credit Invisibles*, CFPB, May 2015, at http://files.consumerfinance.gov/f/201505_cfpb_data-point-credit-invisibles.pdf.

[85] The CFPB estimated some additional information about these groups by age, income, and race. See Kenneth P. Brevoort, Philipp Grimm, and Michelle Kambara, *Data Point: Credit Invisibles*, CFPB, May 2015, at http://files.consumerfinance.gov/f/201505_cfpb_data-point-credit-invisibles.pdf.

be scored by some models might still have the ability to be scored by other models; thus, the state of being nonscorable may depend upon the credit reporting data records and scoring models used.

Borrowers with missing or impaired credit histories may be able to improve their ability to get reliable credit scores by using credit building loans, such as secured credit cards that require either security deposits as collateral for the amount of the line of credit or links to checking or savings accounts, thereby allowing lenders to recover funds if payments are missed.[86] The security deposit is refunded if borrowers do not miss payments. Secured credit card lending can help borrowers build or repair their credit histories, assuming that the more favorable customer payment activity is reported to credit bureaus. In addition, the use of alternative credit scores may also help the credit invisibles because other types of consumer payment activity (discussed below) may be predictive in regard to how borrowers would manage credit. In short, options that increase the ability to calculate scores for the invisible or currently nonscorable consumer groups could allow lenders to better determine the quantity and scope of financial relationships they can establish with such groups.

Alternative credit scoring models could potentially increase accuracy by including additional information beyond that which is traditionally included in a credit report. For example, some credit score models do not distinguish between unpaid and paid (resolved) tradelines.[87] Most credit scores are calculated without utility and rent payments information. Arguably, including this information would benefit the credit scores for some individuals with limited or no credit histories, potentially increasing their access to—and lowering their costs of—credit.[88] Conversely,information about medical debts has often been included in credit scores, but the unevenness in medical reporting, as previously discussed, and possibly the consumers' lack of choice in incurring medical debt raises questions about whether medical debt tradelines should be considered reliable predictors of creditworthiness or

---

[86] For more information on the impact of credit builder loans, see CFPB, *Targeting Credit Builder Loans: Insights from a Credit Builder Loan Evaluation*, July 2020, at https://www.consumerfinance.gov/data-research/research-reports/targeting-credit-builder-loans/.

[87] The treatment of paid and unpaid collection tradelines varies among different credit scoring models. See "New FICO Score Model Could Boost Credit for Millions—Medical Bills in Focus," *NerdWallet*, August 8, 2014, at http://www.nerdwallet.com/blog/health/2014/08/08/new-fico-score-boost-credit-medical-bills-focus/.

[88] Experian, *New Study Shows How Alternative Payment Data Helps U.S. Consumers' Credit Profiles*, February 25, 2015, at https://www.experianplc.com/media/news/2015/alternative-data-to-credit-reports-utilities-and-rent-2015/.

credit performance.[89] For this reason, some newer versions of credit scoring apply less weight to medical debt.[90] In short, developing credit scores with new information might allow lenders to find new creditworthy consumers.

Regulators and Congress have considered the potential for alternative credit scoring. In 2014, theFederal Housing Finance Agency (FHFA) directed Fannie Mae and Freddie Mac—the government-sponsored enterprises (GSEs) that purchase mortgages in the secondary market—to consider using more updated credit scoring models in their mortgage underwriting.[91] Under P.L. 115-174, FHFA is required to define, through rulemaking, the standards and criteria the GSEs will use for validating credit score models used when evaluating whether to purchase a residential mortgage.[92] If enacted, H.R. 3621 would direct the CFPB to report to Congress on the impact of using nontraditional data on credit scoring.[93]

Full implementation of newer versions of credit scoring models, however, may not occur quickly.[94] In the mortgage market, upgrading automated underwriting systems is costly for the GSEs, FHA, and loan originators. Not all originators will choose to update their automated underwriting systems.[95] Even if alternative credit scoring models were widely adopted, the creditscore is not the only variable considered during the underwriting process. Just as several factors are included in the development of a credit score, a credit score is only one of several factors included in an automated underwriting model

---

[89] See Kenneth P. Brevoort and Michelle Kambara, *Data Point: Medical Debt and Credit Scores*, CFPB, May 2014, at http://files.consumerfinance.gov/f/201405_cfpb_report_data-point_medical-debt-credit-scores.pdf.

[90] See Bev O'SheaMay, "FICO Score 9: What You Need to Know," *NerdWallet*, May 5, 2020, at https://www.nerdwallet.com/article/finance/fico-score-9.

[91] See Kevin Wack, "Fannie, Freddie to Evaluate Alternative Scoring Models," *American Banker*, September 22, 2014, at http://www.americanbanker.com/issues/179_183/fannie-freddie-to-evaluate-alternative-credit-scoring-models-1070140-1.html.

[92] Specifically, the law allows Fannie Mae and Freddie Mac to employ alternative credit scoring models when purchasing mortgages rather than rely exclusively on the FICO scoring model. See Federal Housing Finance Agency, *FHFA Announces Decision to Stop Credit Score Initiative: No Decision in 2018; Focus Shifts to Implementing New Law*, News Release, July 23, 2018, at https://www.fhfa.gov/Media/PublicAffairs/Pages/FHFA-Announces-Decision-to-Stop-Credit-Score-Initiative.aspx.

[93] H.R. 3621, §501.

[94] See Mary Ellen Podmolik, "Rollout is Slow for FICO's New Credit Scoring Model," *Chicago Tribune*, October 14, 2014, at http://www.chicagotribune.com/classified/realestate/ct-mre-1019-podmolik-homefront-20141014-column.html.

[95] See Adrian Nazari, "How FICO's New Credit Score Will Impact Consumers," Huffington Post, September 19, 2014, at http://www.huffingtonpost.com/adrian-nazari/how-ficos-new-credit-score-will-impact-consumers_b_5844530.html.

(also referred to as an underwriting scorecard).[96] The debt-to-income ratio, for example, may still be an important variable for mortgage underwriting. Higher levels of medical and student loan debts may still affect mortgage underwriting decisions.[97] Hence, the use of alternative credit scores may help some borrowers close to a threshold or borderline, yet still not translate into significant changes in credit access across the board.

Data Protection and Security Issues

Congressional interest in data protection and security in the consumer data industry has increased following the announcement, on September 7, 2017, of the Equifax cybersecurity breach that potentially revealed sensitive consumer data information for 143 million U.S. consumers.[98] CRAs are subject to the data protection requirements of Section 501(b) of the Gramm-Leach-Bliley Act (GLBA).[99] Section 501(b) requires the federal financial institution regulators to "establish appropriate standards for the financial institutions subject to their jurisdiction relating to administrative, technical, and physical safeguard—(1) to insure the security and confidentiality of consumer records

[96] An underwriting scorecard may include information such as income, assets, and employment history obtained from the borrower's application not taken into account while preparing the credit score. See Federal Deposit Insurance Corporation, *Credit Card Activities Manual, Chapter VIII.-Scoring and Modeling*, March 2007, at https://www.fdic.gov/regulations/examinations/credit_card/pdf_version/ch8.pdf; and Cary Collins, Keith D. Harvey, and Peter Nigro, "The Influence of Bureau Scores, Customized Scores, and Judgmental Review on the Bank Underwriting Decision-Making Process," *Journal of Real Estate Research*, vol. 24, no. 2 (2002), pp. 129-152.

[97] Carrying higher levels of debt may become an equally or, under some circumstances, a more important factor in mortgage approval decisions relative to other factors in light of recently adopted mortgage underwriting requirements. See "How the New FICO Score Model Will Affect Banks," *American Banker*, August 13, 2014, at http://www.americanbanker.com/issues/179_156/how-the-new-fico-score-model-will-affect-banks-1069413-1.html.

[98] See Equifax, "Equifax Announces Cybersecurity Incident Involving Consumer Information," press release, September 7, 2017, at https://www.equifaxsecurity2017.com/2017/09/07/equifax-announces-cybersecurity-incident-involving-consumer-information/. On October 2, 2017, Equifax announced that an additional 2.5 million consumers may have been affected, for a total of 145.5 million. See, "Equifax Announces Cybersecurity Firm has Concluded Forensic Investigation of Cybersecurity Incident," press release, October 2, 2017, at https://investor.equifax.com/news-and-events/news/2017/10-02-2017-213238821.

[99] See CRS Insight IN11199, Big Data in Financial Services: Privacy and Security Regulation, by Andrew P. Scott; and CRS Report R44429, Financial Services and Cybersecurity: The Federal Role, by N. Eric Weiss and M. Maureen Murphy.

and information; (2) to protect against any anticipated threats or hazards to the security or integrity of such records; and (3) to protect against unauthorized access or use of such records or information which could result in substantial harm or inconvenience to any customer."[100]

The CFPB does not have the authority to prescribe regulations with regard to safeguarding the security and confidentiality of customer records.[101] Instead, the FTC has the authority to enforce Section 501(b) as the federal functional regulator of nonbank financial institutions, including CRAs.[102] The FTC has promulgated rules implementing the GLBA requirement.[103] Because the FTC has little upfront supervisory or enforcement authority, the agency typically must rely upon its enforcement authority after an incident has occurred. In addition, in March 2019, the Government Accountability Office released a report that recommended actions for the FTC, the CFPB, and Congress to strengthen oversight of credit bureaus' data security.[104] If enacted, H.R. 3621 would allow the CFPB to supervise and enforce cybersecurity standards for credit reportingagencies.[105] If enacted, H.R. 5332 would allow the CFPB to write rules for credit reporting agencies under the safeguards rule.[106]

Meanwhile, P.L. 115-174, Section 301, requires credit bureaus to provide fraud alerts for consumer files for at least a year under certain circumstances. In addition, credit bureaus must provide consumers with one free freeze alert and one free unfreeze alert per year. The law also established further requirements to protect minors. Currently, many credit bureaus provide consumers services such as credit monitoring for identity theft victims. In general, credit bureaus charge fees for these services, paid for by either a

---

[100] See 15 U.S.C. §6801 and CRS Insight IN10792, *The Equifax Data Breach: An Overview and Issues for Congress*, by N. Eric Weiss.

[101] See CRS Testimony TE10021, *Consumer Data Security and the Credit Bureaus*, by Chris Jaikaran.

[102] GLBA delegated the authority for federal consumer privacy provisions to the federal banking regulators for federally insured depository institutions; the Securities and Exchange Commission for brokers, dealers, investment companies, and investment advisors; state insurance regulators for insurance companies; and the FTC for all other financial institutions. See CRS Report R44429, *Financial Services and Cybersecurity: The Federal Role*, by N. Eric Weiss and M. Maureen Murphy.

[103] FTC, "Privacy of Consumer Financial Information," 65 *Federal Register* 33646-33689, May 24, 2000.

[104] U.S. Government Accountability Office, *Consumer Data Protection: Actions to Strengthen Oversight of Consumer Reporting Agencies*, GAO-19-196, February 2019, at https://www.gao.gov/products/GAO-19-196.

[105] H.R. 3621, §910.

[106] H.R. 5332, §9.

consumer or private company after a data breach incident. H.R. 3621 would expand protections for identity theft victims, including the rightto free credit monitoring and identity theft services.[107] It would require the CFPB to create new regulations to define the parameters for these new consumer benefits, including how long they should be provided and what services should be included.[108]

Appendix. Natural Disasters, Government Shutdowns and the COVID-19 (Coronavirus Disease 19) Pandemic

Many consumers may experience disruptions in their income following unexpected events, such as natural disasters, government shutdowns, or a pandemic and, therefore, are likely to be delinquent or default on loans and other regularly scheduled payments. For example, from December 22, 2018, to January 25, 2019, the federal government shut down for five weeks, raising concerns that federal employees may experience difficulties meeting their scheduled payment obligations that might subsequently affect their credit records and future credit scores. Likewise, a growing number of cases of Coronavirus Disease 2019 (COVID-19) were identified in the United States during the early spring of 2020, significantly impacting many communities.[109] As this situation rapidly evolves, the economic impact is likely to be large due to illnesses, quarantines, and other business disruptions.[110] Consequently, many Americans may loseincome and face financial hardship.[111]

Lenders have various options to mitigate the impact on consumers' credit scores and future creditaccess following disasters or catastrophic events. For example, furnishers may use special codes to report delinquencies due to special circumstances.[112] Financial institutions also may agree to limit late or

[107] Title VIII of H.R. 3621.

[108] H.R. 3621, §808.

[109] For background on COVID-19 (Coronavirus Disease 2019), see CRS In Focus IF11421, *COVID-19: GlobalImplications and Responses*, by Sara M. Tharakan et al.

[110] For more information on the effects of COVID-19 on the U.S. economy, see CRS Insight IN11235, *COVID-19:Potential Economic Effects*, by Marc Labonte.

[111] For more information on financial industry policy issues during the COVID-19 outbreak for consumers having trouble paying their bills, see CRS Insight IN11244, *COVID-19: The Financial Industry and Consumers Struggling to Pay Bills*, by Cheryl R. Cooper.

[112] During natural disasters, lenders have the ability to flag affected borrowers by using special comment codes when reporting to credit bureaus. See CFPB, *Natural Disasters and Credit Reporting: Quarterly Consumer Credit Trends*, November 2018, https://files.consumerf

other fees. Lenders offer forbearance plans, which are agreements that allow extended time for consumers to become current on their payments. However, some of these efforts may be more difficult for some institutions if they require changes in credit contracts. If lenders and consumers enter into loan forbearance agreements, then furnishers have the option to report to the credit bureaus that these consumers are current on their credit obligations.

Congress has also responded to mitigate the financial consequences of an adverse event on consumers. For example, various bills were introduced during the federal shutdown to allow credit restoration for some affected consumers.[113] In addition, on March 27, 2020, in response to the COVID-19 pandemic, the President signed the Coronavirus Aid, Relief, and Economic Security Act (CARES Act; P.L. 116-136).[114] Section 4021 of this bill requires furnishers during the COVID-19 pandemic covered period to report to the credit bureaus that consumers are current on their credit obligations if they enter into an agreement to defer, forbear, modify, make partial payments, or get any other assistance on their loan payments from a financial institution and fulfil those requirements, provided they were current before this period.[115] The covered period starts on January 31, 2020, and extends to the later of 120 days after enactment or 120 days after the national emergency declared by the President on March 13, 2020, terminates. In other words, prior to the CARES Act lenders could choose whether to report loans in forbearance as paid on time. Under the CARES Act, lenders must report such obligations as paid on time. However, some affected consumers may still experience harm to their credit record because lenders generally can still choose whether to enter into an assistance agreement with an individual consumer.

---

inance.gov/f/documents/bcfp_quarterly-consumer-credit-trends_report_2018-11_natural-disaster-reporting.pdf.

[113] For example, H.R. 935, H.R. 799, H.R. 1286, and S. 535. House Financial Services Committee Chairwoman Maxine Waters also released a related draft bill, "Protecting Innocent Consumers Affected by a Shutdown Act."

[114] CRS Report R46301, *Title IV Provisions of the CARES Act (P.L. 116-136)*, coordinated by Andrew P. Scott.

[115] If the consumer was delinquent before the covered period, then the furnisher should maintain the delinquent status unless the consumer brings the account or obligation current. For more information, see CFPB, *Statement on Supervisory and Enforcement Practices Regarding the Fair Credit Reporting Act and Regulation V in Light of the CARES Act*, April 1, 2020, at https://files.consumerfinance.gov/f/documents/cfpb_credit-reporting-policy-statement_cares-act_2020-04.pdf.

The CARES Act grants all consumers a right to request forbearance for many types of mortgages[116] and for federal student loans.[117] In addition, financial regulators have encouraged lenders to work with consumers affected by the outbreak,[118] and many financial institutions have announced efforts to provide assistance to affected consumers.[119] However, for many types of consumer loans, such as auto loans and credit cards, different financial institutions may be subject to different laws and incentives to handle consumer relief requests.[120] Therefore, a consumer's ability to access loan forbearance may vary, and some consumers may still experience harm to their credit records.

CARES Act protections related to the credit reporting system may impact consumers' ability to access credit in the future, possibly in positive and negative ways. Although these CARES Act protections allow consumers with loan forbearance agreements to protect their on-time credit histories, these provisions may also lead to some unintended consequences.[121] Financial

---

[116] 4022 gives consumers the right to request a forbearance and provides a moratorium on foreclosures on loans that are either (1) insured or guaranteed under provisions of the National Housing Act (12 U.S.C. §1707 et seq., 12. U.S.C.§1715z-20); (2) guaranteed under §184 or §184A of the Housing and Community Development Act (12 U.S.C.§1715z-13a, §1715z-13b); (3) guaranteed or insured by the Department of Veterans Affairs or (including those made by) Department of Agriculture; or (4) purchased or securitized by Freddie Mac or Fannie Mae.

[117] §3513 suspends all payments due for loans made under part D and part B (that are held by the Department of Education) of title IV of the Higher Education Act of 1965 (20 U.S.C. §1087a et seq.; §1071 et seq.) through September 30, 2020. Any payment that has been suspended will be treated as if it were a regularly scheduled paymentmade by a borrower for the purpose of reporting information about the loan to a consumer reporting agency.

[118] On Monday, March 9, federal and state financial regulators coordinated a statement to the financial industry, encouraging it to help meet the needs of consumers impacted by the coronavirus outbreak. They stated that "financial institutions should work constructively with borrowers and other consumers in affected communities," as long as they take "prudent efforts that are consistent with safe and sound lending practices." See Federal Reserve Board et al., *Agencies Encourage Financial Institutions to Meet Financial Needs of Customers and Members Affected by Coronavirus*, March 9, 2020, at https://www.federalreserve.gov/newsevents/pressreleases/bcreg20200309a.htm.

[119] Jessica Menton, "Contact Your Mortgage Lender: Payments May Be Deferred as Coronavirus Pandemic Causes Worker Hardships," *USA Today*, March 22, 2020, at https://www.usatoday.com/story/money/2020/03/20/coronavirus-mortgage-payments-may-deferred-amid-pandemic/5073179002/.

[120] For more information on consumer loan forbearance during the COVID-19 pandemic, including the impact of the CARES Act and other federal regulatory efforts, see CRS Report R46356, *COVID 19: Consumer Loan Forbearance and Other Relief Options*, coordinated by Cheryl R. Cooper.

[121] While Section 4021 of the CARES Act requires loan forbearances to be reported to the credit bureaus in the same way, "it does not address how model developers or individual

institutions may find credit scores less predictive of whether a consumer is currently creditworthy, in part due to deferrals being treated the same as on-time payments.[122] This situation could make it more difficult for consumers to access new credit, particularly those currently meeting their loan obligations.[123]

On May 15, 2020, the House passed the Heroes Act (H.R. 6800), and on October 1, 2020, the House passed an updated version of the bill (H.R. 925). H.R. 6800, Division K, Title IV, Section 110401 and H.R. 925, Division O, Title IV, Section 401 would create a moratorium on furnishing adverse information to credit bureaus during the COVID-19 pandemic and for 120 days afterward, as well as for other future major natural disasters.[124] Consumers could request to remove adverse information during the covered period and for 270 days afterward if experiencing economic hardship. Medical debt related to treatments arising from COVID-19 or another major disaster would not be furnished or included in the credit report. New credit scoring models could not be implemented during a major natural disaster period if they would identify a significant percentage of consumers as being less creditworthy than the previous model. Although these provisions would protect consumers from lower credit scores during the COVID-19 pandemic, the removal of information may also reduce credit scores' predictability in the future, which could harm some consumers in the long term.[125]

---

lenders treat any particular variables or information on the back end." See FinRegLab, *Covid-19 Credit Reporting & Scoring Update*, Research Brief, July 2020, https://finreglab.org/wp-content/uploads/2020/07/FinRegLab-Research-Brief-Covid-19-Credit-Reporting-Scoring-Update.pdf (hereinafter FinRegLab, *Covid-19 Credit Reporting & Scoring Update*, July 2020).

[122] Current macroeconomic uncertainties may also make credit scores less predictive of future consumer defaults. See AnnaMaria Andriotis, "'Flying Blind Into a Credit Storm': Widespread Deferrals Mean Banks Can't Tell Who's Creditworthy," *Wall Street Journal*, June 29, 2020.

[123] FinRegLab, *Covid-19 Credit Reporting & Scoring Update*, July 2020, p. 7.

[124] For more information on HEROES Act consumer loan provisions, see CRS Insight IN11405, *Heroes Act (H.R. 6800/H.R. 925): Selected Consumer Loan Provisions*, by Cheryl R. Cooper.

[125] For more information about the policy options and consequences of different credit reporting approaches during the COVID-19 pandemic, see FinRegLab, *Disaster-Related Credit Reporting Options*, May 2020, https://finreglab.org/wp-content/uploads/2020/05/FinRegLab-Disaster-Related-Credit-Reporting.pdf.

Index

D

E

N

O

P

R

W

Y